Conjuring Crisis

Conjuring Crisis

Racism and Civil Rights in a Southern Military City

GEORGE BACA

RUTGERS UNIVERSITY PRESS
New Brunswick, New Jersey, and London

Library of Congress Cataloging-in-Publication Data

Baca, George.
    Conjuring crisis: racism and civil rights in a southern military city / George Baca.
        p. cm.
    Includes bibliographical references and index.
    ISBN 978-0-8135-4751-0 (hardcover : alk. paper) — ISBN 978-0-8135-4752-7
(pbk. : alk. paper)
    1. Racism—North Carolina—Fayetteville.   2. Fayetteville (N.C.)—Race
relations—Political aspects.   3. Fayetteville (N.C.)—Politics and government.
4. Fayetteville (N.C.)—Economic policy.   5. Urban poor—Government policy—
North Carolina—Fayetteville.   6. Urban policy—North Carolina—Fayetteville.
I. Title.
    F264.F28B33 2010
    305.8009756'373—dc22

                                                                        2009036235

A British Cataloging-in-Publication record for this book is available from the
British Library.

Visit our Web site: http://rutgerspress.rutgers.edu

Manufactured in the United States of America

For my mother and father, Betty Knoop and Louis Baca

Contents

Acknowledgments

I am grateful to a multitude of people who have helped me and provided me support through the arduous process of writing this book. Most important were the people of Fayetteville who took the time to teach me about this very interesting and complex city. Without their help, patience, and tolerance this research would not have been possible. In addition to the people who openly encouraged my work, I would like to recognize the residents and community members who remained skeptical and kept me at arm's length. Perhaps it was from these people that I learned the most about racial politics in the ever-changing and dynamic South.

The intellectual ideas that I developed in this book have emerged from discussions and debates from a long line of mentors, friends, and colleagues. I must begin with Chabot Junior College in Hayward, California, where my intellectual career made its rather inauspicious start. As a hapless working student, ill-prepared for the challenges of college, I had the good fortune of taking Introduction to Cultural Anthropology with Professor Susan Sperling. Her enthusiastic teaching was contagious and inspired me to become an anthropologist. During my brief stay at Cal Poly–San Luis Obispo, Professor Nancy Clark had a huge influence on my intellectual development and convinced me I was "graduate school material." At San Francisco State, Professor Philippe Bourgois gave me a crash course in social theory and ethnography; his guidance and support were crucial.

In the writing of the book, I benefited from the expertise and brilliance of many people. Professor Sidney Mintz saw this project through as a dissertation and provided me much insight and expertise in revising the manuscript. Brackette Williams similarly influenced this work and has remained a staunch supporter. Additionally, I want to thank professors Dorothy Holland, Catherine Lutz, and Donald Nonini of the University of North Carolina for inviting me to work on their National Science Foundation-funded project (SBR-954912). They provided me many provocative ideas that challenged me to refine my conceptual framework and engagement with Southern historiography. Upon returning from fieldwork, members of the History Department at Johns Hopkins helped me refine my understanding of Southern history. In particular, Sara Berry, Michael P. Johnson, and Ronald G. Walters guided me through this process.

Over the years many colleagues have lent their help, support, and critical insights. Jason Antrosio showed an amazing amount of patience and was a source of great advice as he read the entire manuscript during many different stages. Sarah Pogell read and provided important questions and advice for editing that greatly improved the text. Arlene Davila read many chapters and gave me the necessary kick in the butt to complete the manuscript. At Rutgers University Press, Adi Hovav, Leslie Mitchner, and Derik Shelor guided this manuscript to completion. Katherine McCaffrey gave me a very critical yet sympathetic reading, which greatly improved the book. Similarly, Kirk Dombrowski carefully read many chapters and helped me clarify my arguments. Also, many other colleagues have read and lent support as I revised. I would like to thank Diane Austin-Broos, Mark Blythe, Dirk Bonker, Dominic Boyer, Kamari Clarke, Colin Dayan, Jean-Paul Dumont, Marc Edelman, Juan Giusti-Cordero, Ghassan Hage, Mike Hanchard, Joel Kahn, Don Kalb, Fred Klaits, Kelly McKinney, Anthony Marcus, Joshua Moses, Mariella Pandolfi, Jonathan Phillips, Elizabeth Povinelli, Joanne Rappaport, Franz Schneiderman, Gerald Sider, Genese Sodikoff, Susan Terrio, and Barbara White. Although many helped, I am responsible for any remaining shortcomings.

Some material in chapter 2 was previously published as "Neoliberalism and Stories of Racial Redemption" in *Dialectical Anthropology* 33 (2008): 219–241.

Conjuring Crisis

Introduction

Against the backdrop of the nation's unceasing preparation for war—most recently highlighted by the War on Terror—Americans passionately dispute the significance of the military on the country's well-being. Supporters of the U.S. military celebrate it as a both a stimulus to the economy and an opportunity for working-class Americans to become upwardly mobile. Facing exclusion, many working-class Americans and minorities have found the military to be a pathway to stable employment; they have parlayed war experience into low-interest home loans, college tuition, and the political capital necessary to transcend racism. Hollywood has spun these military versions of the American Dream into blockbuster films about heroic soldiers defeating Nazism in Europe and then returning home to fight racism and eventually topple Jim Crow segregation.[1] To be sure, nostalgic glorifications of war have not gone unchallenged. Critics of militarization have called on less glorious memories: the Vietnam War, the use of troops to squash urban riots of the 1960s, and the post–September 11th militarization of society that has resulted in the invasions of Afghanistan and Iraq. These egregious acts have embarrassed the Department of Defense and have led many scholars to view the military as an agent of racism, class inequality, and imperialism (see Gill 2004; Lutz 2001; McCaffrey 2002; Sherry 1997).

The U.S. military's effects abroad have often supported or propped up some of the most heinous regimes, regimes that have squelched democracy and halted social reform. However, in the United States the military has had an immense role in shaping the expansion of the American opportunity structure in ways that transcend the dichotomy that would reduce its effects to either "good" or "bad." While both perspectives highlight significant aspects of the military's effect on society, they ultimately short-circuit important questions about how the process of expanding and consolidating military power in the United States is deeply embedded in social reforms in ways that have expanded the nation's opportunity structure, and at the same time has limited reforms within the bureaucracy of the state (Klausen 1998; Light 2003). Fayetteville, North Carolina—the home of Fort Bragg, one of the largest and most important military installations—demonstrates the way federal planners have used military institutions to reorganize local politics in the U.S. South. Since World War II, the U.S. Armed Forces' presence in the historically impoverished eastern portion of the state has been dramatic. Fort Bragg transformed what federal planners at the time considered a southern backwater into a bustling urban center. The changes that followed reflect an intense transformation in the relations between the federal government and southern society. Federal agencies devolved power and authority to southern leaders and sent capital and federal resources to build roads, modernize public health, expand education, and grow the southern economy (Schulman 1991).[2] Seldom commented on, however, is that military-based reforms in Fayetteville and beyond were couched in ways that did not threaten southern politicians' economic commitment to New South development and Jim Crow segregation (see Grantham 1983; Link 1992). Elite southern politicians, so often outwardly committed to opposing federal intervention, became dependent on federal programs and capital, and socially and economically committed to Washington's policy agendas.

Despite the collaboration of southern political leaders with the federal government and its military planners, the increased presence of the military—in the form of training centers like Fort Bragg as well as in the manufacture of military provisions—has promoted social movements and economic enterprises that steadily undermined Jim Crow segregation (Kryder 2001; Myers 2006; Tyson 1999). The flood of federal money, workers, and soldiers from other parts of the country, and a wide array of entrepreneurs, also challenged the preexisting political and economic order. Soldiers, ex-military personnel, and various other "outsiders" associated with the military came to show antipathy toward local political structures. As a result, Fayetteville's image as a southern city today is entangled with the military in conflicting ways. The dominant coalition of political and business leaders in Fayetteville commit great efforts to keep up with the urban growth and have difficulties legitimizing their economic policies in the face of challenges from black and white residents associated with the military. Struggles over political power, economic policy, and racial reform develop along many lines that cross race, class, and regional lines.

This book takes this up historically, and through the lens of a complex series of contemporary events that show how close beneath the surface the tensions of economics, politics, and race remain today. During my ethnographic research, I learned about these very conflicts in dramatic fashion. When I arrived in Fayetteville in January 1997, I haplessly walked into the type of event anthropologist Victor Turner calls a "social drama" (1957, 1974). For Turner, social dramas are public events in which normal patterns of deference and mediation give way to open struggle about a central cleavage that divides society.

Fayetteville's social drama centered on allegations that the police chief discriminated against black officers and retaliated against those who criticized the department's racial climate. After attempts to resolve the controversy failed, leaders from the NAACP publicly accused the police chief of instituting a racially hostile work environment and asserted that the city manager condoned these violations of the 1964 Civil Rights Act. In a shocking turn of events, two white council members departed from the majority of white council members and supported the NAACP's call for an outside investigation. In joining their black colleagues, the "renegade" council members split the nine-member board into two factions: "the Five" and "the Four." Responding to this abrupt shift in power, the city's most powerful white leaders used conspiracy theories to conjure the shift in power into a crisis; over the next twelve months civic leaders mobilized white citizens against the peril represented by the ascendancy of the black community into a dominant political force.

Over the next eleven months, I lived among Fayettevillians as they struggled to define the significance of racism and the meaning of this apparent shift in power. Going beneath the surface images of racial polarization, *Conjuring Crisis* describes the way residents and politicians transformed this rather ordinary conflict about handling racial allegations into a "crisis." By focusing on the narratives Fayettevillians used to produce frightening images of crisis, the following chapters describe and analyze how many groups, constituencies, and political factions shaped this event. Politicians and ordinary citizens openly discussed race in ways that provided an unusual opportunity to study how the military, civil rights reforms, and federal economic policies shape urban America. What becomes clear from these stories is that the rise of civil rights reforms—and expanded rights for African Americans—as they occurred in Fayetteville have collaborated with economic policies that decreased federal spending for public goods like education, transportation, and affordable housing, and actually worsened the conditions for most African Americans in the city. Moreover, the intermeshing of the politics of civil rights and changing social priorities for public spending has been conditioned by the manner in which the federal government used the U.S. Armed Forces to implement racial reforms to narrow and limit black politics within the bureaucratic structures of city, state, and federal governments.

Research

Originally I came to study Fort Bragg and Fayetteville as a research assistant for a National Science Foundation-funded project called "The North Carolina Project."[3] Based in the Anthropology Department at the University of North Carolina, Chapel Hill, we sought to study how economic restructuring had affected local politics in North Carolina. The project framed our research in terms of changing economic policies of neoliberalism, which we took to be the way the U.S. elite have steadily deregulated economic markets, scaled down the social provisions of the state, and expanded the gulf between the nation's wealthy and poor (see Harvey 2005; Holland et al. 2007; cf. Baca 2004). Focusing on five cities—Durham, Fayetteville, Siler City, Boone, and Roanoke Rapids—we developed a comparative framework to study how neoliberalism restructured local politics. My obligation to the project was to study how Fort Bragg and the federal presence in Fayetteville influenced these dynamics.

The North Carolina Project integrated the five research sites with a methodology that focused our ethnographic observations on "dramas of contention," which we took to be "conflicts and differences of opinion that captured public attention" in relation to education and land use (Holland et al. 2007, 14). We sought to use public conflicts to examine the manner in which residents, activists, politicians, and business leaders struggled over public goods and what this told us about American democracy in the "age of neoliberalism" (ibid.). Each researcher went to his or her respective field site to explore the ways in which citizens struggled over policies related to education and the environment.

Before ever setting foot in Fayetteville, though, I learned about a "drama of contention" that made the city unique in relation to the other research sites: the city's scandalous reputation as a military town. Eventually I would come to see that most every recent political battle in Fayetteville is and has been shaped by the way "outsiders" unfairly perceive Fayetteville as a "military town." Local political and business leaders constantly envision and create economic plans that search for ways to ameliorate the city's reputation as simply an extension of Fort Bragg. Curiously, I learned about this dynamic relationship between outside perceptions and local politics while living in

Chapel Hill, North Carolina. During my two-month stay, in preparation for fieldwork, I became sensitized to the infamy that surrounds Fayetteville and Fort Bragg in other Carolina communities. From my very first day in Chapel Hill, shopkeepers, bartenders, professors, and graduate students displayed a collective disdain for Fayetteville as they bombarded me with lurid accounts that depicted Fayetteville as a center of racism, violence, and vice, captured by the slur "Fayettenam." Later it would become clear that Fayettevillians were well aware of this stigma, and constantly sought ways to dull or rebut it.

My time in Chapel Hill overlapped with a dramatic spike in anti-Fayetteville sentiment. At the time an ex-82nd Airborne paratrooper, James Burmeister, was being tried for the racially motivated killing of two black Fayettevillians, Jackie Burden and Michael James. In seeking the death penalty, the district attorney argued that Burmeister murdered his victims as part of a Nazi skinhead ritual to earn a "spider web" tattoo—an emblem that signifies the murder of either a black or a homosexual. These disturbing facts were presented in sensationalist manner. Nightly newscasts flooded Raleigh, Durham, and Chapel Hill with photographs of white supremacists posing in Nazi regalia and brandishing weapons, further burnishing the image that Fayetteville was rife with racial animosity and violence.

Many residents in Chapel Hill construed the racist murders as an example for the type of racial problems endemic to a military city; a conclusion that was much too simple, and which swept under the rug a host of local dynamics of race, federal spending, economic transformation, and social change that were at once part of local–federal interactions, but which could not be reduced to simply the presence of soldiers in the city. The actual source of most of Fayetteville's racial and economic tension was rooted in much more complex processes, which reflect a far broader swath of southern towns than simply those with military bases. Having grown up in a military family in the San Francisco Bay Area, I was familiar with how members of the military are often stigmatized as being slightly dangerous, racist, culturally unsophisticated, and overly nationalistic. Growing up, I watched these class-based conflicts play out as many professionals, who were being priced out of San Francisco, inundated my hometown, which was the home of the Alameda Naval Air Station. Newly arriving residents often had a sense of cultural superiority vis-à-vis servicemen like my father. Such condescension often transformed my father's class disadvantages into cultural predilections. My father, the son of a Mexican typesetter, is typical of many working-class soldiers. He had dropped out of high school and joined the U.S. Navy, put in his time, and today appreciates the pension and stable life afforded by a career in the military. Yet he has complicated political views about the military, racism, war, and inequality. Rather than presenting his service in nationalist terms, he refers to the military as a job, a job he hoped his son would never have to endure.

The anti-Fayetteville sentiment that I observed during my brief stay in Chapel Hill resonated with my childhood experiences in ways that led me to reflect on the ways in which the stigma that is often attached to military servicemen like my father had been imposed on the entire city of Fayetteville. Such misrepresentations in the stereotypes of a violent military town came into striking view when I traveled to Fayetteville to attend jury selection for the Burmeister murder case. News coverage in Chapel Hill made it appear as if the city was awash in controversy about racism and the military. Nothing could have been further from what I witnessed. Neither crowds nor protests were present, and the courthouse was humming along as if it were any other day. Instead of a drama of contention, the murder trial provided the capstone of a ritual of racial solidarity. From the time when Burmeister was arrested, black and white political leaders joined each other across the color-line to condemn the killing of innocent citizens and the perpetuation of the city's unfair image as a dangerous military town. Representing this widespread anger, the district attorney referred to Burmeister as a "son of a bitch" on the local news and promised he would suffer the greatest penalty for his deeds. City government, the Chamber of Commerce, the NAACP, the *Fayetteville Observer*, and Fort Bragg's leadership joined the chorus as they held church events, marches, and peace vigils in ways that produced a sense of shared vision of community that transcended race.

Performances of racial reconciliation provide a more revealing window— far more indicative of how race was made and lived in the South than anything associated directly with the trial—for understanding how military institutions have shaped racism in Fayetteville during the postsegregation era. I would see rituals of reconciliation again in Fayetteville, each time attached to moments in which the actual structure of political economic power had been put on display. Such displays prompt us to look much more closely at the way race is made and remade amid the institutions ostensibly set up to end its effects. To see this requires looking more carefully at how civil rights reforms have redrawn the color-line rather than erased it. After the passage of the Civil Rights Act, for example, authorities in Fayetteville (like the rest of the United States) dismantled legal segregation and repudiated its legitimating ideology of white supremacy. However jarring these reforms were at the time, federal policies created laws and protections that, while seeking to end one kind of racism, simultaneously incorporated African Americans into political institutions in ways that maintained the logic of racism (see Dominguez 1986; Fields 2001). One way it did this was by qualifying the social and political

status of blacks as "racial" and thus distributing to them new rights and responsibilities as minorities. Through such policies, and others, race was realigned
with a new economic and political order, one that had been in the works more
generally, and which had little use for the antique racism of Jim Crow
(Wacquant 1997, 2005).

Taking these racial changes into account, *Conjuring Crisis* focuses on the
ways that racism works after segregation. In this sense, I take racism to be the
ideas and practices that stigmatize African Americans with the innate attributes that disqualify them from being part of the majority and which continue
to portray African Americans as a troubled population that has interests at
odds with the majority. In particular, this book is concerned with the ways
that civil rights laws and color-blind ideology have reconstituted racism
with an idiom that avoids overt racial terminology (Bonilla-Silva 2003;
Mendelberg 2001), but which continues to produce a hierarchy of social priorities and possibilities largely along lines of color. This change has been promoted as a kind of "racial progress" in the South—and certainly gains have
been made. But such ideas too often elide the way that new systems of racism
have supplanted old ones, bringing with them a new, and perhaps more severe,
economic order (Holt 2000).

With these underlying practices of racism at work, ideas of racial progress
and equality break down when black politicians or activists level charges of
racism against mainstream authorities. As the Burmeister trial was winding
down, such an event was taking shape. When the local chapter of the
NAACP publicly questioned the city manager's handling of a racial controversy in the Fayetteville Police Department (FPD), it seemed that almost as
soon as black and white leaders had finished marching in solidarity with the
murder victims, they ran down to city hall to take up opposing positions about
racism in the police department. Adding to the irony was the split between
the then-sitting city manager and the NAACP, allies in the public relations
campaign that followed the Burmeister incident, who squared off against each
other for the next twelve months. In an intriguing turn of events, the
NAACP's leadership actually accused the city manager of condoning racism
and demanded an "outside investigation" of his administration—a far cry from
the rituals of reconciliation that had taken place only weeks before. The city
manager dismissed his former partners in racial harmony by claiming their
demands for an inquiry of his department would jeopardize the "council-
manager form of government" and could spell disaster for the city's well-being.

City manager Jim Thompson's warnings of calamity seemed to come to life
when white council members Tom Manning and Sam Johnson left the white
majority.[4] Joining their black colleagues, the two white council members

believed that there was enough evidence of racism in the FPD and that an objective third party was needed to resolve the problem. Tilting the power to the black city council members, the biracial alliance pushed for an outside investigation of the FPD. Powerful business and political leaders suddenly found themselves holding the "minority" position on city council and were powerless to stop the new council majority as it pursued the NAACP's call for an outside investigation.

Coming to Fayetteville with a methodological focus on dramas of contention, I found the city's turmoil about racism an ideal though unfortunate test bed. I watched the key protagonists as they used racial principles with dramatic flair and sought to present themselves as standard- bearers of the most cherished values of democracy, and to impugn their enemies as dangerous threats to justice.[5] Such strategies are a departure from the way in which race is normally disputed. Generally racial conflict in the United States is sublimated by customs and practices that obscure the underlying issues of conflict and inequality in the ambiguous term "race relations," which assumes a natural hostility between groups. By eliding the issue of power and inequality, racial discussions reduce racism to merely an attitude (Steinberg 2007, 17). In this instance, however, Fayettevillians displaced the routine patterns of racial deference, and performances of interracial harmony, with open hostility whereby blacks and whites discussed their anxieties and animosities surrounding racism in terms that invoked structures of governance, local political power, and economic difference.

By the time I arrived, the battle lines had been drawn and the bimonthly city council meetings had become the heart of the public performances of racial enmity. Before racially segregated audiences, the city manager and the NAACP blamed each other for causing racial hostility and destroying the community's values. I started collecting the material for this book at the beginning of the struggle. From the meetings I followed the way that black and white media interpreted and presented the conflict, and how these claims were struggled over and reformulated among the many competing groups and factions. Beginning with the many partisans, politicians, and city bureaucrats I met at the council meetings, I traced the conflict to other struggles over economic policy, neighborhood improvement, public education, and crime, to name a few. Eventually my research fanned out into a variety of social and political gatherings: informal meetings at bars and barbershops, in addition to every possible political meeting, rally, and church gathering I could find. I came to know the many residents and politicians in their lives beyond the conflict, and Fayetteville residents in the context of their everyday lives. Furthermore, I started to see how preexisting conflicts within the so-called "white" and "black" communities shaped the event, and how this event was similar and different from those that occurred before the civil rights movement, before Fort Bragg, and before the imposition of a New South economy by the federal government from the 1940s onward. In this way, I came to understand how the battle about racism brought many actors into the fight who had broader political interests that complicated the image of racial polarization. Keeping one eye fixed on the way politicians and citizens were narrating the conflict, I traced the workings of government into the community in ways that allowed me to develop rapport with a wide network of political groups and residents. In this way, I ethnographically connected the event with the broader issues of urban politics, racism, and the military, and with the history of race and racism, in Fayetteville and beyond.

Politics of Crisis

Ideas of crisis have emerged as a central framing device in contemporary politics. Ordinary citizens, scholars, and political functionaries often appeal to the term to explain modern-day problems—everything from underfunding of public schools to terrorism—in a dramatic fashion that then seems to demand immediate action. In this way the idea of crisis does not merely describe change, it seeks to intensify *perceptions* of change (Koselleck 2006, 1998). Anthropologists have increasingly paid attention to the symbolic qualities of public events, and have showed the ways both political actors and citizens invoke the idea of crisis to express anxieties and fears about political changes, increasing instability, and the breakdown of social institutions (Brash 2003; Lomnitz 2003a; 2003b; Mbembe and Roitman 1995; Redfield 2005).

Despite the ubiquity of crisis rhetoric, it is actually a rare occasion when perceptions of crisis succeed in mobilizing fear in ways that compel ordinary citizens to take decisive action against a threat. *Conjuring Crisis* describes and analyzes one of those moments, when Fayetteville's white business and political leaders succeeded in transforming their political defeat into a general crisis. By using rumors of racial conspiracy they were able to construct the power-shift that took place in city council as an object that necessitated decisive action (Blyth 2002; Hay 1996, 1999). Moreover, these same perceptions of crisis resulted in an equally compelling image of the majority—a code for white people—who had the power to intervene and return the city to order.

Understanding how moments of crisis emerge requires the examination of the rhetorical strategies whereby a problem or event is narrated as if it represents a dangerous turning point in history that portends disaster. Most calls of crisis fall on deaf ears. From news reports about the nation's crumbling

infrastructure to the plight of inner city youth, people in the United States are
rarely compelled by routine appeals to the term *crisis*. For a problem to emerge
as a full-scale crisis, it must be constructed in ways that mobilize anxieties and
sources of uncertainty that resonate with a multitude of people, much like
September 11th.[6] In Fayetteville, civic and business leaders constructed
images of crisis that recruited the anxieties and fears of many people (Hay
1996). As described in chapter 1, the narration of the "Five–Four" crisis not
only found but also *created* points of resonance with a multitude of
Fayetteville's white residents (Hay 1999, 321). The events and actions of the
city council were used toward this end. As a frightening image of racial division, the "Five–Four" split was presented by the members of the Fayetteville
elite as what anthropologists call a spectacle. Spectacles are symbolic displays
of power that seek to simultaneously present an image of the world and enforce
the order (Goldstein 2004; Handelman 1990, 2004; Wedeen 1999). As a
system of symbols and sacred meanings about race and order, the "Five–Four"
publicly represented Fayetteville's dominant coalition of political and business
leaders' understanding of governance and a strategy to impose their dominance. As a form of political action, spectacles, much like other public events,
do not merely reflect society's cultural principles. The performances of crisis in
Fayetteville sought to act upon and shape the city's racial ideas and structures.
Moreover, spectacles produce a compelling representation of the tensions,
fears, and hopes that define a particular epoch (Wedeen 1999, 13).

Spectacles of crisis have a long and deep connection to racial politics in
the United States. Much like the event I describe in this book, conspiracy
theories have formed an important part of racial knowledge that organizes
American politics (Roediger 1999; Rogin 1988). From the period of slavery
until the contemporary time, white authorities and factions, as they vie for
power, have often used conspiracy theories to speculate about threats to the
community that seek to upset proper relations between blacks and whites
(Carter 1976; Simon 1997). Originally emerging during the colonial period,
rumors and racial conspiracies have outlasted slavery. And despite many
changes in race and racism, racial conspiracy theories have retained a similar
plotline about African Americans being corrupted by harmful influences.[7]
The narrative, as it emerged while I was in Fayetteville, presumes blacks to be
naturally docile and complacent. However, under the influences of corrupt
whites and a small number of troublesome blacks, the masses of African
Americans become aroused into dangerous and violent beings. Racial politics,
accordingly, have been constructed in terms of shielding ordinary African
Americans from negative influences—often in the image of renegade whites
and/or the uppity black who did not know his place—that would bring
African Americans to rise up against whites. Such visions of crisis imagine an

empowered black community as vengeful, seeking to turn the tables on whites with humiliation and abuse. Against this threat, an awakened and unified white community would turn the tables back on the deceitful blacks and restore order (Simon 1997).

Chapter 2 describes the evolution of this symbolism of racial conspiracy to explain how civic and political leaders have found new ways to orchestrate racial fears to compel poor whites into accepting the authority and economic agendas of white elites, as a way to turn back the tide of racial vengeance. As racial ideas and laws have changed, one constant that remains is the way civic leaders have appealed to racial fears in order to present their own programs, policies, and agendas as if they represented a white culture that transcends class divisions (Hartigan 1999, 2005; Roediger 1999). In this light, we will see that the local elites' response to the "Five–Four" represents a broader phenomenon of public events: flashpoints when anxieties about racial changes become ignited to create frenzy. Such periodic displays of power and anxiety are a key characteristic of North American racial politics; during these moments of change, authorities project their hopes and fears, and manufacture race along with consent. Rather than merely reflecting racial norms, these frenzies are created by political groups to shape political institutions and define proper relations between blacks and government, and poor whites and their elite leaders.

Racial panics in the United States have always been about more than controlling African Americans; racial fears entwine with class politics that have pitted many whites against each other about economic policy and public projects (Carter 1976; Cecelski and Tyson 1998; Johnson 2001). In the face of political division, racial fears divert attention away from factional and class struggles among whites and blacks. Politicians and economic leaders found racial fears a powerful way to demand conformity to racial orthodoxies, particularly the allegiance of all whites to the greater importance of race superiority. As seen in chapter 2, authorities in Fayetteville came to manipulate these fears to discourage political dissent among whites, leading to never-ending fears of conspiracy, often where conspiracy did not exist. Politicians and planters used alarm to demand all whites conform to racial orthodoxy and commit to racial superiority as part of their duty to search out those who threatened society.

Myths of Racial Progress and Neoliberalism

Yet while much of the story of the "Five–Four" crisis is local in origin and execution, the events speak to a far wider set of social processes that have sought to make a New South, and unmake an old one. Indeed, contemporary forms of racial fear and crisis highlight the puzzling relationship between racial reforms that have created privileges for some African Americans and economic policies that have worsened living conditions for the majority of blacks (Cohen 1999; Gregory 1998). As such, the events in Fayetteville put on display two seemingly contradictory ideas that dominate political discussions of race and economic policy in the United States. In the first, Americans of various political positions believe in the idea of racial progress. From dismantling Jim Crow to the election of Barack Obama as the first black president, most Americans feel that race relations have improved because of the changes collectively labeled "the civil rights movement." Indeed, civil rights laws have outlawed overt racism and greatly expanded black middle classes. Indeed, African Americans no longer suffer overt forms of racial violence, their numbers in the middle classes have grown exponentially, and they hold greater positions of power and authority. Yet when Americans shift their focus to broader issues—often presumed to be beyond "race"—of economics, public education, and civic life, they embrace a second and seemingly opposed narrative of *decline*. In this way, social scientists have combined an image of social decay into ideas of neoliberalism, which they take to be the state's steady disinvestment in public goods (Baca 2008).

Social scientists have developed this narrative of decline into theories of neoliberalism that dramatize how the state's disinvestment in public goods like education, healthcare, affordable housing, and transportation acts as a rupture in the social contract that stemmed from the New Deal (see Harvey 2005). As a trope of decline, the idea of neoliberalism presumes a rupture with the past—often viewed through an idealized Fordist State and its so-called compromise between capital and labor (Baca 2004). This sense of crisis presumes a general decline that has worsened the condition for most African Americans and is to blame for new forms of racism (see Mullings 2005). In this form, neoliberalism unwittingly relieves civil rights institutions of responsibility for current conditions in the United States by taking attention way from how federal agencies and local politicians have implemented racial reforms.

Rather than viewing neoliberalism as a rupture that has retrenched the nation's commitment to racial reform, *Conjuring Crisis* describes the political structure that has emerged in Fayetteville from the simultaneous expansion of civil rights protections for African Americans and federal cutbacks for the provision of social goods.[8] As discussed in chapter 3, the federal government's cutbacks for public education, social services, transportation, and affordable housing created great challenges for city governments throughout the United States (Eisinger 1998). In the face of decreasing federal support, city governments—under the pressure of having greater responsibility for providing basic urban services—began to reorganize government. Most notably, city managers forged closer links with private capital in order to promote economic development and envisioned city government as an economic development tool (Davila 2004; Hackworth 2000).[9]

In Fayetteville, city management designed public projects around the needs of land developers and the merchant coalition in ways that connected such things as education and crime prevention in black neighborhoods. City management opened the city's administration to the needs and interests of the business community and sought a close relationship with ostensibly private business groups like the Chamber of Commerce, the downtown revitalization group, and the Fayetteville Economic Development Corporation. Increasingly, civic leaders associated the use of public money with cleaning up the city's image and economic development, aimed at growing the tax base, improving the quality of life, and expanding urban services. Fayetteville's political leaders also expanded the city's authority at the time—expanding its use of outside resources and access to state and federal aid—by connecting city government with the needs of various community groups and the business community, advocating "public-private partnerships" as a means of meeting what had formerly been primarily city government responsibilities.[10]

These changes in government were simultaneously shaped by the increasingly negative publicity the city received in relation to the unpopular Vietnam War. As the antiwar movement put Fort Bragg under the spotlight, Fayetteville's reputation suffered as many of its urban problems became linked to the notoriety of the armed forces, resulting in the epithet Fayettenam. Reorganization of the city government in Fayetteville thus became framed in terms of the city's negative reputation, as civic leaders sought to forge a new image of Fayetteville as a metropolitan center. Increasingly, civic leaders associated the use of public money with cleaning up the city's image and economic development.

The new forms of governance that emerged revolved around city management and its ability to coordinate disparate political and economic groups into a workable and enduring coalition, what political scientist Clarence Stone calls an "urban regime" (Stone 1989). Here the concept of urban regime is used to describe the ways that Fayetteville's politicians and bureaucrats use informal relationships to bring the machinery of formal government to meet the private needs of capital. In this sense, urban regimes are neither rigid nor monolithic entities. Instead, Fayetteville's urban regime involves a steady process whereby city management constantly seeks to build and maintain the coalition. And as elsewhere in the United States, Fayetteville's city manager plays a crucial role in forming, maintaining, and expanding the regime's power. Rather than commanding, city managers seek to create productive relations between competing interests by pursuing an overarching policy agenda to promote common economic and political projects (Stone 1989). Though many members of the municipal coalition hold conflicting and competing interests, they share a commitment to the city's policy agenda, and seek to rationalize their own interests in its terms, rather than against it. City management maintains the dominant coalition by holding leverage over earmarking municipal funds for transport, urban renewal, suburban subdivision, and shopping malls, at each step reinforcing its progrowth ideology by rewarding one constituency or another.

Such a shift of focus—to urban regimes and the coalitions they produce—has important theoretical implications. My concept of municipal coalition draws from the pioneering work of Clarence Stone (1989) and most recently from Matthew Lassiter (2006). Yet despite the strength of these works, they do not use their case material to theorize beyond urban politics in the United States. Rather than being interested in local politics for its own sake, the approach taken here aims at a more general understanding of the relationship between state level and local level power and authority. In particular, I am interested in how local political structures represent an important part of the larger structure of the nation-state. Drawing on the work of Phillip Abrams (1988 [1977]) and Claudio Lomnitz (1992, 2001), I am interested in how local struggles of power indicate the ways central authorities mutually engage local actors. Rather than trying to dominate local politics, state power often seeks to engage local power in ways that set the broader terms, leaving local power to struggle within itself over the actual means and implications of the agenda. In such an approach, the expansion of power requires that we focus on how the central state delegates power. With the connections to the central-state in mind, the idea of urban regime allows us to focus on the role of culture in forging political dominance, or the process that Antonio Gramsci's called "hegemony" (Gramsci 1971 [1929–1935]). Like Stone, Gramsci conceptualized political dominance as a process that transcends coercion. He uncovered the ways that dominant groups produced authority by creating conditions for subjects to consent to dominance. In this sense, urban regimes in the United States express their power with persuasive ideas that present their world view as if it were common sense. Hegemony is expressed through a wider alliance of classes by fusing economic projects, governmental institutions, cultural beliefs, and ideology, which results in the union of forces Gramsci called "historic bloc" (Gramsci 1971 [1929–1935], 366). Forming a historic bloc requires the active spreading of cultural arrangements in ways that bind conflicting social, class, and (in the United States) racial groups into a political organization. Achieving hegemony, in Gramsci's view, requires the establishment of moral and intellectual leadership in social life by diffusing one's "world view" throughout the fabric of society as a whole, thus equating one's own interests with the interests of society at-large (Eagleton 1991, 116).

Far from simple coalition-building and negotiation, the concept of hegemony uncovers the cultural processes that surround and complement formal government to produce a dominant vision. Such processes are readily apparent in the history of Fayetteville. Since the late 1940s, federal agencies have used racial reforms to reinterpret the embarrassing history of racism as a story of progress throughout the United States. As federal agencies began the long and gradual process of desegregating U.S. institutions, the federal government promoted racial changes as a tale of national redemption and racial progress (Dudziak 2000). Most important for understanding the connections between neoliberalism and racial reforms, the federal government organized its reforms in the view that American democracy and economic liberalism was the only viable path to racial "reconciliation." In the process, federal agencies instituted racial reforms in ways that limited black politics to formal equality and discredited black political groups that offered broader criticism of the American economy and politics (ibid.).

Myths of Progress

Tales of racial progress are among the type of stories that anthropologists call myths (see Lévi-Strauss 1979; Malinowski 1922; Turner 1967). They are not fictitious stories. Instead, they are powerful presentations that reinterpret the past in ways that sustain the social order. With romantic recollections of popular resistance to racism in the post–World War II era—from decolonization to the U.S. civil rights movement to the fall of apartheid—political officials have appropriated triumphal narratives of how after years of civil rights struggle the underprivileged have asserted themselves politically. More than merely coopting popular movements, reform policies defused struggles for liberation as they recuperated the energy of these struggles into the maintenance of liberal forms of power (Baca 2006).

Myths of racial progress represent a global politics whereby political officials throughout the world have reconstituted racial domination by recognizing past atrocities of slavery and colonialism. The "cunning of recognition," as anthropologist Elizabeth Povinelli describes this maneuver of power, recognizes the history of racial inequality in ways that secure and reinvigorate the state and its core values (2002, 29). Accordingly these forms of multiculturalism use national rituals of apology for past subjugation of subordinated members of society not to transfer power or change the actual social order, but to rebirth the state in a postracial world (Trouillot 2000). In this way, racial reforms, from attempts at reconciliation in Australia to civil rights in the United States to the truth and reconciliation in South Africa, function as narratives of national redemption that maintain the logic of the racism they ostensibly seek to remedy (Dominguez 1986).

Myths of racial redemption have maintained the idea that the majority's best interest is represented by white culture. The ideal of whiteness conditions racial reforms in ways that demand black political leaders and activists must tailor their agendas to the majority's will. In this way, whiteness stands as a symbol of privilege and power which remains unmarked (Brodkin 1999; Lipsitz 1998). Whiteness, much like crisis, cannot be taken at face value. As analyzed in the last half of the book, the construction of crisis and fears about the NAACP's alliance with white council members Tom Manning and Sam Johnson did not represent something we can call "white culture." Instead, images of the majority's will—against a threatening racialized other— represents a site of cultural struggle between competing groups of people and interests that are divided along the lines of class and status (Arnesen 2001; Hartigan 2005). Symbolically, supporters of the city manager used the universal language of professional government to promote a "unified view of white people as a collective order sharing a common cultural identity" (Hartigan 2005, 188). Indeed, the white civic and business leaders promoted the idea of crisis in order to produce this very idea of "whiteness" as a culture that represented the majority's interests.

The proliferation of myths of redemption and racial progress has guided the processes whereby city governments and their urban regimes have incorporated civil rights organizations like the NAACP into their political administrations (Reed 1999a). By incorporating the NAACP and Urban League, city managers in the United States have expanded the legitimacy of their urban regimes by providing black politicians, citizens, and activists access to the machinery of government (Reed 1999a; Stone 1989). In this way, *Conjuring Crisis* describes the ways that black Fayettevillians participated in, and gained some of the spoils of, Fayetteville's urban regime. Yet such gains were not an unmixed blessing. As will be seen in the chapters that follow, such channeling of participation into acceptable forms greatly narrowed black politics and harnessed a number of quite different interests to the urban regime's policy agenda. Such processes, I argue, highlight the ways that a confluence of civil rights reform and neoliberal economic policies have helped reproduce, rather than cure, a disturbing pattern of poverty, crime, and hopelessness among working-class blacks.

Conjuring Crisis follows on other studies that have demonstrated that rising opportunities for middle-class African Americans have often accompanied the worsening social conditions for working-class African Americans more generally, placing a second analytical lens on the politics of race and racism as it affects the internal relations and class struggles among African Americans (Cohen 1999; Gregory 1998; Pattillo-McCoy 2007). Over the last fifty years, black middle classes and political leaders have become engaged in political struggles in ways that illustrate how political structures that represent minority needs can also deprive poor blacks of the economic and social resources they need to participate actively in the decision-making that most directly affects their lives (Cohen 1999). This reality has expanded the behavioral distance between the black middle class and working classes that are at the core of most "cultural" conflicts between these groups (Gregory 1998; Pattillo-McCoy 2007). Yet an examination of the tensions within the African American community is not sufficient to explain the difficult situation that black leaders (in and out of the middle class) face. Thus chapter 5 takes up how changes in black politics have led to a popular discourse that presumes a bifurcation of middle- class and poor blacks. However, the bifurcated model that counterposes black middle classes with the poor actually simplifies and distorts the complicated ways that racism and class power interact (Jackson 2005).

In Fayetteville, amid fragmentation and stratification that was being negotiated and put in place by the response to the "crisis," issues of the black community were most prominently framed by more privileged members of the black community. Where such forms of politics centered on the fact that blacks have legal citizenship and are due the sorts of rights that go with that (contrary to Jim Crow-era attempts to remove them), with neoliberal reforms, black Fayettevillians gained legal rights and access, but found themselves in a situation of civic estrangement. As a result, today the workings of racism are more opaque, hidden, and cloaked in political correctness, and as such, much harder to confront. As John L. Jackson points out, with the prohibition of racial discrimination, more subtle forms of racism have flourished and can be easily imagined, in what he calls "racial paranoia." Updating Richard Hofstadter's theory of conspiracies as a "paranoid" style that emerged on the fringes of American society, Jackson focuses on the way all Americans confront social differences in their lives. The type of racial distrust that emerged in the conspiracy theories mentioned above has shifted with the structural changes in the power relations between blacks and whites, and between minorities and the machinery of the nation-state (2008). He points out how the workings of racism are more subtle and difficult to discern than when racism was explicit. *Conjuring Crisis* builds on these insights to describe the manner in which ordinary black citizens use conspiratorial thinking to discuss the manner in which some blacks contribute to the politics that harm the majority of African Americans.

Military Power

It is from the context of neoliberalism and civil rights reforms that we can begin to understand the importance of military power in Fayetteville and perhaps the United States more generally. In Fayetteville, it is difficult to speak of the federal government and race without broaching the issue of military power, but the relationship between these three is often far from simple. Recently anthropologist Catherine Lutz has provided one view of the connections between the military and U.S. society in her book *Homefront: A Military City and the American Twentieth Century*. Using the history of Fayetteville, she largely focuses what she calls the "wounds of war" as she surveys the city's landscape to describe what she takes to be military- inflicted injuries in the form of crime, poverty, racism, and urban sprawl, as well as a small tax base and a lack of urban services. Lutz uses this record of damage to refute "the now widely entrenched idea that war is the health of the nation" and that military spending yields positive benefits for either the economy or society. Moreover, she contends that war has allowed the U.S. government to enlarge the state "while shrinking the rule of law" (2001, 1–2). Similar to other American critics of war, Lutz presumes an ideal moment when the rule of law was untainted by the forces of militarization.[11]

Rather than being the foregone conclusion of militarization, *Conjuring Crisis* begins with the suggestion that Fayetteville's social problems stem from the collision of southern political forces with the vast expansion of federal power. This expansion came in the form of the military, but also as in the form of national economic policies, and in civil rights laws. From this perspective, it is clear that military power has represented a powerful tool for the federal government to reshape social and political institutions in Fayetteville. Yet by paying attention to how the expansion and consolidation of Fort Bragg (and its role in the regional economy) benefitted from and provided the basis for a host of other federal initiatives, a different picture than Lutz's Fayetteville comes into focus. Rather than imposing itself at will, the federal government and the architects of its expanding state power have skillfully used military facilities to expand its authority into the impoverished and stigmatized southern region of the United States, bringing with it a host of interests that go beyond the military itself—economic and social interests on a much more broad scale.

It is important to remember that in this story, at the beginning of the twentieth century, southern politicians and business leaders were a formidable power. They were actively reorganizing a region that suffered much poverty, and seeking to overcome a political order largely imposed from outside. Their success and the system they produced represented an obstacle to political and economic interests outside of the South. As a result, the federal government could ill afford not to have them contribute to national policies and economic goals. At the same time, southern elites, including those in Fayetteville, recognized the opportunities provided by federal resources, and faced the economic threat of their self-imposed isolation. Reflecting this tense dialectic (a dialectic felt by both sides), the federal government developed economic policies to which southern leaders would consent. Southern leaders played along as they actively sought to minimize the sorts of changes that these same policies intended. As a result, the military policies that established Fort Bragg dovetailed with southern interests in economic growth and retaining white supremacy. Yet, military investments also threatened the same structure and the privilege it entailed. Thus, Fayetteville's political leaders had an influential role in shaping Fort Bragg's development during the twentieth century, constructing mutually formative social relations with federal power to produce what came to be the military town Lutz describes. Chapters 2 and 3 describe how many of the problems that Lutz associates with the military actually grow much more clearly from the collision between southern political forces of the New South and the expansion of the federal government (see Phillips 2002).

Throughout the twentieth century, the expanding presence of the military resulted in tighter connections between Fayetteville and the national economy, economic development, and racial reforms that contributed to the civil rights movement.[12] Many people from the military, or those who were attracted by business created by the military, came to the South and challenged many of its norms and customs. Most obviously, African Americans joining the service began to behave in ways that challenged the status quo. Moreover, white servicemen often challenged that authority as well, bringing their own forms of race, politics, and economic priorities. Eventually, the expansion of the economy and population overwhelmed local authority.

In *Conjuring Crisis*, these contradictions are described in the manner in which middle-class retirees from the military came to challenge local authority during the events of the "Five–Four." Though the idea of a crisis framed the conflict on city council, many whites, a significant number of whom were retirees, were not compelled by the narrative. Many residents who self-identified as "the military" believed the racial anxiety expressed by the leading political and business figures revealed the backwardness and ineptitude of the city's political leaders. Moreover, these critics accused the dominant coalition of using racial fear to divert attention from its economic policies. In this way, "the military" emerged as an aggressive political force and a critical faction that has reshaped the urban regime.

By focusing on these conflicts, *Conjuring Crisis* provides an interpretation that is at odds with liberal social criticism that often takes for granted what *should* be done. Following Bent Flyvbjerg, the subsequent chapters reorient the discussion of militarization to "what is actually done" (Flyvbjerg 1998). By viewing democracy in relationship to the creation and reproduction of inequality, *this book* opens up questions about how the federal government and Fayetteville's local leaders have used military power to not only reform racism but to legitimize it in ways that reinforce class power. In the South, military institutions have contributed to policy reforms sought by the federal government in ways that complicate the workings of military power and reveal multiple currents and interests in the state itself. Neither Fort Bragg nor the more general processes of the federal expansion of power have one-sidedly determined Fayetteville's present- day problems of racism, crime, urban sprawl, and inadequate public schools. Instead, Fayetteville's particular experience of these national problems stems from how local power brokers and business leaders used federal policies, from militarization to civil rights, to control local affairs, and how those same policies in turn altered the ground on which those struggles took place.[13]

Outline of the Book

Conjuring Crisis uses the police department controversy that prompted the "Five–Four Crisis" to examine the relations between military power, economic policy, and racial politics. Chapter 1, "Narrating a Racial Crisis," introduces the reader to the conflict that eventually engulfed city hall for an entire year. This chapter describes how the dispute between city management and the local chapter of the NAACP became understood as a "crisis," and in turn, the way that powerful civic and business leaders mobilized racial fears to transform their loss of power into a crisis. In so doing, the dominant municipal coalition appealed to racialized ideas of "the majority," shifting the question of racism to a question of "self-government." By stigmatizing the NAACP's interests as marginal to the concerns of the wider public, white businesses and civic leaders created fear about how biracial alliances could threaten the integrity of local governmental control of civic life and the city's putative best interests.

Chapter 2 relates the "Five–Four Crisis" and its rhetoric of racial conspiracy to the broader history of racism in the Atlantic world. Periodical rituals of white solidarity in Fayetteville and beyond stem from the politics of plantation agriculture, whereby planters used fearful images of marauding slaves to enforce—and redraw—racial relations, just as they mobilized collective images of whites to transcended class and status differences. As the region's plantation economy expanded, white political factions began to express their political anxieties and fears in a political ritual, the slave insurrection panic. Slave panics became a powerful way in which contending white factions sought to mobilize white solidarity, normally against currents and divisions within the existing power structure. This chapter shows how the importance of these rituals increased after manumission, as periodic displays of racial fear became a key feature in North American race relations. During moments of political conflict, authorities have used these events to project their hopes and fears and to redefine racial relations, even as they sought to alter or maintain control over the economic forces of which they were a part. Rather than merely reflecting racial norms, authorities have used periodic frenzies of racial fear to reorganize racial politics and define the proper relations between majority and minority members.

Chapter 3 shows how business leaders during the twentieth century adapted slavery's racial patterns of fear into a ritual of racial reform, a response to new political forces unleashed by the expanding of the War Department and the founding of Fort Bragg in 1918. This chapter uses the history of Fort Bragg to show how the federal government used military power to intervene into southern politics and society. Yet rather than imposing itself unilaterally, the federal government devolved power to local politicians and business leaders. In turn, local political forces used municipal power to mediate the federal government's influence on the local economy and race relations, seeking to channel new initiatives into forms that could maintain the status quo. Yet over the years, a municipal coalition of real estate, home building, and retail used federal authority and resources to produce its own dominant regime, and complied with civil rights laws in ways that strengthened its own control over African Americans and the city government. An emerging civil rights leadership developed, along with the federal government's gradual withdrawal of funds from local governments across the nation. This chapter brings the reader to the eve of the "Five–Four" conflict, when the municipal coalition was embroiled in three ambitious projects—the continuous annexation project, a $28 million revitalization project, and an $87 million school bond—which profoundly shaped the developing conflict.

Chapters 4 through 8 return to the "Five–Four" to show how these political and economic forces shaped urban politics. In chapter 4, "Performing Crisis," I describe how political and business leaders used their informal relations to mobilize public and private power to produce a powerful image of social protest on behalf of "the majority," which in turn connected their interests in the city management's policy agenda to a wider public image of local control and sovereign government. Stake-holders in the city manager's regime used rituals of protest and populist rhetoric to present their interests in the urban regime as if it represented all white people and most of Fayetteville's citizens. Illustrating the power of crisis rhetoric, they recruited members of the community to their image of the public.

Chapter 5, "Threatening Images of Black Power," digs beneath the visions of crisis to describe how ordinary black residents understood the event. I will focus on the disagreements and conflicts among African Americans. From these discussions I will analyze the way the rhetoric of crisis hid these conflicts. Moreover, I will show how black leaders engaged these struggles within the community and projected the community's authority to powerful white leaders.

Chapter 6, "Power Shift," carries the theme of conflict to that among whites. While the dominant civic and business leaders were focusing their attention on racial conspiracies, a group of retired military, called "Fayetteville Taxpayers for Financial Responsibility," attacked the urban regime with the hopes of ousting the dominant coalition. Several black politicians joined these retirees in their effort to expose the rhetoric of a "Five–Four" crisis as merely an attempt to move an agenda of downtown revitalization and assert greater control over the city by Fayetteville's urban regime. By highlighting corruption and racism in the plans for downtown revitalization, these black and white residents revealed the biggest danger to the dominant elite: the possibility of dissenting white groups coming together with black voters for a common cause.

Chapter 7, "Outsiders and Special Interests," examines how city management used the criticisms launched by the NAACP and the military faction to strengthen its control of power. Behind the scenes, city management reformed its policies in response to the criticisms of downtown revitalization. Rather than representing a fatal blow to the municipal coalition, the NAACP's criticism of the police department and Fayetteville Taxpayers for Financial Responsibility's attack on downtown revitalization alerted the municipal coalition to its weaknesses. City management responded by revising its racial policies and downtown revitalization so as to appeal to key segments within the black and military communities. These plays of power illustrate how bureaucratic power played a determining role in the rituals of democracy, and vice versa—including both periodic protests as well as electoral politics.

Chapter 8, "Single Shot," develops the discussion of class conflicts among blacks. This chapter uses the "Five–Four" to analyze how black leaders and elected officials carefully calculated their moves in relation to connections with the municipal coalition. It then describes how many black residents challenged black leaders in ways that erupted into a full-fledged battle over electoral strategy, which resulted in division and nasty debates between African American citizens and politicians.

The concluding chapter pulls these themes together by describing how civic leaders succeeded in using the election to "resolve" the crisis. The urban regime's dominance led to postmortem discussions among black leaders about "what went wrong," while victorious white leaders sought to "heal" the community. Yet the central contradictions within the municipal coalition—its inability to control large segments of the military and black community—became ever more visible and continue to reverberate to this day.

Chapter 1

Narrating a Racial Crisis

W HEN I ARRIVED in Fayetteville in February 1997, the dispute over racism in the police department had divided city council into two factions—the Five and the Four. Many white citizens shared with me their anger and anxiety about how white council members Tom Manning and Sam Johnson, who, as a white man told me, "fell in with the niggers" on city council and transformed the otherwise powerless bloc of black council members into a controlling force.[1] Although Fayetteville's most powerful civic and business leaders avoided such overt racial language, they were equally anxious about the danger represented by this alliance, which they called a "conspiracy." During my first morning in town, the sense of racial polarization revealed itself on my doorstep when I grabbed the *Fayetteville Observer* off my porch. The editorial board rebuked the "new" council majority for worsening racial tensions. It asserted that the council majority's quest for an "outside investigation" represented "an assault on the council-manager form of government" and could cause irreparable damage. The editorial pleaded with the deadlocked council to "end this dangerous experiment."[2]

Despite these explosive appearances of a sudden shift in political power, this chapter will show how the explosion of animosity was framed and narrated by key players in the drama. The chapter describes how white political leaders and the NAACP strategically used ideal images of racial norms to create the appearance of a violation in racial customs that would, if not corrected, threaten the well-being of the city. The opening stages of this event illustrate the way crisis situations create the appearance of a sudden and polarizing jolt to normal relations (see Turner 1974; Ginsberg 1989). Rather than a sudden or abrupt deviation from normal racial patterns, the schism on city council grew from a broader history of conflict over the implementation of civil rights reforms. Members of city management and the leaders of the NAACP drew from this history of racial struggle to create narratives that presented the controversy in a dramatic fashion—as an abrupt violation to the city's racial laws and customs. Central to these competing images of a breach in racial norms were rumors, ideas of conspiracy, and symbols of crisis. Politicians and citizens on both sides of the debate used these cultural terms to contest and reformulate the meaning and significance of racism in Fayetteville. Most importantly, this chapter will draw attention to the manner in which powerful white politicians succeeded in defining the event. Thus, as we will see, turmoil did not result from a natural conflict between blacks and whites. Instead, we will see how specific actors and groups created the sense that the controversy represented a dangerous breach in healthy race relations, thus redefining the debate in terms of crisis.

A Little Problem Downtown

The controversy in the police department focused the public's attention on issues of racism in ways that heightened the anxiety many whites experience about how civil rights reforms have redistributed rights and privileges to African Americans. Indeed, the dispute grew from longstanding struggles in the Fayetteville Police Department (FPD). Like many cities in the United States, Fayetteville has struggled to desegregate its institutions, and the FPD has been a crucial battleground. Although the FPD began hiring African Americans during the late 1960s, controversy broke loose in 1971 when nine black police officers sued the city for racial discrimination. Ruling in favor of the aggrieved officers, a federal judge issued a consent decree in 1974 that ordered the FPD to raise its number of black officers to 30 percent.

After twenty years of increasing the numbers of African American officers, the department never fully complied. In 1996, less than 30 percent of line officers and only four of twenty-seven sergeants were black. Moreover, the city manager and police chief were lobbying to disband the consent decree, as they believed it was reverse racism.

As city management was working behind the scenes to break up the consent decree, racial tensions surfaced in 1996 when white officers began talking about how many of their black colleagues felt the department had racial problems. Eventually, stories of disgruntled black officers complaining about discrimination reached police chief Dan Proctor, who was white. The chief was floored by such hearsay. After all, city council had hired him in 1983 with the mandate to clean up the beleaguered department. After experiencing several embarrassing setbacks in its already fragile image, city leaders had sought to replace the notorious Chief Bobby Richardson, whom many black and white residents remembered as a racist who compensated for what he lacked in police training with what many observers called "knuckles and know-how." His tenure came to an end when a resident named Jimmy Simms charged the FPD with police brutality. Sims had been beaten while in police custody and suffered a damaged testicle. Mr. Simms sued the City of Fayetteville for $800,000, precipitating the ouster of Chief Richardson.

By all accounts, Proctor's administration signaled a new era in Fayetteville's police department, which resulted in a more positive relationship with African Americans. Coming from Rock Island, Illinois, the chief brought a clean image and new police techniques, like community policing, modern equipment, and a keen sense for public relations. Under his leadership, the department finally received national accreditation. Civic leaders praised him for professionalizing the police force, and he received many awards for community service, including the Fayetteville NAACP's service award. Part of his popularity drew from the unprecedented way he reached out to the black community, building close relations with black neighborhoods through community policing, forming a club where he taught poor children judo, and creating a rock band of Fayetteville police officers called the "Rollerz" that played in the city's schools.

With his successes, the chief also collected his fair share of enemies. He matched his reputation as a reformer with notoriety as an outspoken and confrontational boss. Opponents considered him an authoritarian. His supporters recognized his strictness but preferred to characterize him as a no-nonsense guy with a hands-on management style. Chief Proctor complemented his toughness and heightened his confrontational style with a panache for public relations. Using charm, he skillfully fed news reporters stories, held press conferences, and wrote letters to the editor to deal with his enemies. He often divulged embarrassing facts about his enemies to further his agenda.

Shortly before the dispute over discrimination became public, Proctor had been involved in such a controversy with several lawyers about "driving while intoxicated" cases. The chief believed many of his department's DWI arrests were being overturned by corrupt judges and lawyers, whom he and his supporters called "the fix-the-ticket crowd." Several lawyers had become specialists in getting DWI arrests overturned. Fed up, he called a news reporter at the *Fayetteville Observer* and tipped her off about how lawyers specializing in drunken-driving cases had "a racket." He spoke on the record about how DWI lawyers made backroom deals with district court judges and assistant district attorneys. He backed his claims with a study that reported a dramatic decrease in DWI convictions between 1990 and 1995.[3] Chief Proctor used this publicity to create new rules banning lawyers from speaking with officers in the court-house's back halls. The district attorney followed suit with reforms that required his personal approval of each dismissal for drunken driving.

When black officers raised the issues of discrimination, he confronted them in a similarly aggressive fashion, minus the public denunciation. For many who knew him, this reaction was not entirely racial. He was well known for his dislike of criticism. When the criticism came from his own officers, he equated it with insubordination no matter what their skin color. Believing that their opinions of racism harmed the department's morale and sense of unity, he ordered Major George Moses and Captain Robert Chambliss—his two highest-ranking African American officers—to interview all sixty-eight black officers to see if they experienced racial discrimination or if they knew of discrimination. Though he later argued that the interviews were intended to help rectify the racial problems, many black officers thought the interviews were designed to squash dissent. Moses and Chambliss delivered a report showing that seventeen officers complained of racial problems.[4] Proctor took the names of the officers to the head of the Office of Professional Standards (OPS) and ordered him to interview the seventeen officers. He also con-fronted some of the officers individually and personally demanded that they provide specific instances of prejudice and provide names of black officers who could corroborate their statements. He held meetings with officers who told Chambliss and Moses that race figured in promotion, assignments, and train-ing opportunities.

Racial Discrimination and Public Perceptions

After Proctor's investigation of black officers, some of the subjects of his indig-nation hired lawyers and filed complaints with the U.S. Equal Employment Opportunity Commission (EEOC). In light of the impending EEOC investiga-tion, the city manager— who directly supervises the police chief—asked the leaders of the NAACP to help him resolve the conflict in the FPD. Official dis-cussions of the discrimination cases developed between Richard Ross, the pres-ident of the NAACP, and the city manager. Ross, a thirty-one-year veteran of the army, had been active in the local chapter of the NAACP for more than twenty years. From the outset, city manager Thompson set the terms of debate. He agreed to share information with President Ross but demanded that the negotiations be confidential and outside the view of the public. Negotiations, however, did not go smoothly. After several months, city manager Thompson received a letter from President Ross that demanded the police chief apologize to the aggrieved officers for "singling them out for investigation." Second, Ross asked the chief to set up an Equal Employment Opportunity Committee in the police department. Finally, he requested that the FPD rescind all punishment to the officers that the management had reassigned, terminated, or suspended for voicing concerns about racial discrimination.

The city manager seemed to ignore President Ross's demands. Eventually the NAACP leadership came to the realization that the city manager was unwilling to resolve the issue. So President Ross changed his tack. Like other minority representatives who have failed to resolve cases of discrimination through bureaucratic channels of government, the NAACP's leadership faced a dilemma: either let the issue die or take it into the public arena and risk angering white residents. Though the passage of the Civil Rights Act provided the NAACP the agencies necessary to fight for the aggrieved officers, it also reorganized racial politics in ways that created new limitations for black politics (see Reed 1999a). To be sure, formalizing protocols for dealing with racial discrimination dealt a blow to informal and arbitrary means for meting out punishment and coercion. However, it also made many political strategies and tactics illegitimate and has steadily confined racial discrimination cases to behind-the-scenes negotiations, outside of the public realm, and discouraged open protests and direct action (Smith 1996). Officials from the NAACP faced this catch-22 when it became clear the city manager would not meet the organizations' requests.

By the time the NAACP leaders had decided to take the issue to the city council, Floyd Yarborough had replaced Richard Ross as president of Fayetteville's NAACP.[5] As Richard Ross receded into the background, the local media focused attention on Floyd Yarborough.

Yarborough's biography draws attention to the ways the military shapes politics in Fayetteville. Most people in Fayetteville identify as "local" or as part of "the military." The contrast is important among whites as well as blacks. Many African Americans believe "locals" are more deferential to political authorities and unwilling to fight for racial equality than those who have served in the military and come from different parts of the country. Yarborough was unique in this regard. He was born in Fayetteville and retired from the army. Coming from Redbone, one of the city's older black neighborhoods, Yarborough escaped the deprivations of Jim Crow by joining the army. Oddly, Yarborough's retreat from the South's racial segregation took him no further than Fayetteville's city's limits— to Fort Bragg. Yarborough's life has spanned the city's Jim Crow segregation to the dismantlement of legal segregation. Fifty years of changes in the army and Fayetteville have shaped Yarborough's perspective and made him optimistic about the future of race relations. Yet he, like many black and white residents, believes Fayetteville's racism was especially harsh and unyielding. He still has vivid memories of local authorities strictly adhering to Jim Crow laws even after World War II, when soldiers from all over the country flooded the city, and of how the Ku Klux Klan had posted a billboard that welcomed visitors to the city as late as the early 1970s.[6]

Entering the council chambers, Yarborough and his two colleagues—Attorney William Wilson and civil rights adviser Bill Frederick—were prepared to face off against these forces whom they believed carried the seeds of resistance to racial reforms. He addressed the mayor and city council in a frank but cordial manner: "I would like to start by thanking you for the opportunity to address some very serious concerns that have been identified in the Fayetteville Police Department. However, before we do that, I would like to correct some of the statements that were printed in the *Fayetteville Observer*. . . . The paper quoted Chief Proctor as saying that he had not been apprised of any specific incidents of mistreatment. That is not correct."[7] Yarborough told council of the two letters his predecessor sent the city manager. Carefully navigating the racial codes, he clarified, "we are not here this evening to assess blame, nor are we pointing fingers. Instead, our purpose is to put the City Council on notice of the problems affecting African American officers and ask the council to join in our efforts to have these matters amicably resolved." He asserted that the department's "racially hostile work environment" was part of a broader pattern of "systemic" racism. He pointed out that the FPD not only failed to carry out the 1974 Superior Court consent decree but was seeking to dissolve it.[8]

Yarborough's claim of a racially hostile work environment was based on the cases of three officers: Alvin Harms, Sharon Jones, and Michael Sweeney. During questioning, investigator Sweeney told Proctor and the head of the Office of Professional Standards that the best avenue for African Americans to advance was in narcotics and vice, departments often associated with black crime. Officer Harms accused several white officers of being prejudiced against blacks; because of their prejudice, he reasoned, they passed him over for promotion. Sharon Jones told management the department discriminated against blacks and preferred whites. Following the interviews, Proctor punished all three officers: he transferred Sharon Jones to the night shift, moved Michael Sweeney to narcotics, and fired Alvin Harms. These officers responded to the disciplinary actions by hiring lawyers and filing complaints with the EEOC.

Attorney William Wilson elaborated on Yarborough's comments with fiery and damning rhetoric. Like his colleague, Wilson grew up in Fayetteville. He was much younger and did not speak with cordiality or deference. He owned a modest law practice and was the only lawyer willing to take the case, as most of the more prominent black firms stayed as far away as possible. Having little to lose, he blasted the police chief by equating his practices with the terrorism that characterized Jim Crow:

> There are major concerns that African-American officers are not promoted, are denied training opportunities, are denied work opportunities, and retaliated against when they attempt to raise issues about their working environment. More specifically, when an African-American officer has brought issues concerning the treatment of African-Americans in the department to the attention of management within the department, the adverse results against those officers complaining has been investigations, suspension, dismissals, involuntary transfers, and other forms of overt intimidation. This department has instituted a system of terror on African- American police officers that can only be rivaled by the inhumane treatments and tactics not experienced since the 1960s. African-American officers have been brought in by the department and interrogated, given lie detector tests, and intimidated for doing nothing more than stating that African Americans were not being treated fairly. . . .
> The United States Supreme Court observed that Title VII is violated when the work place is infiltrated with discriminatory intimidation, ridicule, and, or insults that are sufficiently severe or racist.[9]

Leaders of the NAACP closed their presentation by recommending a plan that would allow the city to comply with the Civil Rights Act. First, they urged the police department to stop all disciplinary actions taken against officers who exercised their Title VII rights. Second, they insisted that the FPD not use its Office of Professional Standards to intimidate officers who raised issues of discrimination. Third, they asked the city council to conduct an outside investigation of the department's personnel practices and to evaluate the department's progress in fulfilling the 1974 court decree.[10]

Haymount Hill

The NAACP's presentation connected the police department controversy to Fayetteville's history of racism. Implicitly, Yarborough and Wilson drew on local ideas of power. Despite Fayetteville's reputation as a "military town," most Fayettevillians look beyond Fort Bragg when they assess the city's racial problems and focus on the small neighborhood overlooking downtown called "the Haymount." Recent arrivals and local working classes—black as well as white—believe that the Haymount elite dominate politics. Regarding the controversy about racism in the FPD, many African Americans viewed it as deriving from the Haymount's hold on power. In local political discussions, the term *Haymount* refers to people who trace their ancestry to the city's origins and the prestigious neighborhood to the west of downtown. As the city's trade grew during the late eighteenth century, its expanding elite built large houses on the hill overlooking downtown and the neighborhood became synonymous with power.

Much like the aristocrats of Indianola, Mississippi, described by anthropologist Hortense Powdermaker in the 1930s, most people identified as "the Haymount" are not directly related to founding elite or a southern aristocracy. Though the aristocrats of the antebellum period mostly left the South, the idea of a southern aristocracy was important to the emergent authorities that built the New South on the vestiges of an old, aristocratic South (see Powdermaker 1939 [2010]). In Fayetteville, opponents of the dominant political structure used a similar image of an untouched aristocratic and insular elite entrenched in southern traditions. Indeed, many residents view Haymount Hill as the political establishment's core identity, thereby blocking out Fayetteville's more recent history with Fort Bragg. Invariably, all political discussions invoke the idea of "the Haymount"—also called the Haymount Crowd, the Hill, Olde Fayetteville, and the FFFs (First Families of Fayetteville). Most Fayettevillians believe that this small portion of their community wields too much power; and they blame it for the city's problems, from racism and crime to poor urban planning and badly performing public schools.

Defining the Threat

Fayetteville's white politicians and city administrators are used to having their decisions and programs reduced to southern stereotypes associated with the mythical Haymount. Longtime mayor J. G. Dawson saw this coming. After listening to President Yarborough, he attempted to nip that line of reasoning in the bud. Instead of southern tradition or values, he appealed to the formal principles of local government when he responded to the NAACP's presentation: "Of course I think everyone's aware of the council-manager form of government and I think that's pretty evident and pretty clear about that. And there are channels to go through . . . it's pretty clear cut on personnel matters the oaths that this city council takes."[11] The seemingly mundane declaration was crucial in the development of the controversy. He appealed to the symbolism that shrouds the mechanics of local government in the United States in two complementary ideals: democratic government and professional administration. Accordingly, the mayor held that city council serves a legislative role and to intervene into the implementation of policy would be an encroachment on the city manager's authority. He subtly questioned the legality of the NAACP's demands and countered the idea that "the Haymount" was making arbitrary decisions. Instead, he placed Thompson above the political fray, as the symbol of the community's values, which included a commitment to racial equality.

After the mayor's allusion to the principles of government, city manager Jim Thompson took the opportunity to explain his side of the story. Unable to hold back his frustration, he explained: "I was involved in the two meetings with the Fayetteville Branch of the NAACP. Let me first say that I have always, in the past, had the utmost respect and regard for the local chapter of the NAACP. I believe that we had expressed a willingness to sit down and discuss specific issues. I can tell you quite frankly that the tone that was expressed here tonight was not the tone that was expressed in those [previous] meetings. And I am a bit taken back by that." Conveying that the NAACP leadership betrayed him, he said that he offered the NAACP the opportunity to sit down and meet. He continued: "That offer stands. As far as rescission of any disciplinary action . . . I cannot and will not rescind disciplinary actions on the basis of complaints that have been filed by an *outside agency* when I have not even been given those specific complaints. We have procedures within the city. We have the grievance process, the personnel review board process. That process has been working and continues to work." He then laid out the basis of the dispute with the NAACP: "If city council has concerns about personnel matters, those matters need to be discussed with the manager."[12]

Though the NAACP's criticism of the city manager did not violate the council-manager form of government, this view spread through the media and became conventional wisdom. Against this sense that the NAACP sought to cut corners and skirt proper procedures, the notion of professional government emerged as the legitimate counterpoint to the claims of racism in the police department. By presenting the city manager as representative of the will of the people against minority threats, politicians and civic leaders created an image of the white majority, which sought to link all whites to a collective position of superiority (Hartigan 2005). Most important to this image of the majority was the way the NAACP was characterized as an "outside group" that held opposing interests. This maneuver, what sociologist Eduardo Bonilla-Silva calls "color-blind" language, heightens the sense of racial threat without overt racial language (Bonilla-Silva 2003).

Such images of whiteness, and its use of color-blind forms of racism, became compelling because they resonated with middle-class residents and business leaders who were committed to city manager Jim Thompson's policy agenda. As will be discussed below, since the 1970s Fayetteville's civic and business leadership has reorganized city government and its policy agenda to help diminish the city's notoriety as the military town captured in the term "Fayettenam," of which Thompson had been a central figure. Illustrating this sense of struggle to improve the city's image, the *Fayetteville Observer* quoted a fuming Chief Procter, who drew on this story of progress when he accused the NAACP of having "done more in ten minutes to destroy the reputation of this department than it took 13 years to build, and that's a shame."[13]

A great source of legitimacy for the city manager came from the *Fayetteville Observer*. The day following the NAACP's presentation, the editorial board added credence to the belief that the civil rights group was handling the issue of racism in a destructive manner: "If there is a 'racially hostile work environment' in the Fayetteville Police Department, as officials with the local chapter of the NAACP contend, all fair-minded people want it corrected. It's an awful charge, right up there with graft and police brutality. It is unreasonable, however, for the complainants to expect the department to accede to their demands, or even to acknowledge the existence of a problem, on the scant information made public so far."[14] The editorial illustrates important contours of racial politics after segregation. It embraces the ideal of racial equality and sympathizes with the issue of discrimination while it simultaneously exploits racial anxieties (see Bonilla-Silva 2001, 2003).

The city manager's position was further emboldened on talk radio. The morning radio show represented a venue for politicians and business leaders to rally support for the city manager and as a conduit to mobilize opposition to the NAACP. Like the *Fayetteville Observer*, WFNC Radio, also associated with an old Fayetteville family, played an important role in Fayetteville politics. Since businessperson Henry Rawls founded the station in 1940 and introduced talk radio to Fayetteville in the early 1970s, WFNC has been the mainstay of local politics.[15]

Its show *Top of the Morning* was a staple of politics, providing citizens and politicians with an interactive arena in which to debate local issues. *Top of the Morning* magnified the conflict as its hosts, Susan Jacobs and Scott Simpson, heralded the formal principles of the council-manager form of government as if it were naturally representative of the community. Presuming objectivity and an interest in only the facts, the hosts took the city manager's authority for granted as they assessed the NAACP's conduct.[16] Using race-neutral language, they were suspicious of the individual officers' characters and downplayed allegations of systemic racism in Fayetteville. Many callers used this logic to denigrate the "complainers" and to criticize the NAACP for "playing the race card." Information about the three police officers in question started to circulate in the media during the next two weeks, as supporters of the city manager and the police chief portrayed the black officers as inept and insubordinate. Media reports depicted one police officer in particular, Alvin Harms, as bungling, as well as immoral. News stories presented Harms's work record as a series of reckless transgressions; he was guilty of sexual harassment and denied promotion to motorcycle patrol because he "dropped his bike forty-one times during a two-hour [motorcycle training] session." In many of my own conversations about these claims of discrimination, opponents of the NAACP pinpointed specific failings in Harms's personnel record, especially "dropping the motorcycle forty times," to discredit the NAACP. Citing such faults as threats to public safety, many white Fayettevillians rationalized Chief Proctor's treatment of the officers and questioned the NAACP's motives.

Following two weeks of debate and rumor about the dispute in the police department, residents packed the council chambers. At 6:30 P.M., citizens, police officers, and members of the NAACP began flooding into the council chambers. The crowd was so big that the fire chief opened the auxiliary room, where the overflow watched the meeting on television. Producing an image of racial polarization, blacks filled the right-hand side of the chamber as they lined up behind the NAACP, while whites lined up behind the city manager. The segregated crowd anxiously awaited the city manager's official response to the complaints and city council's decision.

City manager Jim Thompson stepped before city council and began by criticizing the NAACP for its "inflammatory" rhetoric and personal attacks, which he believed were "creating racial animosity" in the community. Regarding the substance of the complaints, he refuted the claim that the FPD "harbored a racially hostile work environment." Instead, Thompson praised Chief Proctor's sterling record of fairness and the department's "aggressive affirmative action."[17] He also commended Chief Proctor for his "honest attempt" to resolve the issue of discrimination. Rather than presenting the dispute as a racial issue, he described it as a managerial problem that included investigating and disciplining white officers.[18] He reported that the three black officers in question had been "untruthful" and summed up:

> I really think it boils down to this: Yes, we have standards in the
> police department. And I think one of the standards we have to have
> for a police officer is a standard of truthfulness. We require police
> officers as part of their job, as a part of their duties, in fact, they're the
> only city employees that as a part of their job description is required
> to testify in court. We give these individuals the power of arrest and
> we give them the ability to use deadly force. . . . I think the facts of
> the case boil down to this: none of these three officers received any
> adverse treatment due to their race. If they received any adverse
> treatment at all, it was adverse treatment based upon their own

actions. This was not an issue of race; quite frankly it was an issue of character. With regard to any outside investigation of these maters: when we met with the representatives of the NAACP, we were informed that all *complaint ensuers* who came to the NAACP were referred to EEOC, Equal Employment Opportunity Commission.[19]

He concluded by assuring council that the EEOC was looking into the complaints, which he believed sufficed for an outside investigation. Thompson asserted: "we have a police department that has a solid record not just of equal opportunity and fairness but a solid record of affirmative action."[20] Turning Martin Luther King on his head, Thompson asserted that the controversy did not have to do with the skin color of the complaining officers, but with the content of their characters. He assured city council and the citizens of Fayetteville that their rights were being protected; he reminded the audience that the EEOC was looking into the complaints, which he believed was the type of third-party investigation that the leaders of the NAACP requested. He concluded: "We have a police department that has a solid record of affirmative action."

Thompson's rebuke of the NAACP set the stage for Milo McRae, a seventeen-year veteran of city government who traced his Fayettevillian ancestry to the antebellum period. As the drama unfolded, McRae played the role of the hard-liner. He was an enormous man who spoke with a distinct eastern North Carolina drawl and often antagonized black leaders.[21] Unnerved by the NAACP's accusations, he fired back. McRae had missed the previous meeting because his wife had undergone surgery. After reviewing a video of the meeting, he sought to explain to the citizens what was really going on: "I saw you all on TV trying to discredit him [Jim Thompson] by saying he knew about these things. Certainly he knew about them if he took part in the discussion, but he did not know the specific cases they were talking about." In reference to black city council member Frederick Walker, McRae said: "I think he wants Mr. Thompson's job. I saw another one who would like Chief Proctor's job. I mean maybe we should fire all these guys and let these council members take over their offices." He scolded his black colleagues and the NAACP for "trying to smear the Fayetteville Police Department." He closed by saying: "Mr. Mayor, I personally would like to make a motion, I would like to make a motion that we ask the three officers involved if they would permit us to print all this information. If they won't, then I think we need to talk to Mr. Boswell [the city attorney] about going ahead and doing it anyway. . . . I believe what I've seen substantiates the investigation by the police department, by the city manager, and I think everybody in this town needs to know who's right on this and who's not right."[22] Although many Fayettevillians associated him with the city's racist past, his appeal to the EEOC as "politically neutral" draws attention to major changes. In sharp contrast to the massive resistance of the 1950s, he was willing to give this federal agency the authority to decide this dispute.[23]

Though McRae had raised the stakes, as he attempted to widen the sense that the NAACP had run afoul, black council member Frederick Walker challenged him by presenting a substitute motion that would order the city manager to release "all relevant information" about the three officers in question, of which the results would be "binding on the City staff and the affected departments."[24]

With the substitute motion on the table, council debate intensified as the meeting passed midnight. Council members Janet Chaney and Gerald Hodges backed McRae. They added eloquence to his point as they attempted to be less polarizing in manner. As a professor of political science at Methodist College, Chaney argued that "we are elected representatives of the citizens and we certainly have a responsibility to do our part in governing the city." After a "very careful reading" of the documents, she concluded: "We have seen evidence of a tight ship in the police department . . . we have an outside, unquestionably unbiased agency, the EEOC, already coming in to investigate this. . . . I don't see discrimination. I see unhappy employees and employees being held to a standard. I don't feel comfortable in voting to take this any further. . . . I encourage council to think that we aren't investigators; we are here to use information that we have. We have channels to go through and let's stay with the channels. As far as an investigation, it is being done."[25]

Reinforcing Chaney's more moderate position, Mayor Pro-Tem Gerald Hodges began his argument by acknowledging President Yarborough and his wife, Annie, as friends of twenty years. He asked why both sides could not agree. He then alluded to a "rumor" about a group of lawyers out to get the chief. To clear up the political struggle, he sought to distinguish "political accountability" from "political interference." He continued: "But evidently there's perception in the management of the police department that some folks are out to get them, and also that this may be a guise for the real agenda. I hope that's not the case. I'm here to listen about a complaint or complaints represented by the NAACP of this county. I'm not here for any other agenda item. And if there is a hidden agenda, I would be, as I already stated to the press yesterday, very, very disappointed."[26]

Bringing Hodge's fear to life, white council member Tom Manning argued that the documents showed that the FPD had a serious problem that required an objective and professional review. He also warned that the EEOC is not a third party. Instead, he argued, the EEOC would sue the city. An outside investigation could mitigate the suit, he said, recalling the incident in which Sims sued the city for $800,000. Along with Tom Manning, white council member Sam Johnson bolted from the white majority and joined his black colleagues Larry Allison, Edna Harrington, and Frederick Walker. Suddenly, Fayetteville's most powerful civic and political leaders had lost control of the board. Now, the new majority—who would be known infamously as "the Five"—controlled city council, which launched the black council members into the dominant position of authority. To many, it appeared as if black council members Allison, Harrington, and Walker were in control of city government.

Conspiracy Theories

With white council members Tom Manning and Sam Johnson joining their black colleagues to create a "new majority," rumors of the hidden agenda and conspiracies exploded.[27] As far as the supporters of city management and the police chief were concerned, the cat was out of the bag. Chief Proctor responded to the power shift by telling reporters that the courthouse faction he had been warring with about DWI cases was behind the transfer of power. He said these allegations of racial discrimination were a pretext to force him out of office so they could retake control of their DWI industry. Leading the faction, according to his story, was Billy Manning, an attorney who had been vocal in condemning the chief's new tactics regarding drunk driving cases. Giving the rumors of conspiracy resonance, Billy Manning was the brother of council member Tom Manning and brother-in-law of council member Sam Johnson. Rumors spread of Billy Manning orchestrating the "Five–Four" split.

Reporting and editorials in the *Fayetteville Observer* supported the rumors. In an article entitled "Ex-Judge Wants Proctor's Ouster: Conspiracy Suspicion Denied," the newspaper reported that attorney Manning wanted Chief Proctor out of office and underlined his connection to council members Manning (his brother) and Johnson (his brother-in-law), and stated that he was running for district attorney. In the article, Billy Manning candidly discussed his dislike for the chief, saying "he should go" because he had lost his effectiveness. He believed "the citizens of Fayetteville would be better served by a new police chief." However, he denied that "his dislike of the chief constitutes a conspiracy."[28]

Manning's denial seemed to validate the conspiracy theories as they gained force. Conspiracy theories are a powerful way for residents to understand the complex plays of power that characterize urban politics in a large city. Conspiracy theories about the Manning family made intelligible a complex set of forces that came together to produce a shift in power. As many anthropologists have pointed out, conspiracy theories are an integral type of cultural knowledge in modern states that give people a way to understand the opaque workings of power (Boyer 2006; Briggs 2004; Silverstein 2002). In this case, Fayettevillians learned about the shift in power in a powerful and unambiguous way. As the theory explained, Billy Manning had put his brother and brother-in-law in office so that they could unite with the blacks and take control of city council. The three black council members, as the story went, agreed to get rid of Chief Proctor if the Mannings replaced the city manager with an African American. Additionally, William Manning would serve as counsel for two of the officers who brought their concerns to the NAACP.

Rumors of conspiracy supplanted the NAACP's complaints about racism with hysteria about the Manning family's hidden agenda. Most importantly, it mobilized perceptions of crisis in ways that diagnosed the uncertainty: unscrupulous white politicians were using the black community (and its power derived from the successes of the civil rights movement) to take control of the city. The tale diagnosed the problem in terms of the threat this biracial alliance unleashed. Protagonists used rumors to tell a troubling story about how the normally powerless black council members, under the negative influence of Tom Manning and his cronies, had taken control of the city government. Such conspiracy theories are illustrated by a retired postal worker's explanation of the drama to me: "See, you have a lawyer, Billy Manning, who wants to be DA. He was a judge and is an enemy of Chief Proctor. So he put his brother, Tom Manning, and brother-in-law, Sam Johnson, on City Council to get rid of Chief Proctor. Normally the blacks are a farce on city council, but when these two boys fall in with the niggers, you got power! That's what all these folks are mad about: the Manning boys are using the blacks for their personal gain."

Conspiracy theories about the Manning family and DWI lawyers manipulating the black community mobilized perceptions of crisis.[29] Moreover, tales of conspiracy widened the sense of breach represented by the NAACP's demands that putatively jeopardized the council-manager form of government. The rumors exaggerated the power of these enemies by conjuring a secret group of trial lawyers who had used the black community to assert their control over the city and subvert self-government. By transforming the Mannings into enemies that had undermined the majority's will and unleashed the black community, conspiracy theories underwrote the city manager's authority and his policy agenda. The complexities of city government, civil rights laws, and economic concerns of city government were mapped into a coherent narrative: the master plot of the Manning Boys.

The conspiracy theory was compelling because attorney Billy Manning and the chief had been feuding. Moreover, attorney Manning had represented two of the black police officers who had accused Police Chief Proctor of racist personnel practices. Supporters of the police chief and city manager easily made the connection between the attorney's presumed ambitions and his brother and brother-in-law's support of the NAACP. The *Fayetteville Observer* ran a series of editorials that developed this theory. On January 14, it increased pressure on the new council majority by publishing a piece entitled "Marked Deck: Two Councilmen Should Recuse from Probe." The editorial asserted that the council was incapable of "delivering what the local chapter of the NAACP says it wants: an 'impartial' inquiry" into complaints of discrimination in the police department; thus "the Five's" two white council members should recuse themselves from the investigation:

> Fayetteville lawyer Bill Manning, a candidate for district attorney, has represented two of the officers whose files the Council agreed to review. In the past four months, Manning, who is candid about his eagerness to oust Chief Dan Proctor, has represented those two and three other complainants. Manning says he has discussed it with every member of the council—including his brother Tom and Tom's brother-in-law, Sam Johnson. Both of them voted to have the council investigate matters that had already been brought to the attention of the Equal Employment Opportunity Commission. Yet Lawyer Manning says that this doesn't make for a conspiracy. . . . For the record, Tom Manning and Sam Johnson were not at liberty to abstain from voting once the proposal to investigate came before the council, although there was no rule requiring them to vote as they did. But they can recuse from participation in the investigation. They should. Otherwise, there is little likelihood that the council's investigation will be impartial, and none at all that it will be perceived as such.[30]

The alliance between the Mannings and the black council members weakened the NAACP's claims, the newspaper argued, since the Mannings' quest for power had nothing to do with fighting racism. News reporting and rumors came together to transform the Manning family into an enemy that threatened the city's well-being.

Conclusion

The NAACP's complaint about racism in the police department stemmed from a history of struggle to implement civil rights reforms. Civic and business leaders countered these claims by presenting their public criticism of racism as a breach in the proper forms of race relations. Using color-blind language and the ideals of civil rights, they raised the specter of racial unrest to oblige the NAACP to follow the proper channels of government. As the NAACP continued on its quest and convinced a biracial majority of city council to uphold their concerns, civic leaders and administrators focused their attention on the two white council members who supported them. Using the idea of conspiracy, they transformed their loss of power into a specter of crisis whereby the Mannings had transgressed proper modes of race relations and given the black community an inordinate amount of power. The city manager and his supporters on city council used the idea of race to naturalize his political regime and the decisions he made, as if they transcended politics. He used the bureaucratic language of professional government to connect his political decisions with a deeper collectivity represented by race. Most importantly, this showed how racial ideas are equally concerned with policing white behavior and regulating cross-racial relations.

Chapter 2

Conspiracies and
Crises on Cape Fear

Rumors of the Manning conspiracy sent shock waves through Fayetteville as white civic and business leaders presented their loss of power as a dangerous alteration in the normal workings of government. By presenting the sudden ascendance of black council members into the majority as if it represented a dangerous turning point that could threaten the city, white civic and business leaders drew upon a rich political tradition of cultivating and mobilizing white racial fears, a tradition that extends back to the era of slavery. Cities like Fayetteville, throughout the plantation zone of the Caribbean and southern United States, have been continuously rocked by racial hysterias since their founding. Racial fears developed in relation to the slave laws that restricted people of African descent to servility and agricultural labor. Despite all-encompassing slave laws, authorities never fully dominated slaves. No matter how degraded, slaves held an independent consciousness and were often aware of weaknesses in authority (Davis 2003, 6–7). Authorities had to contend with the fact that slaves were humans who exercised their own volition and sought many ways to resist their condition.

Awareness of slave resistance was complicated by other political problems involving non-slaveholding whites. Slaveholders and political authorities faced constant dissent from poor whites as well as other competing white factions. At moments of heightened conflict or economic uncertainty, white political factions often resorted to fears about slave rebellion to create a powerful image in order to unify whites across class divisions. This chapter will describe how fear about slave insurrection gradually developed into a political ritual whereby competing white factions periodically appealed to fantasies of plotting slaves, reckless abolitionists, and untamed free blacks to produce frightening images of crisis. This chapter describes the evolution of this ritual form, highlighting how, at each new historical juncture following slavery, civic and political leaders found new ways to orchestrate racial fears to compel whites to look past class differences and accept their authority and economic agendas. In this light, we will see that the "Five–Four" represents a broader phenomenon of public events: flashpoints when anxieties about racial changes become ignited to create frenzy. Such periodic displays of power and anxiety are a key characteristic of North American racial politics; during these moments of change, authorities project their hopes and fears. Rather than merely reflecting racial norms, these frenzies are created by political groups to shape political institutions and define proper relations between blacks and government.

Racism and the Rise of Cape Fear

Politics of racial fear, exemplified by the Manning conspiracy theories, must be placed in the context of Fayetteville's history of slavery. The city's formation started about one hundred miles away, at the mouth of the Cape Fear River, when powerful plantation owners from South Carolina began building a port town in 1725. North Carolina had remained largely untouched by plantation slavery until the colonial governor of North Carolina granted Maurice Moore, a wealthy plantation owner from South Carolina, 325 acres near the mouth of the Cape Fear River. Coming from one of the wealthiest families in South Carolina, Moore brought considerable plantation capital, slaves, and political power to his endeavor to economically develop the Cape Fear Valley. He and his brother Roger used their land grants to build an ocean-going port. Naming their settlement Brunswick, the Moores envisioned a great seaport that would unlock the Cape Fear Valley, and its hinterland, to the lucrative trade with the British Isles and the West Indies (Wood 2004, 15–16). Brunswick, where the Cape Fear River empties into the Atlantic Ocean, provided North Carolina its last hope for building an ocean port. Commerce would follow the path of the Cape Fear to its navigation head at Fayetteville, and the river became North Carolina's primary channel of trade (Brewer 1949, 6–7).

In launching Cape Fear society, the Moore family vigorously promoted Cape Fear as a slave colony and recruited wealthy plantation owners from South Carolina and the Albemarle Sound of North Carolina. With the plantation as the central mode of settlement and economic development, the Cape Fear Valley developed with a distinct social and economic structure. As sociologist Edgar Thompson argues, plantations represented a highly specialized organization for the production of commodities of coffee, sugar, tea, and cotton for an overseas market (Thompson 1932 [2010]). As an economic institution, the plantation unleashed an "industrial dynamic" on the lands, as it organized land and labor systematically. More than commodity production, plantations were also political institution that colonizers like the Moores used for settling and distributing a new population throughout the hinterland of North Carolina. Edgar Thompson points out that plantations operated as small states, with an authoritarian structure, whereby plantation owners claimed a monopoly of violence over the life of the people who lived on the plantation. These features came together in its role as a cultural institution as it systematized the political and economic functions in a way of life where hierarchy was organized ethnically and racially, which led Edgar Thompson to argue that the plantation was a "race- making situation" (1975 [1955], 31–38; see Trouillot 2002, 115–117; Mintz and Baca 2010).[1]

Following this pattern of political and economic development, plantation owners from South Carolina brought large teams of slaves as they gobbled up massive tracts of land at the mouth of the Cape Fear River. From the beginning, slaves were part of the pioneering group of settlers. Due to poor soils, however, the Moores failed to duplicate the grand rice and indigo plantations that made the South Carolina lowcountry very profitable.[2] Gradually, planters turned their attention to the Cape Fear Valley's vast pine forests for the production of "naval stores"—tar, pitch, and turpentine. Britain's maritime empire required large amounts of tar and pitch to preserve ships from decay. Significant quantities of longleaf pine, large numbers of slaves, and the desperate need for exportable staples promoted the Lower Cape Fear's rapid growth (Wood 2004, 187).

As planters used slaves to transform the pine barrens of North Carolina into an industrial- like zone of production, they implemented racial ideas and legal codes to systematize people of African descent with plantation labor (Fields 1990). Racial ideas were used to make black servility as if it were a fact of natural history. Authorities used these ideas to not only define Africans as "different" from Europeans, but crucially, they characterized Africans as the opposite of the Enlightenment ideal of humans as bearers of universal rights (Trouillot 1995, 77–94). With this historical development in place, race and racism, accordingly, cannot be viewed simply as an aberration or a moral dilemma in American history. Instead, racist ideas were crafted to make slavery congruent with liberty by ascribing moral and intellectual features to a phenotype that disqualified people of African descent from otherwise unalienable rights (Fields 1990).

Inferiority of blacks became captured in the image of Sambo: docile yet irresponsible. The slave's loyalty was constantly compromised by laziness, dishonesty, and silliness. Such moral and intellectual deficiencies required special rules and regulations.[3] Institutions were built on the ideal of a paternal relationship between master and slave—one of utter dependence and child-like attachment. The other side of the equation was the fear about slaves when they were not properly cared for (see Davis 2003; Trouillot 2002). Elaborating this side of racial stereotypes were the slave codes that preceded the settling of Cape Fear, as planters in the northeast of the state—the Albemarle Sound—had created North Carolina's slave code. North Carolina authorities made their first attempt to formalize restrictions on slave behavior amid the political struggles with the French and Spanish governments when some colonists suggested arming slaves to help defend the colony against hostilities. One planter helped create a sense of alarm when he warned, "there must be great caution used, lest our slaves . . . might become our masters" (Crow 1977, 19). Such fears of "Negro Domination" were codified in the 1715 statute "An Act Concerning Servants and Slaves," which represented colonial North Carolina's first of many attempts to codify constraints on black conduct. Slave codes would change over the years; yet, in their many forms, they always asserted that peaceful relations, morality, and prosperity required careful guidance and control of blacks (ibid.). Slave codes forbade slaves from traveling outside the planter's authority, outlawed miscegenation, discouraged manumission, and forbade slaves from gathering.[4]

Racial beliefs of the plantation system structured the development of the Cape Fear economy in ways that transcended black behavior as thousands of poor whites began pouring into the valley. Within a decade of its founding, Brunswick was being challenged by the rival port town of Wilmington. Located fifteen miles closer to the backcountry, Wilmington surpassed Brunswick and became the center of Cape Fear's mercantile system. Such commercial success inspired Wilmington's merchants and planters to sponsor settlements further up the Cape Fear River. Using the river's far-reaching network of waterways, Highland Scots poured into the Upper Cape Fear and built modest farms and settlements throughout the longleaf pine country, reaching more than one hundred miles upriver.[5]

Massive settlement of Scottish immigrants led to the emergence of Cross Creek, later renamed Fayetteville in honor of the French partisan of the American Revolution, Marquis de Lafayette. Fayetteville attracted many settlers, farmers, and merchants who joined the expansion of the Cape Fear plantation economy from the northern colonies of Virginia, Maryland, and Pennsylvania. Lacking decent roads, much of the North Carolina hinterland sent its goods and commerce to South Carolina, as the inland farmers largely traded with merchants in Charleston. The colonial assembly encouraged the expanding commercialism by aggressively building roads, communication networks, and other infrastructure that would allow trade with North Carolina's Piedmont farmers (Merrens 1964). New roads linked the Cape Fear River to the Piedmont, making Fayetteville and Wilmington the "nucleus of the state's industrial and commercial structure" (Brewer 1953, 155). Together the merchant and plantation elite in both cities represented a powerful coalition, deeply committed to the system of slavery that would dominate North Carolina politics throughout the antebellum period.[6]

Haitian Revolution and Slave Insurrection Panics

Fantasies of content and complacent slaves came crashing down in 1791, when the slaves of Saint Domingue revolted and launched the Haitian Revolution (1791–1804).[7] To be sure, the revolution was a watershed in the Americas, with far-reaching effects on racial politics and revolutionary movements. As slaves destroyed France's most profitable colony, they also tore down the mythology that slaves were naturally accustomed to slavery (Trouillot 1995, 72). However, the extraordinary feats of the black revolutionaries did not challenge the intellectual bases of racism. Rather, the events became interpreted as an orgy of violence, rape, and destruction. To see it as anything else—let alone part of the broader movement that produced the French and American Revolutions—was "unthinkable" (ibid.). Though the slave revolt was at odds with the deeply held beliefs about the sub-humanity of Africans, the planters did not abandon their conviction. Instead, plantation owners and authorities throughout the Americas crafted new interpretations of slave behavior that forced the reality of the Haitian Revolution back within the scope of these beliefs (ibid.).

Over the next fifty years, proponents of slavery devised "new formulas to repress" the horrifying threat of the slave revolt "and to bring it back within the realm of accepted discourse" (Trouillot 1995, 72). Rather than accepting that slaves had the intellectual capacities for attaining their freedom, Western onlookers came to view the Haitian Revolution as an "unfortunate repercussion of planters' miscalculations" or the result of the negative influences of "outside agitators" (Trouillot 1995, 90–91). In such a way, the news of the events generated rational fears as well as fits of paranoia among slaveholders. Fearful images of marauding slaves became used for a variety of arguments that led to a more anxious and reactionary approach to policing slaves.

Many researchers have examined how the Haitian Revolution inspired black politics in the hemisphere.[8] An equally important yet less talked-about result of the Haitian Revolution was the way in which slaveholders, their enemies, and governmental authorities in the New World responded to the

events. As the first stories of slave revolution circulated through the trading
and communication networks in the Atlantic World, authorities focused on
the events of Saint Domingue. In the U.S. South, embattled planters began
seeing threats to their authority everywhere. Many newspapers began spreading fearful stories about the volatility of Fayetteville's and Wilmington's large
slave populations, and, as historian Rosser Taylor pointed out many years ago,
such narratives dominated North Carolinian politics: "A casual perusal of the
public prints of North Carolina from about 1792 to 1808 will convey unmis-
takably the conviction that the whites of Eastern Carolina entertained the
liveliest fear of West Indian negroes. The negro insurrection in Haiti and San
Domingo in the 'nineties of the eighteenth century, attended as it was by the
most horrible atrocities, thoroughly alarmed the whites, not only of North
Carolina, but of all the seaboard slaveholding states" (Taylor 1928, 29).
Despite these fears, Taylor points out: "As to insurrections in North Carolina,
there were none; as to conspiracies, there were a few; but, as to rumors of conspiracies and insurrections, there were a multitude" (ibid.).[9]

The rumors of conspiracies and insurrections that Taylor identifies point
us to the way new forms of prosecuting black insurgency developed.[10] Fear of
slave revolts became increasingly pervasive as it became a political tool for
creating white solidarity. Amid deep political divisions among whites, political leaders periodically used fear of slave rebellion to rally white citizens into
frenzied vigilance against enemies of the community, resulting in the ritual
pattern known as "the slave insurrection scare" (Carter 1976; Wyatt-Brown
1982). Many historians have taken these rumors of conspiracy as proof of how
"whites" were "haunted" by the specter of slave revolt. Rather than revealing
white fears, these episodes of agitation were conditioned by political struggles
between white factions and political classes. Slave panics entwined with
planters' fears from other quarters of slave society—non-slaveholding whites,
free blacks, reformers, and abolitionists. Using horrific images of slaves killing
and raping, authorities could mobilize whites across class lines to a frenzied
vigilance against enemies of the community, diverting their attention from
bitter conflicts about economic policy. Authorities manipulated these fears to
produce a standing ambience of fear that discouraged political dissent among
whites, leading to an endless fantasy of conspiracy, often where it did not
exist. Politicians and planters used alarm to demand that all whites conform
to racial orthodoxy and commit to the racial superiority as part of their duty to
search out those who threatened society (Wyatt-Brown 1982).

News of the Haitian Revolution led to significant political changes in
Fayetteville. In 1792, white citizens became incited by fears of a looming
slave rebellion. Although there are few records of the events, Fayetteville and

North Carolina authorities changed laws and created new institutions to deal with the threat and created the Fayetteville Independent Light Infantry (FILI), and the federal government responded to this heightened concern of slave insurrection by setting up a small federal arsenal (Parker 1990, 42). Throughout the South, these types of local militias proliferated and served largely as slave patrols (Hadden 2001).

Panics would recur throughout the 1790s and inspired vast legal changes.[11] Lawmakers restricted immigration of West Indian slaves, believing revolutionary events in the Caribbean had poisoned slaves with such ideas of *liberté* and *égalité*, the mottos of the French Revolution.[12] In 1794, the state legislature banned importing slaves into North Carolina and gave the FILI new authority to police slave behavior. The law stipulated that patrollers should increase their scrutiny of black quarters and granted them new powers to punish blacks who were off of their owners' land without papers (Taylor 1928, 21; Hadden 2001). Although North Carolina authorities sympathized with white refugees of Saint Domingue, they viewed slaves from the West Indies as "particularly objectionable for the reason that they were liable to be inoculated with ideas of freedom and, once in the State, might prove incendiary in an otherwise peaceable Negro population" (Taylor 1926, 25).

Such legislative action contributed to the further propagation of conspiracy theories. Rumors of conspiracy could engulf the entire South at moments of political uncertainty, economic depression, or divisive struggles among whites. For example, the slave revolt scares of 1800–1802 developed at a time when blacks were becoming increasingly assertive and as white dissenters associated with the Great Awakening were pushing for reforms in slavery (Crow 1980). In the case of the famous Denmark Vesey conspiracy, an economic depression related to the decline of cotton yields was deeply dividing whites in Charleston, South Carolina (Johnson 2001). It was in the face of political division that local and state authorities commonly focused on slave behavior, both to divert attention away from factional struggles and to create a sense of crisis, allowing them to better mobilize the various white factions with calls for white solidarity. Politicians and planters, relying on fear, could demand group conformity and particularly the allegiance of all whites to the greater notion of race superiority as part of their obligation to discover and weed out those who threatened society. Unsurprisingly, authorities usually discovered that the originators of imagined conspiracies were their traditional enemies: abolitionists, nonconformist white southerners, and free blacks (Carter 1976, 350).

Each slave insurrection panic, much like the "Five–Four," emerged suddenly, polarizing the community along the lines of good and evil. In this sense, slave panics materialized as the type of events that anthropologist

Victor Turner calls social dramas (Turner 1957; 1974). As public events, slave insurrection panics came together as events from *perceived* breaches. Rather than following from a structural logic, political actors created these images of breach during political struggles. As a social drama, slave insurrection panics often started from rumors about slaves conspiring to overthrow and kill whites. Such rumors often fell flat when poor non- slaveholding whites would volunteer information. Slaveholders and the dominant authorities often doubted and despised lower-class whites. During moments of conflict between white political factions, however, rumors of conspiracy seem to have been more likely to be accepted as true.[13] The panic and excitement associated with the mobilization of slave patrols, which included marching and beating of drums, helped to escalate the sense of breach to the level of crisis. Patrols heightened concern and anxiety among whites and terrified blacks. The slightest perception of insolent behavior, show of lack of deference to whites, or advance in black rights could trigger such suspicions. Sensational—even if improbable— stories of elaborate plots to assassinate whites, of stockpiles of weapons, and of organized regiments of slaves waiting to pounce on the community were able to acquire credibility in an atmosphere of anxiety (Baca 2009).

Such hysteria could rapidly spiral out of control and threaten the slaveholders because the widening sense of panic gave poor whites license to harm or even kill slaves, inflicting real property damage upon the planter class. With the rise of panic, authorities sought to halt the frenzy and reassert control over the situation in the name of tradition and community values. Once patrollers uncovered the plot, however exaggerated and unlikely, they brought the conspirators to justice: the authorities initiated what Victor Turner (1974) calls redressive mechanisms—actions designed to provide an authoritative explanation of what occurred and assert a view of the relationship of insurrection to the community. Accordingly, authorities acted both to contain the threat of whites panicking and to project an image of unified action against the conspiracy, often "[staging] a theater of public power" in which they "magnified both the strength of the state and the impotence of the captured conspirators" (Sidbury 1997b, 123).

Racial Panics after Freedom

After the Civil War, the slave insurrection panic became modified to meet the new demands of a world without slaves. Fayetteville's power grew during the war because the city's transportation linkages were crucial to the Confederate war effort (Watson 1991). When the state of North Carolina captured the federal arsenal in 1861, Fayetteville became an important arms supplier for the Confederate Army (Barrett 1963, 24–27). A week before the takeover of the arsenal, the Confederate Army seized a federal gun factory in Harper's Ferry, Virginia, and sent the confiscated weapon-producing machines to Fayetteville, where the Confederacy could better protect the state-of-the-art equipment. By October of 1861, the Confederate Army had converted the Fayetteville Arsenal into a gun factory, rendering the plant into the Confederate States of America's Arsenal and Armory (ibid.).

During the notorious "March to the Sea," General William T. Sherman made Fayetteville pay for its actions during the war and sent sixty-five thousand Union troops to the city and its surrounding Cumberland County. As one account described, the Union troops "dynamited the arsenal, burned the *Fayetteville Observer* office, and sacked the town."[14] In total, the war destroyed the city's major roads, bridges, and mills, driving capital away and inaugurating a long period of instability, violence, and poverty.

As local authorities struggled to rebuild the city's economy, wealthy whites faced major challenges from newly enfranchised slaves. With Fourteenth and Fifteenth Amendment rights, African Americans held the promise of becoming a significant political force. Representing 50 percent of Fayetteville's population, they indeed held the balance of power in terms of electoral politics. Responding to this reality, dominant white political leaders began reviving slave codes and enforcing city ordinances forbidding blacks to meet in public (Parker 1990, 81; see Kousser 1974). Using fraud and intimidation, political authorities restricted black electoral power in order to form a coalition of poor whites, medium-size planters, and businessmen, as well as the wealthiest families in Fayetteville and Cumberland County.

Refashioning of racial ideas for the new demands of free labor and industrialization manifested in new conspiracy theories as competing white factions actively refashioned slave insurrection panics into new narratives of racial threat. Postwar rumors of conspiracy replaced the old enemies of slavery (abolitionists and free blacks) with a new coterie of enemies: federal agents, carpetbaggers, and scalawags contaminating blacks with ideas of freedom and social equality. In the place of the slave rebel arose the black rapist who focused attention on white women. Anxieties and frustrations erupted in racial panic in 1867, when Fayetteville authorities arrested a black drayman, Archie Beebe, for assaulting a young white woman, Elvina Massey. A large crowd formed around the Market House during a magistrate's hearing. When a sheriff escorted Beebe from the hearing, an "unknown hand" left Beebe dead (Parker 1990).

These new forms of racial fear played a decisive role in the elections of 1868. Mobilizing against the federal occupation, Fayetteville's Conservative

Party created a racial panic with rumors about how the freed slaves had caused the failures of the southern economy and Reconstruction reforms. Revised rumors of racial fear coupled with the language of religious redemption to mobilize perceptions of crisis in the form of rumors of power-hungry blacks being empowered and emboldened by conniving carpetbaggers. In the face of these threats to civility and order, Conservatives promised to redeem the state. Underlying the calls for racial solidarity were planters' and industrialists' attempts to restore their fortunes and reduce freedmen to the servility of slavery. In addition to the racial scare, authorities fine-tuned another element from the slave insurrection crises, vigilantes. Conservatives used the Ku Klux Klan as the successor of the slave patrol and as its terrorist wing (Hadden 2001).

Despite the racial panics of 1867, the Republican Party won most of the North Carolina votes in 1868, striking fear into the Democratic elite (Kantrowitz 1998, 102). Moreover, the Republicans won in Cumberland County, sending a sobering message about the difficulties of creating white solidarity amid the poverty and depression that plagued the county. Decades earlier, slaveholders had labeled abolitionists as dangerous extremists who incited blacks into becoming vicious insurrectionists. Now, many white southerners, who suffered poverty and experienced horrible deprivations, were increasingly more willing to ally themselves with blacks (ibid.). They viewed the Republican Party as a biracial alternative to the ex-slave aristocracy's Conservative Party.

Over the next three decades, North Carolina Democrats successfully used racial fears of rebellion to deny blacks the vote. They devised "racial settlement" to wipe out hostile class-based political groups by disfranchising African Americans and poor whites (Kantrowitz 1998). Economically dependent on black labor, Fayetteville's leaders embraced these designs as they rejected African American citizenship rights because of their purported threat to racial balance. If the southern elite allowed African Americans to have citizenship rights, then they would hold the balance of power between contending groups of white people. If authorities succeeded in stripping blacks of their rights, they would control competing white factions. Settling the future of African Americans in the New South inevitably also meant settling the future of white people (Fields 2001).

Racial Redemption and Riots

Fear that blacks, if not held in their place, would create disorder and violence remained the centerpiece of the emerging Democratic Party's control of North Carolina's legislature. Democratic leaders used racial fears as a cover for their policies and legislation that protected the agrarian elite of southeastern counties like Cumberland County from class-based alliances (Prather 1984, 34–5). Nevertheless, Democratic authority remained flimsy in many places like Fayetteville, as poverty drove many white farmers, sharecroppers, and even small planters out of the Democratic Party and to the Populist Party in the 1880s. Populists searched for new alternatives to laissez-faire policies and even sought federal intervention into the southern agricultural economy. Realizing that success would require crossing racial boundaries, the Populist Party created alliances with black Republicans in what they called the "Fusionist strategy" for the 1894 elections.

In Cumberland County, Cyrus Murphy, an ex-Confederate soldier, chaired the county's Populist convention and organized the plan for fusion with the Republicans (Parker 1990, 86). Fusionists swept every office in Cumberland County and triumphed in many parts of the state. In power, the Fusionists tore apart the Democratic Party's electoral mechanisms that disfranchised poor whites and blacks; they restored local elections and reintroduced popular elections (Prather 1998, 18–19). In 1896, strengthened by a considerable number of black voters, the Fusionists swept the major offices statewide as well as the governorship.[15]

North Carolina's Democratic leaders endeavored to industrialize the state, and they viewed the Fusionists as their key obstacle. Anxious to retake control of state government, a dynamic group of leaders prepared for the 1898 election by devising a strategy that would destroy the biracial solidarity that dominated state politics. Leading the way, the Democratic Party's chair, Furnifold Simmons, enlisted Josephus Daniels, the editor of the *Raleigh News and Observer*, to orchestrate a statewide white supremacy campaign. Drawing on the underlying racial fears that remained in the minds of many followers of the Fusion Party (see Gaither 2005), Daniels spread stories that presented the Fusion government as a dangerous conspiracy that unleashed black violence. Focusing the media blitz on eastern North Carolina's black majority counties, they published stories of insolent Negroes disrespecting whites in public (Prather 1998, 21). By flooding the state with tales of "Negro Domination," Simmons and Daniels carefully framed Fusionist reforms as a crisis in government that unleashed chaos.[16] They used these stories to create horrifying images of marauding blacks, drunk with power, invading white homes and assaulting the sanctity of white women (Gilmore 1998).

Fayetteville's Democratic Party supported the white supremacy campaign as planters and industrialists sought to end their ongoing conflict with the farmers in the western portion of the city and county—the backbone of the Fusion alliance. Joining the bandwagon of white supremacy, Cumberland

County Democrats raised fears of "Negro Domination" to bring rural whites back into the party. In February of 1898, the *Fayetteville Observer* claimed itself as "the leading advocate in North Carolina of the policy of turning out the present Goldbug-Fusion Government, now disgracing the state, by a reunion of whites whom [former Governor Zebulon] Vance led to victory. It is for WHITE REUNION against BLACK FUSION" (cited in Phillips 2002, 104–106).[17]

As the white supremacy movement gathered momentum throughout North Carolina, Democratic leaders finally found an instance of black inso‐ lence that allowed them to create a powerful image of racial crisis. In August of 1898, Alexander Manly—the publisher of the black newspaper in Wilmington—wrote an editorial decrying the famous Rebecca Felton. Felton had written about the black threat and she implored white men to protect their women; she asserted the threat to white women was so great that white men should "lynch a thousand times a week if necessary" to protect white women from black men. Manly rebuked Felton in an editorial. He agreed that "if the alleged crimes of rape were . . . so frequent . . . her plea would be wor‐ thy of consideration." He pointed out, however, that not every white women who cried rape told the truth, nor was every sexual contact between black men and white women rape. In fact, many black men were "sufficiently attractive for white girls of culture and refinement to fall in love with them, as is well known to all" (Prather 1998, 23).

Democratic leaders pounced as they reprinted Manly's editorial. Distorting its meaning, they added such sensational headlines as "Negro Editor Slanders White Women," "Negro Defamers of White Women," and "Infamous Attack on White Women" (ibid.). Fayetteville's Democratic Party participated in spinning Manly's editorial to alarm whites. On October 20, 1898, Cumberland County's Democratic leaders used this sign of black threat to rally whites across class lines. Crowds of white residents filled the streets, producing the image that all whites of the Upper Cape Fear had "left the plow, the machine shops, the kitchen, nay, the very neighborhood schoolroom," to rally against Negro Domination.[18] South Carolina's Senator Benjamin Tillman, leader of the white supremacy campaign that disfranchised the state's blacks, joined Fayetteville's Democrats (Kantrowitz 2001). With the Red Shirts, his terrorist group, he helped raise the ire of whites. Fayetteville's mayor, Democratic chair, and the editor of the *Fayetteville Observer*, welcomed Senator Tillman (Prather 1998, 24–25). Arriving amid the boom of cannons, the master of ceremonies introduced Tillman to the crowd as "the liberator of South Carolina." Thanking the audience for the warm welcome, Tillman bitterly railed against President Grover Cleveland, Alex Manly, blacks,

Republicans, and Fusion politics, lumping them all together under the rubric "Negro Domination." Tillman declared that the threat of Manly's article was a danger to the women of North Carolina, and he asked: "Why didn't you kill that damn nigger editor who wrote that?" He continued: "Send him to South Carolina and let him publish any such offensive stuff, and he will be killed."[19]

Illustrating the power of crisis that I described above, North Carolina's Democratic Party displayed its strength by transforming its loss of power into a general crisis. By defining Manly's editorial as black insolence that threatened white women, the Democratic Party held the key to resolving the problem. They connected the belief in black threat to the Fusionist regime. In removing the corruption of black political participation, they promoted "good government" and the return to Anglo-Saxon rule as the way to ensure the safety of white women and to promote civil behavior among blacks. They used this scare to suppress Fusionist voting in the November 8 election (Cecelski and Tyson 1998).

The upshot of the racial crisis took place in Wilmington, where victory at the polls was not enough. With municipal offices up for election in off years, Fusionists remained in control. Two days later, a group of Conservatives carried out a plan that they envisioned would guarantee that African Americans would never again be a factor in North Carolina politics. Led by Alfred M. Waddell, an army of whites destroyed Alexander Manly's press and burned one of the few black-owned newspapers in the country. The militia went on to terrorize blacks as they shot many bystanders who happened to be on the streets.[20] After securing the town, Waddell's band of soldiers forced Wilmington's officials to resign their positions. His coup resulted in his taking the mayor's office himself. Waddell led the Conservatives in driving their opponents into exile. "We have taken a city," the Reverend Peyton H. Hoge boasted from the pulpit of First Presbyterian Church. "To God be the praise."[21]

Civility and Order

Violence in Wilmington set the tone for policing the color line by projecting a powerful image of the dangers of interracial cooperation. Following the racial terrorism of 1898, the Democratic Party returned to dominance in North Carolina. Like in the aftermath of other racial panics, Democratic leaders followed violence by appealing to the well-being of blacks. Strategically they presented their goodwill by seeking to reform black education. North Carolina's elite understood the benefits in fashioning a moderate image of its racial order. With the commitment to black education, the white establishment portrayed itself as more "civilized, enlightened, and tolerant" than the rest of the South, in what historian William Chafe calls "North Carolina's progressive mystique" (Chafe 1980, 7–8). Chafe captures the essence of the progressive self-images of the North Carolina elite as an active policy that restricted black behavior in terms of industrialization. Against fears of what they perceived as dangerous blacks, the elite viewed education as they way to cultivate black leaders who could shepherd the black masses in civil ways, which meant accommodation to white supremacy. North Carolina's white elite made public pronouncements about its responsibility for the well-being of blacks, an outpouring of concern that cloaked a patron-client relationship between white benefactors and black petitioners and attempted to reduce legitimate African American leadership to merely seeking specific favors. Overtures to "friendship" and concern for blacks became the basis for North Carolina's paternalistic ethos, captured in the idea of civility, which preserved the status quo more efficiently than violence (Chafe 1980).

Tellingly, North Carolina's new image of moderate racial politics sought to lay the groundwork for disfranchising blacks. Proponents of disfranchisement argued that racial harmony could only be achieved by removing blacks from the political process, an action they said would ensure the well-being of both races. They envisaged a new period of moral and material progress through good government (Kirby 1972, 11). By stripping African Americans of the vote, they promised to "clean up" politics, establish "good government," and foster civic progress.[22] Reformers viewed black voters as merely "a political resource" for "corrupt office seekers plotting to capitalize on power conferred to Negroes." The fear of corrupt politicians conspiring to take control through the "instrumentality of stolen Negro vote" dominated the will of the white elite as they struggled to control southern society and build a New South (Kirby 1972, 11).[23]

North Carolina Democrats argued that legitimate government would allow law-abiding and industrious blacks to flourish. The editor of the North Carolina Presbyterian captured the emerging racial paternalism: "When the negro learns to take the advice of Booker T. Washington, the greatest man of his race today, and devote himself to industrial pursuits; when he learns that his white employer is an infinitely better friend of his than the demagogue who wants his vote, a better day will dawn for both races. And it will be both wise and becoming for the leaders among Negroes to follow Booker Washington's example."[24] Commitment to civility anchored these relations between blacks and whites, which projected the values of courtesy, concern about the poor, and a personal grace that "smoothes contact with strangers and obscures conflict with foes" (Chafe 1980, 8). As such, the ideal of civility emphasized racial etiquette, in terms of "good manners," and ignored substantive issues about racial inequality. Civility, therefore, encompassed all the other themes of the progressive mystique: abhorrence of conflict, courtesy toward new ideas, and generosity to the unfortunate (ibid.). White politicians devised black politics in terms of the ideal of racial cooperation and civility, which demanded that blacks remain outside of politics, segregated and deferential to whites. Such cooperation was based on the veiled threat that unraveling this settlement could ignite a race riot.

Following the violence, a group of North Carolina black leaders accommodated the new era of civility and good government. Prominent among them was James Seabrooke from Fayetteville. The group reminded whites of the faithfulness of blacks. White authorities sought and cultivated teachers who were followers of Washington to take charge of educating blacks. Black leaders sought the protection and sympathy of the state's elite. In turn, white authorities supported black education and charitable and social welfare institutions. Rather than being Uncle Toms, these leaders knew the meaning of civility and that on the other side was the "chilling power of consensus to crush efforts to raise issues of racial justice. As victims of civility, blacks had long been forced to operate within the etiquette of race relations that offered almost no room for collective self-assertion or independence. White people dictated the ground rules, and the benefits went only to those who played the game" (Chafe 1980, 9). When the color line was threatened, North Carolina's leaders were prepared to demonize and to unleash violence. Progressivism went hand-in-hand with the use of caricature, hysteria, fear, and violence to retain the racial status quo. White leaders would, when needed, evoke the specter of conspiracy to ring the alarm bells that would mobilize a solid phalanx of white resistance to change. Most notably, southern politicians used racial codes to stifle interracial alliances that could challenge their political plans, such as the populist movement alliances of the 1890s. As a result, southern politicians and business leaders rebuilt their economy around two mandates: reconciling southern politics with the national government and consolidating control over black labor.

Conclusion

The hysteria and fear that followed the rumors of the Manning conspiracy are part of Fayetteville's history of racial struggles. Beginning with the settling of the Cape Fear region, dominant authorities have created a democratic tradition that envisions blacks as not only inferior but dangerous to whites. With racial codes, white authorities codified fears about blacks that presumed white solidarity to be sacred to a moral order. The ascendance of slave insurrection fears following the Haitian Revolution led to the development of political rituals that transformed potential challenges to political authority and its racial conventions into crisis situations. In the form of the slave insurrection panic, periodic racial hysterias outlasted slavery and became a ritual of white solidarity. The remnants of the old planter class and the emerging industrial elite refashioned the slave rebellion scare to meet the political challenges presented by industrialization. Most importantly, such rituals of crisis targeted cross-racial alliances, conveying them as taboo. After the violence of 1898, North Carolina's ruling elite redefined its image of race with social reforms that resulted in its image as a progressive southern state, showing how reforms and racial moderation proved to constrain black behavior and protect white supremacy better than violence.

Chapter 3

The Cunning of Racial Reform

From plantation slavery to the present, dominant political groups and governmental authorities in Fayetteville have repeatedly exploited fear about African Americans to forge white solidarity across class lines. Despite the continuing importance of race and racism that these traditions of racial crisis reveal, everything about racism—except for the way Americans think about it—has changed.[1] One cannot take those changes in racial patterns as simply good or bad. Instead, the types of political changes that followed the Wilmington race riot led to a comprehensive reorganization of politics that emphasized reforms geared to economic growth and industrialization. This chapter develops this insight by describing the ways the establishment of Fort Bragg set in motion political and economic changes that reorganized politics and led to mounting modifications in racial patterns that eventually led to the dismantling of Jim Crow segregation and the discrediting of white supremacy. On the one hand, I will clarify the relations between local political forces and military power by focusing on the way the federal government used military power to intervene into southern politics and society. Rather than imposing itself unilaterally, the federal government devolved power to local politicians and business leaders. In this way, Fayetteville's dominant political and business leaders shaped the manner in which federal policies—from military planning to the Civil Rights Act—developed locally. At the same time, Fort Bragg's development promoted economic and social forces that challenged local authority, which I will describe in terms of ongoing struggles over racial and economic policies. Racial politics developed in relationship to these changes in ways that defy a simple explanation of progress. Indeed, federal agencies and local politicians implemented reforms in ways that created the sense of "progress" at the same time as they limited and narrowed black

politics within the ideological confines of the dominant economic development schemes. Most importantly, the era of civil rights reform was also the
so-called age of neoliberalism. This chapter will describe the municipal coalition that emerged. The last sections of the chapter will describe the ways that
the civil rights and neoliberal policies have reorganized political power and
reconstituted racial politics. I conclude the chapter by bringing the reader to
the eve of the "Five–Four" conflict, when the municipal coalition was
embroiled in three ambitious projects—the final phases of annexing 60,000
residents, a $28 million revitalization project, and an $87 million school
bond—all of which profoundly shaped the developing conflict.

Southern Progressivism, the Military, and the New Nationalism

The ways contemporary racial reforms intersect with economic policy stem
from the political arrangement discussed in the previous chapter. Violence in
Wilmington was the crowning moment of the white supremacy movement,
broadcasting to all whites the peril in interracial alliances (Cecelski and
Tyson 1998, 5).[2] Wilmington's massacre supplanted the labor- intensive
approaches to keeping blacks from voting—such as literacy tests, stuffing
ballot boxes, and face-to-face intimidation—with absolute disfranchisement.
What the Mississippi state legislature began in 1890, the North Carolina
white supremacists finished in 1898, pronouncing its new order as "permanent
good government by the party of the White Man."[3]

White supremacy's words and violence, however, cannot be reduced to
racial hatred. The movement of 1898 represented North Carolina elites'
attempt to impose their industrial development policies on the entire state
(Luebke 1998, 79). And while such a plan necessarily involved disfranchising blacks, it did not mean to drive them from the state. Far from it. Black
labor would play a key role in the industrial development planned for the
region. Thus, after purging the Fusionists from office, industrial planners from
the Democratic Party built roads, schools, and urban services that connected
the agricultural regions of the east and west with the growing industrial centers of Raleigh, Durham, Winston-Salem, and Charlotte. Industrialization of
the Piedmont helped secure North Carolina's reputation as the most progressive state in the South. Beneath the surface of its progressive mystique, North
Carolina's Democratic Party led an "aggressive aristocracy of manufacturing
and banking" that represented what political scientist V. O. Key calls a
"progressive plutocracy" (1949). Public policies protected and advanced the
manufacturing elite and supported the large employers in the tobacco

industries, allowing them to form a corporate oligarchy that dominated state politics (ibid., 211).

The rise of North Carolina's corporate elite only worsened the economic problems for Fayetteville. Like in other antebellum merchant towns, the city's economy stagnated and remained deprived of capital during the early 1900s (see Doyle 1990). By World War I, the Civil War's destruction was still very noticeable, as buildings downtown were charred, most of the county was a wasteland of pine barrens, destroyed by three centuries of producing forest products like tar, pitch, and turpentine (see Outland 2004), and the city's population, at five thousand, was barely larger than it was on the eve of the Civil War (Parker 1990).

Such social and economic devastation was common throughout the South and drew the attention of federal planners, who sought to find ways to develop the southern economy, reform its social policies, and ameliorate its poverty. The outbreak of war in Europe provided Woodrow Wilson's administration an opportunity to intervene in the region. Based on the idea of a "new nationalism," Wilson promoted "military preparedness" as the key to safeguarding and building democracy in America and the rest of the world (Gaughan 1999). By expanding the military, Wilson's administration provided numerous economic opportunities to capital-starved cities in the South. With the dreams of military dollars, southern political leaders began looking to the long-hated federal government for capital investment, as the expanding military industrial complex promised huge contracts for the building of munitions factories and training centers.

Following this pattern for New South economic development, Fayetteville's Chamber of Commerce turned toward the War Department in its efforts to recruit capital. By advertising the city's prime geographical location, railroad access, water routes, good climate, and "proper" labor conditions, local boosters succeeded. In July of 1918, the War Department chose Fayetteville to be home of a new post, which the Chamber of Commerce bragged would become the "world's largest artillery range" and bring in $17 million.[4] Unexpectedly, the city's vast expanse of exhausted pines, often viewed as a wasteland, became a valuable commodity to the War Department. By summer's end, the War Department began building Camp Bragg ten miles northwest of downtown, from which the training center extended westward for twenty- three miles to Southern Pines.

The establishment of Camp Bragg represents a broader pattern of political power that centralized the national state into the South. Rather than hostile expansion of state power, federal planners devolved power to local leaders in places like Fayetteville, ensuring that even before the arrival of the military post, military preparation policies dovetailed with the economic and social concerns that preoccupied southern leaders. In Fayetteville, the local elite used federal programs associated with the war to expand its power through building public services needed for commercial growth, laying the foundation for the federal-local partnership that historians define as "Southern Progressivism" (Grantham 1983; Link 1992). Through these new relationships to the federal government, municipal coalitions throughout the South increased their power and authority by controlling federal agencies, such as the National Council of Defense and the Department of Agriculture; local authorities used federal agencies to consolidate control over local politics. For example, the Fayetteville Chamber of Commerce and city administration, by implementing the war mobilization efforts around Camp Bragg, gained new resources and authority to pursue the prewar business goals framed during the Wilmington race riot: economic development and white supremacy.

Despite contributing to the policies and agendas of southern progressives, World War I resulted in far-reaching political changes in the South. Military growth and expansion of the War Department drew African Americans into the military and industrial labor, raising their wages and power. Part of this was encouraged by black leaders, even radicals like W.E.B. Du Bois, who persuaded blacks to close ranks with the nation. Participation of African Americans in the war effort challenged the meaning of democracy, as the call to war resulted in the mobilization of 200,000 black men—one-fourth of whom saw combat in segregated divisions (Singh 2004, 48). In the end, black mobilization was challenged by powerful whites, who resisted any attempt to change the political status of African Americans. Moreover, by the war's end, southern authorities, with the expanded powers of the federal state, increased their political control over blacks. Rather than praising blacks for their sacrifice, southern authorities (as well as Woodrow Wilson) became suspicious of black soldiers as conduits for Bolshevism, leading to a political policy that linked the civil rights struggle to anti-Americanism (Singh 2004, 31).

Mythologies of Racial Progress

Camp Bragg closed in the late 1920s, and the Fayetteville elites' dream of economic ascendance would be deferred until the outbreak of World War II. By 1940 the U.S. War Department had resumed building up its forces and reopened the training center at Camp Bragg. Renamed Fort Bragg, the post became home of the U.S. Army's Ninth Infantry Division training center and underwent a significant expansion. This decision to expand Fort Bragg must be related to the broader context defined by the New Deal programs and policies in which President Franklin D. Roosevelt's *Report on Economic Conditions in the South,* a scathing indictment of southern society, labeled the region the nation's "Number One economic problem" (Schulman 1991, 51). With this commitment to improving the region, the federal government made this investment in Cumberland County in order to jump-start the economy in an effort to replace its "backward" social structure with democracy and economic prosperity.

In expanding the training center, more than $44 million of federal money flowed into the city, and the War Department embarked on a massive construction plan that attracted more than 30,000 construction workers. Fayetteville once again became a bustling economy, which created an immense housing shortage. Homebuilders, land developers, and construction workers descended on the city. Also, bankers and merchants were equally attracted by the more than 92,000 soldiers who would pass through the gates of Fort Bragg over the next several years.[5]

Mobilization for the war promoted economic growth and created many jobs in the civil service, war-related businesses, and the military, which pushed Jim Crow to its limits. Many African Americans gained relative amounts of economic independence and enhanced social status with industrial and governmental jobs, while the presence of black soldiers—the ultimate symbol of civic equality—continued to besiege the mythic tenants of Jim Crow segregation. Improved social standing resulted in new forms of black activism and the tremendous growth of the NAACP as African Americans increasingly fought for citizenship rights; membership in North Carolina's NAACP doubled as it swelled to 10,000 (Crow, Escott, and Hatley 1992, 151).

Racial changes were more dramatic in Fayetteville, as local whites had to get used to seeing blacks not only wearing military uniforms but also carrying guns and patrolling soldier bars and hangouts, providing a strong and sobering message to local authorities. By 1941, Fayetteville had become known as "Uncle Sam's Powder Keg,"[6] as thousands of black artillery trainees overwhelmed the city's Jim Crow institutions (the city lacked adequate recreation and transport facilities for black soldiers). Each payday, Fayetteville's downtown would be full of African Americans wearing military uniforms, drinking, and milling around.

Like the Democrats of 1898, many whites in Fayetteville and in North Carolina in general responded to the images of black soldiers by raising the specter of miscegenation and racial violence (Tyson 1998, 254). Many authorities accused black activists of using the war emergency to advance racial equality, with the authorities exaggerating the degree of change to create panics about a coming race war, which led to the explosion of racial violence on military posts throughout the United States (Burran 1977; Kryder 2001). Following the pattern of the slave insurrection panic, many white southerners told fantastic stories about blacks using their newfound prosperity to stockpile weapons. UNC sociologist Howard Odum collected these rumors of race violence, including ones that told of blacks using newfound wealth to stockpile ice picks in preparation for a coming race war (Odum 1997 [1946]).

In southern cities without military posts, things were no better for activists and those who advocated racial reforms as antiblack hysteria grew after the war. Black soldiers returned from the war to face violence, intimidation, and in extreme cases lynching. For the U.S. State Department, the contradiction of black soldiers helping to vanquish the xenophobic regime of Hitler only to face racist persecution in the South was an international embarrassment (Dudziak 2000). Responding to this public relations nightmare, the federal government issued Executive Order 9981 to desegregate the armed forces, which in part led to *Brown v. Board of Education* and the gradual dismantling of Jim Crow in the South (Dalfiume 1969).

In conjunction with these moves toward desegregation, federal agencies began creating a narrative of American racial progress (Dudziak 2000). Exemplified by the pamphlet *The Negro in American Life*, representatives of the government argued that great changes in the United States stem from the superiority of its democratic form of government. The pamphlet recognized the history of slavery, as the baseline from which African Americans emerged to be free, and transformed it into a story of progress. It used these improvements to argue that "American democracy was a form of government that made the achievement of social justice possible, and that democratic change, however slow and gradual, was superior to dictatorial imposition" and thus superior to communism (Dudziak 2000, 13).

As federal agencies decidedly turned against Jim Crow, the government used the myth of racial progress to limit the sorts of changes it proposed for African Americans within the framework of American democracy and the cold war (Dudziak 2000). Business leaders in the South began to put their belief in segregation on the back burner, as they understood that creating stability and economic growth required more progressive policies and the relinquishing of violence and Jim Crow. And so, instead of openly defying federal orders, southern politicians found new ways to retain the social order. In the face of greater involvement with federal economic policies, North Carolina politicians, led by Governor Luther Hodges, invented laws to resist federal laws on such hallmark issues as school desegregation.

In a move reminiscent of the current link between neoliberalism and civil rights-era progress, Luther Hodges earned a positive reputation as a progressive southern governor as he led the North Carolina legislature to policies that would diversify the economy—to move beyond textile industry-driven development. Though a believer in segregation, Hodges felt the issue was not important enough to risk positive standing with the federal government and the economic development that it could bring. Therefore Hodges developed the Pearsall Plan, with the help of an integrated committee that included African American James Seabrooke of Fayetteville State University (Murphy 1960). The plan was a way to continue school segregation by offering "local choice" to individual citizens without openly defying the federal government's ban on legal segregation (Chafe 1980; Luebke 1998).

By balancing commitments to the federal government on the one hand and the racialized status quo (via the Pearsall Plan) on the other, Hodges allowed Fayetteville's local government and others throughout North Carolina to present themselves as open to racial progress even while pursuing white supremacy policies and liberal economic development. Contributing to this vision of racial open-mindedness, Dr. W. P. Devane, a black physician, won a seat on the Fayetteville city council in 1949, which the *Fayetteville Observer* hailed as proof that blacks have full opportunities in America (Covington and Ellis 1999, 100).

Economic growth related to Fort Bragg changed local patterns in terms of an expanding consumer and real estate market among African Americans. Responding to growing consumer demand, Fayetteville authorities made new compromises, granting limited forms of economic progress and political access for economic expansion and social quiescence. White developers and merchants adjusted their views about African Americans as they recognized the new wealth among blacks. In April 1952, local white developers showcased "fifty modern homes in the Holly Springs section of Fayetteville."[7] While the Broadell Homes remained racially segregated, the *Fayetteville Observer* celebrated the development: "it may well be a pattern for other communities throughout the Southland to follow." Indeed it was.

Black leadership in the U.S. South developed within these confines of cold war politics and commitment, representing a particular, marginal, and largely identifiable group, with distinct interests from the general working-class and poor blacks. And over time, black leaders expanded the political capital gained in this process, gradually assuming the position of being able to speak for the so-called black community. In so doing, the emerging black elite had new opportunities to expand their power and rights for African Americans. However, the increased repression of the state required that they relate black progress to the cause of anti-communism.

Frontier Town

In Fayetteville, the dialectic of racial fears and myths of racial progress were shaped by the city's peculiar form of urbanization. The expansion of Fort Bragg fueled tremendous growth of the population and economy. However, the city lacked the tax base and urban structures to regulate and plan growth, a weakness that was exacerbated by the U.S. government's control of the 23-by-8-mile swath of pine forest that constitutes Fort Bragg. In building the training center, the federal government took one-tenth of Cumberland County's area off the tax rolls, and intensified the county's revenue shortfall. Military investment in Cumberland County aggravated economic conditions that distinguished eastern North Carolina cities from the Piedmont's industrialized cities, like Raleigh, Durham, Charlotte, and Greensboro. Fayetteville lagged behind these Piedmont cities in both tax base and urban infrastructure. To this day, politicians refer to Cumberland as a low-wealth county, an urban area with a rural tax base, which makes it difficult to build the proper infrastructure to handle urban problems and economic growth.

With many opportunities to make money, and few regulations, land developers and homebuilders rushed into Fayetteville. To meet demands for affordable housing, developers built subdivisions and strip malls in unincorporated areas outside city limits to avoid building ordinances, zoning laws, and city taxes. Land speculators bought options from farmers and worked with homebuilders and mortgage bankers to take advantage of federal urbanization policies and the growing demand for housing. Until the late 1970s, the real estate market grew with little or no intervention from government agencies, which became an increasing burden on city government. Fayetteville came to resemble, as many Fayetteville residents described to me, a "frontier town." Expressing this sense of a free-for-all, the newly built subdivisions were self-contained entities outside the city's authority. Developers supplied homeowners with minimal services: nominal health and safety standards, septic tanks, private water companies, and volunteer fire departments. Developers, therefore, created their own organization for urban services, which resulted in the volunteer fire departments becoming centers for county politics and bastions for developers' resistance to the city. Fire departments had their own tax base and therefore had an interest in opposing the city's attempts to expand its authority into the county.

Homebuilders and land developers grew to be a powerful force and fought with civic leaders and merchants about the city's authority, taxes, and building regulations. By the late 1940s, many civic leaders and merchants started to support civic growth and the expansion of the city through annexation.

Authorities sought to annex the subdivisions to increase the tax base, control urban development, and create amenities for economic development. Facing strong resistance, city officials tried to encourage developers to accept the city's authority by promising them access to water, sewer, and other urban services. Homebuilders and developers resisted these efforts. Calling on southern traditions of laissez-faire economic policies and anti- government rhetoric, developers condemned the city for abusing its power. Critics often accused the local government of holding the unincorporated areas hostage to force homebuilders to pay city taxes before they could use the city's water and sewage lines. Land developers were notorious for resisting the city's dictates.

The case of Jimmy Gladwin, a prolific developer known for thwarting the city's efforts to expand its authority, illustrates the "frontier-like" behaviors of developers. As a retired developer recounted, "Jimmy Gladwin was a very independent guy" who started the Lafayette Village subdivision: "He went to the city and said 'I'm going to build this subdivision and I want you to supply me with water.' Jimmy, a huge fat man, hated the government in any form. When the city demanded that they annex the subdivision before they would supply water and sewer, he said: 'the hell with you' and built his own water company. It's only in the last few months [thirty-five years later] the city has annexed Lafayette Village. Soon every homebuilder and land developer created his own individual water company. We had about twenty different water companies."

Conflict between developers and city government erupted in 1959, when the North Carolina state legislature passed an annexation law. City managers throughout the state, representing industrial developers, designed the law to give cities with a population over five thousand the authority to annex urban areas outside city limits. Political leaders used the law in order to increase their tax base, develop comprehensive economic development plans, and strengthen public services to cope with the growth of suburbs. Civic leaders, merchants, and the *Fayetteville Observer* supported the annexation law; they believed the legislation would help modernize the city and help expand the urban services necessary for economic development. Such optimism was dashed when House Representative John Henley spoiled the plan. Drawing support from rural interests in Cumberland County, he placed Fayetteville on a list that exempted it from the new law. To this day, civic leaders speculate about the mysterious ways in which the legislature excused Fayetteville from the law. They blame the exemption for "holding Fayetteville behind," and John Henley lives in infamy as "the guy that kept Fayetteville from growing."

Excluding the city from annexation kept Fayetteville's population at about 50,000, whereas the surrounding urban areas were more densely populated, with 60,000 residents and—most terrifying to city planners—over 35,000 septic tanks. Urban expansion to the west drained revenue from the city as developers became wealthy. Fayettevillians understand this history through the story of one of the city's wealthiest developers. Local legend has it that P. J. Middleton, a former rural mail carrier, became Cumberland County's largest real estate developer by tirelessly buying options on many small farms. He accumulated a huge expanse of farmland four miles to the west of downtown. Eventually the Middleton Development Company sold the land to a Charlotte-based development firm, which built a million-square-foot shopping mall—the Cross Creek Mall. Opening in 1976, the Cross Creek Mall became the keystone of a network that linked six shopping centers and commercial strips covering two square miles—the largest in-one-place commercial zone in North Carolina, according to the 1990 U.S. Census. Before its grand opening, Cross Creek Mall had already signed on most of the downtown's largest department stores, including Belk's, Sears, and J. C. Penney. The most conspicuous casualty of this economic realignment was Fayetteville's downtown business district.[8]

Stories of developers becoming wealthy at the city's expense shape political debates. Residents from the military often call on the exploits of Middleton and other developers to impugn local government for being dominated by a miserly group of developers who have little concern for the city's well-being or its civic life. As the argument goes, they seek to make easy profits by building houses and selling goods to the military. Instead of using the wealth generated by Fort Bragg to build Fayetteville into a metropolitan center, many residents from the military argue that Fayetteville's power brokers have concentrated their civic efforts on Haymount Hill, creating an upper crust, "a city on the hill," that features the exclusive Highland Country Club, as well as Highland Methodist, Haymount Presbyterian, and Snyder Memorial Baptist Churches.

Black Officialdom and Neoliberalism

From the white supremacy movement of 1898 to both world wars, Fayetteville's local government developed racial ideas as a political instrument for governance. Increasingly, political leaders and governmental officials used ideals of racial progress to contain and limit black political demands within the confines of economic development. Despite these resourceful uses of racial institutions, the growing momentum of the national civil rights movement finally broke apart Jim Crow segregation in its more sophisticated forms, such as the Pearsall Plan. Students at Greensboro A&T sat at the lunch counter and launched the national sit-in movement, and in nine days the protest spread to Fayetteville State University when several students took seats at the downtown lunch counters, leading to intermittent marches and demonstrations over the next three years.

In a move reminiscent of past and future strategies of inclusion, Fayetteville's mayor responded to the protest movement at FSU by reforming city government. He negotiated with student leaders and prominent black leaders, and the city government agreed to hire African Americans and to integrate appointed boards and commissions in exchange for halting the student protests. In a calculated move, the mayor put several prominent Fayetteville African Americans on policy-making boards in local government and formalized these policy changes by creating the Human Relations Commission in 1963. In this way, city planners provided African American leaders an official channel through which to voice their concerns, rather than leaving it to students or "outside agitators" to organize direct action protests.[9]

Many other racial reforms became formalized with the passing of the Civil Rights Act in 1964 and Voting Rights Act in 1965. Political enfranchisement, desegregation of public schools and public accommodations, and federal investment in antipoverty programs indeed inaugurated a new structure of racial politics. However, racial reforms became compromised by the larger economic problems that beset Fayetteville (as well as many other cities in the transforming South). By the early 1970s, federal demands to desegregate public institutions were made alongside decreasing federal contributions to public goods like education, transport, and affordable housing (Prashad 2006).

In the vacuum left by federal government cutbacks, city governments began taking on greater responsibility for providing basic urban services and physical infrastructure. City managers sought to meet these challenges by forging closer relations with private capital and interests to promote economic development as an alternative to federal support, and through this rhetoric, to build a dominant coalition of civic leaders and business interests. Changes under way earlier culminated in the move by Fayetteville's business leaders and public officials to envision local government as primarily an economic development tool whose provisioning responsibilities are driven by economic development plans.

These changes in Fayetteville were deeply shaped by the negative publicity the city received in relation to the unpopular Vietnam War. As increasing numbers of Americans became disillusioned with the U.S. military, Fayetteville's reputation suffered. People throughout the South began defaming the city with such nicknames as "Fayettenam," reducing the city's problems to Fort Bragg. Visitors to Fayetteville and news reports about the city

often confirmed these stereotypes. Fort Bragg Boulevard, the main thorough-
fare between the post and the city, evoked the clichéd images of a "military
town," with seven miles of strip bars, pawnshops, used car lots, and military
surplus stores. Downtown's Hay Street was the jewel in the crown of soldiers'
debauchery. Throngs of strippers, prostitutes, and drug dealers found buyers
on Hay Street. Sales of these goods and services filled the void left by many
businesses that, since the late 1950s, had retreated to the western portion of
the city and county. For most military personnel, Hay Street was Fayetteville.
The city had little else to offer in terms of recreation and cultural activities.
The 500 block alone had as many as twenty strip clubs, adult movie theaters,
and tattoo parlors.[10] The once-elegant Prince Charles Hotel turned into what
some soldiers claim was the South's largest brothel, with most of its rooms
rented out by the hour.[11]

Seeking to erase the notoriety of the town's "Fayettenam" label, business leaders focused the city's economic policy agenda on mitigating its bad
reputation and targeting what leaders believed to be the epicenter of the
problem: the 400 and 500 blocks of Hay Street. In 1981 the winning may-
oral candidate ran on a program of "destroying" the old image of Fayetteville
by closing "adult businesses" downtown, which he described as "a cancer in
this city."[12] By the fall of 1983, city council began its own attack against
Fayettenam by banning strip bars and condemning downtown buildings, and
even staging a media event of bulldozing the buildings on the 500 block of
Hay Street.

These city-backed projects represented both the transformation in political power as well as the culmination of processes under way for several
decades, as business and political leaders began connecting the city's reputation with projects designed to attract investment and grow the economy.
They designed public projects around the needs of land developers and the
merchant coalition in ways that connected such things as education and crime
prevention in black neighborhoods. City management opened the city's
administration to the needs and interests of the business community and
sought a close relationship with ostensibly private business groups like the
Chamber of Commerce, downtown revitalization groups, and the Fayetteville
Economic Development Corporation. Increasingly, civic leaders associated
the use of public money with cleaning up the city's image and with economic
development, aimed at growing the tax base, improving the quality of life,
and expanding urban services. Fayetteville's political leaders also expanded
the city's authority—increasing its use of outside resources and access to state
and federal aid—by connecting city government with the needs of various
community groups and the business community, advocating "public-private

partnerships" as a means of meeting what had formerly been primarily city government responsibilities.

This informal arrangement among political officials and private interests represents what political scientist Clarence Stone calls an "urban regime," a municipal coalition of many business and middle-class interests (Stone 1989). Stone developed the urban regime concept in his study of Atlanta's politics to describe and analyze the informal arrangements that surround and comple- ment formal government. His model emphasizes "civic cooperation," the informal practices that coordinate political efforts across institutional bound- aries. In Fayetteville, since the 1980s, an identifiable urban regime—a coali- tion of political and business interests—has evolved. Civic leaders have formed the coalition to promote economic and political projects in the face of decreased federal support and greater scrutiny of racial reforms. In a complex environment like Fayetteville, no single group or entity has complete control. Thus, the urban regime matured under the guidance of city manager Jim Thompson, who was at the center of the controversy introduced in chapter 1. Rather than commanding, Thompson led the urban regime by managing con- flict in ways that built a lasting coalition. Members of the regime share an interest in a single policy agenda to promote common economic and political projects. Working in the regime, political and economic leaders reach across institutional boundaries to produce the capacity to govern.

Romantic images of civil rights struggle and the often patronizing ideals of multiculturalism conceal how bureaucratic links have made black leaders dependent on top-down racial management. Rather than representing the interests and demands of particular constituencies among the black popula- tion, black leaders have become subordinate partners within the urban regime. In Fayetteville, city management and the Chamber of Commerce worked (and continue to work) closely with the local chapter of the NAACP, contributing to the building of a new system of black politics. Growing from the racial politics that developed during segregation, under the ideology of racial uplift, civil rights laws have formalized what was once an informal rela- tionship between elite whites and black leaders (Reed 1999a). Fayetteville's business and political leaders often appeal to black officials and the NAACP for assistance with everything from settling complaints of racial discrimina- tion to gathering support for such initiatives as passing bonds for public schools, crime fighting, and economic growth. In this way, the NAACP and black political officials have become a conduit for connecting the city manager's policy agenda to neighborhood groups and other advocacy organi- zations. This connection has expanded Fayetteville's dominant economic development coalition into black neighborhoods, mainly via the Community

Development Division of the city planning office. Under the Community Development Division, Fayetteville's city management has assigned an African American assistant city manager to direct projects that extend affordable housing, urban services, and public safety to poor neighborhoods. While such programs remain necessary, the means through which they are put in place and the limited say of local residents over how and where public monies will be invested in their neighborhoods represent a significant narrowing of the political field.

These corporatized forms of black politics have developed in the vacuum created by the federal government's decreasing role in providing for social programs, discussed above. Black leaders and representatives contribute to strengthening and maintaining the urban regime by bestowing legitimacy to the economic policies that have diverted funds from black neighborhoods to build and expand middle-class neighborhoods. Over the same period of the consolidation of civil rights, Fayetteville's black neighborhoods of Wilmington Road, Savoy Heights, and College Heights became increasingly rife with crime and unemployment. Increasing social isolation of the poorest black residents has resulted in these types of political institutions that are designed for the management of impoverished residents. Black political leadership reflects as well as manages the increased political differences among blacks—especially differences between elected officials and their constituents. This chasm is the product of the process whereby African Americans gain leadership positions, which emphasizes connections to Fayetteville's dominant white institutions—for example, the Democratic Party, the county courthouse, city hall, and the North Carolina state legislature. Black church leaders and neighborhood activists are valuable to political networks when it is time to mobilize voters. However, the development of political careers necessitates that individuals redirect their energies so that "black issues" are mediated by the larger concerns that the urban regime defines as the community's best interest.

Despite this control over black politics, Fayetteville's dominant coalition of business and political leaders continues to fear black political power and seek ways to limit and dilute black electoral power. An example of these fears emerged after the Justice Department passed the 1982 Civil Rights Act. Seeking to remedy the failures of the 1965 Voting Rights Act, the new law required U.S. cities to create "majority-minority" voting districts to ensure accurate levels of black representation. Attempting to bring this law to bear on Fayetteville, a group of black activists lobbied to create single-member districts to bring black electoral strength in line with the population, which was almost 40 percent black. Responding to federal mandates and local pressure from African Americans, city management formulated a new plan that would minimally satisfy the amendment with a "mixed system." This plan provided for three minority districts, three majority districts, and three at-large districts. At-large voting districts effectively diluted black representation, ensuring that the downtown coalition would control city policy by a 6-to-3 margin. As one activist described the outcome: "They [Haymount Hill] expanded city council with three at-large [seats] so that it put the power in the hand of the man that had the dollar and not the hand of the man that wanted to serve the community. They [wealthy whites] could run at-large and pay the money. Because of economic conditions, blacks could not run at-large and pay the money." In a sense, it is this safeguard that Tom Manning and Sam Johnson upended when they voted to support the NAACP.

New Fayetteville

Fayetteville's voting plan illustrates how local politics simultaneously trades on the idea of racial progress while limiting the impact of black voting. At-large voting limits the degree to which black representatives can form competing coalitions that would challenge the urban regime's policy agenda. This control of black voters was central to the way city manager Jim Thompson used public policy to coordinate the interests of the Chamber of Commerce, industrial development, homebuilders, and many civic groups into a durable coalition. Most notably, Thompson designed the annexation program to expand the urban regime's reach into the outlying urban areas. After years of struggle, in 1989, the city of Fayetteville finally succeeded in persuading the North Carolina General Assembly to grant it the authority to begin annexing 60,000 outlying residents into the city. Thompson's business allies touted annexation as fundamental to the city's modernization as well as an opportunity to produce a "unifying vision" for Fayetteville. Like many of the urban regime's policies, this one was controversial and faced much opposition from whites, especially those associated with the military. As one city planner explained, there is a strong sense of division between the city of Fayetteville and the military subdivisions. She explained that resentment is strong because the city's boundaries did not change until after 1989. She traced this antipathy back to the anti-annexation law created by Henley in 1959. Because of this law, she believed the "communities" had "never meshed, as it would have if the city were allowed to grow." She felt that it boiled down to civic participation and explained that if people in the subdivisions had either been elected to, or participated on, governmental boards and commissions, that their would be less antagonism toward city government and its development policies.

Instead, Fayetteville is a "densely" urbanized area that lacks a "heart. It is a big suburb with no identity."

The type of conflict that has developed between people in the military and city government is somewhat unique to Fayetteville. Normally, military families are notorious for remaining aloof from local politics and community concerns in the cities that host military bases. Often soldiers will carry out their duty and will be transferred to another military post within a few years. Fort Bragg is one of the exceptions because it is home to the 82nd Airborne and there are few places for this sort of training. Oftentimes, soldiers will spend the majority of their careers at Fort Bragg, what is known as "homesteading." In Fayetteville, many of these "homesteaders" live in the subdivisions that have been targeted for annexation. Feeling distant from the city, these residents have bitterly opposed annexation into the city. Part of the sense of alienation stemmed from they way their neighborhoods were poorly linked up with the city. Moreover, opponents of the urban regime connected annexation with raising taxes for downtown projects that had little relevance for them. In addition to taxes, residents had to pay thousands of dollars to hook up their homes to city water and sewage lines. North Carolina's annexation law required cities to extend water, sewer, storm drainage, and fire and police protection to the areas they incorporated within city limits. New city residents would share the cost of annexation with city taxes.

Strong and vocal opposition to annexation did not surprise city officials and their allies in business. The military community is known for being opposed to civic projects and downtown politics. City planners believe that many active-duty and retired military have a "myopic" view because they cannot see beyond their neighborhood and the post. Business and political leaders have tried to devise ways to include representatives of the military into their policy agenda of economic growth, which in 1989 led to the creation of "MetroVisions." The group sought to formulate an "inclusive" initiative for a "unified" Fayetteville. Eventually the Chamber of Commerce absorbed MetroVisions and used it to compile data on the "community's needs." As the director of MetroVisions explained to me, "We are a nonpolitical and nonpartisan organization that gathers data about the city's quality of life." MetroVisions sees its job as collecting data from the "grass roots" and presenting its findings as "unbiased" information on the "community's wants." They use longitudinal studies to track "quality of life indicators," which are published in an annual "state of the community" report evaluating the community's progress in different social services, from public health and education to crime prevention and economic development. Engaging in policy debates with government officials, the Chamber of Commerce uses the data to "induce change through informed participation."

MetroVisions highlights one of the many ways the dominant business and political coalition expands its power. By identifying conflicts and political factions, public and private members of the coalition seek ways to incorporate different groups and interests into the broader policy agenda. As it expands its control, allies and partners of the downtown coalition increase its capacity to promote public projects like education, transport, and other urban services necessary for economic development.

Members of the urban regime have used the reform-oriented tendency to present the regime as having evolved from, and as an alternative to, the "old guard." Projecting itself as progressive and forward looking, the urban regime attempts to transcend Fayetteville's negative reputation associated with the epithet "Fayettenam" and replace it with a new vision of progressive government. Despite the infamy associated with the military, many residents— including members of the urban regime—see the military as being the scapegoat. Even a member of the Chamber of Commerce described the city's problems in the way "Old Haymount" responded to the growth of Fort Bragg:

> Because of Fort Bragg's build-up in the 1940s, money was flowing on
> the streets and developers and businessmen got accustomed to that.
> The community was built on that. These few Fayettevillians made a
> conscious decision not to build the city. They didn't want annexation,
> I-95, or more generally *foreigners* coming into "our insular world."
> For example, look at Highland Country Club, when was it established?
> 1946! Think about it? A few good ole boys who were making money
> off of Bragg and said, "Let's bind together here. It doesn't include
> 'foreigners' or people from the 'other side.'" They don't want any
> competition; it's Dumb Money. Now Fayettevillians see the need for
> public spending on schools, libraries, and urban amenities.

Representing its transcendence of "dumb money," MetroVisions and the Chamber of Commerce began mobilizing for downtown revitalization in 1994. At the time, attempts to resurrect downtown had been discredited because they were associated with a group called "Olde Fayetteville," which was viewed as representing the insular and provincial views of Haymount insiders. Leaders from the Chamber of Commerce worked with city management to adopt revitalization and make it part of its economic development policies. In this effort, city management and the chamber formed a group to hire Robert Marvin, a landscape architect from South Carolina, to design the "Master Plan for a Complete Fayetteville Once and for All." In a gala event at the civic auditorium in June of 1996, the architect unveiled what became known as the "Marvin Plan," which consisted of a forty-five-acre park built around an artificial lake, lakeshore houses, and an arts district.

Fayetteville's most prominent developers hailed the plan as providing the city a "new heart." Indeed, Marvin's presentation captured the support of the many competing constituencies that form Fayetteville's urban regime. As one city staff member described the event: "You had old guys stand up yelling. It was dramatic. Even scary. I was waiting for Jim Jones to pass out the Kool-Aid. . . . It was a very flashy presentation. People stood up and started saying, 'We are the problem.'" Playing on this new attitude toward public money and civic commitments, supporters tried to lighten the blow of its $28 million price tag. A new heart, as supporters argued, would require Fayetteville to change its ways. Many of the city's land developers, known for being fiscally conservative and the creators of the urban problems that stemmed from unregulated growth, criticized policies that avoided raising taxes as they campaigned for the use of public money.

Once city management adopted the Marvin Plan, supporters formed a nonprofit organization that would mobilize public support and private capital for the project. For this purpose, civic leaders revamped Olde Fayetteville to become an "action agency" and renamed it the "Fayetteville Partnership," hoping the reorganization and name change would help revitalization gain appeal among a wider set of residents. In addition, business leaders formed a separate and private group called the "Once and for All Committee" to drum up support among private interests and to shield the project from a certain amount of public scrutiny. By defining itself as both private and non-profit, the committee sought to keep "politics" out of the process. Although the effort was coordinated with the city management's economic policies, the Once and for All Committee tried to "take the spotlight off elected officials" for committing millions of dollars to the project. Although limiting public scrutiny was an important function of the Fayetteville Partnership, business and civic leaders used the revitalization campaign to elaborate the city's policy agenda in terms of economic development.

For city management, downtown revitalization became the keystone to its overarching policy framework for expanding the city's business infrastructure. City manager Jim Thompson used revitalization to coordinate Cumberland County's representatives in the U.S. Congress and the North Carolina legislature—not to mention the Department of Defense—to leverage state and federal money. An important player in North Carolina state politics was Cumberland County's Senator Frank Edwards, who secured a $50 million grant from the North Carolina Housing Finance Agency to construct housing in the downtown district. The grant was contingent on a commitment from local developers and a city-sponsored revitalization plan.[13] Meeting the Housing Agency's criteria lent further support to the downtown revitalization coalition, as the Marvin Plan would provide the necessary infrastructure. As we will see below, Senator Edwards's network of power had long tentacles. Most local initiatives and plans, from annexation and revitalization to neighborhood-level plans to reduce crime or build parks, called on Senator Edwards's support, which resulted in his legendary status as the "godfather of Fayetteville."

In the following months, the Fayetteville Partnership and city management enlisted the North Carolina Housing Authority, the Fayetteville Public Works Commission, the Cumberland County Commissioners, and the U.S. Army. The Public Works Commission committed $10 million to redevelop downtown; the county commissioners established a downtown revitalization fund, with monies coming from the sale of downtown buildings donated to the county; and First Citizens Bank donated a ten-story building at the corner of Hay and Green Streets, valued at $154,000.[14] The U.S. Army, through its Capital Venture Initiative, sought to develop houses according to the Marvin Plan's call for "mixed use" development.

Downtown revitalization illustrates city manager Jim Thompson's leadership role in building and maintaining a vast network of political and economic interests that included local land developers, real estate agents, educators, and Fayetteville State, as well as state, federal, and military agencies. Most significantly, Thompson built and maintained the urban regime through an informal but stable agreement to create a coherent policy agenda and his coalition of public and private interests. Fayetteville's urban regime has taken shape over the past three decades as a collaborative arrangement between city government and private parties to assemble a workable coalition with the object of creating, maintaining, and expanding its capacity to govern. The collaboration influenced the hysterical reactions to the new council majority, and these relationships and imperatives defined the city's race relations.

Conclusion

Racial fears about the Manning conspiracy and an empowered black community stemmed from the political struggles that Fayetteville's dominant coalition of business and political interests faced as they embarked on the downtown revitalization project. City manager Jim Thompson's administration grew from the expansion of Fort Bragg after the Second World War. Growth of the economy and its military community collided with the preexisting power structure, which resulted in the city's contemporary political structure. This evolution highlights important elements of power that shaped the "Five–Four." First, it shows how civic and political leaders adapted racial institutions stemming from slavery and Jim Crow to the tremendous political and economic changes that followed the post–World War II boom, the civil rights movement, and the decreasing role of federal government in governing cities. The most important aspect of racial politics has been how reforms helped maintain this structure of power. Political and civic leaders used racial reforms to legitimize their authority and policy agenda. Following the mythology of racial progress, Fayetteville's political leaders fashioned a black leadership structure that celebrates the civil rights movement at the same time that it increases bureaucratic control over the black population. Applications of racial reforms were limited by the way the federal government simultaneously cut back public funding of education and social services. Fayetteville's political leaders redesigned local government to simultaneously comply with the Civil Rights Act and adapt to decreases in federal grants-in-aid to cities. Political and business leaders used the government to build a dominant coalition that would reform racial politics in ways that would legitimize its policy agenda, which increasingly used public money for business interests. On the eve of the "Five–Four," Fayetteville's dominant coalition was a heterogeneous group—including black and white middle-class and business interests—that was committed to the city government and its management team. These political and economic commitments to increasing the economy and transforming the city's military image would have a dominant role in shaping the event.

Chapter 4

Performing Crisis

Oₙ ᴛʜᴇ ᴇᴠᴇ ᴏꜰ Tom Manning and Sam Johnson's shocking turn against the city council's white majority, city manager Jim Thompson and his regime partners were actively mobilizing public support for the audacious Marvin Plan. More than merely a cosmetic change, the revitalization plan had become the hub of the city's economic policy agenda. Civic leaders did not view the black community as a threat to revitalization. Several prominent black leaders had endorsed it and there was no sign of black opposition, except for council member Edna Harrington. Instead, members of the urban regime braced themselves for strong opposition from the many thousands of residents who identified with the military and lived in the parts of the city that had been, or were targeted for, annexation.

It is from this context of struggle between competing white factions that we can better understand the full force of the NAACP's allegations of racism in the police department. By challenging the city manager's authority, the NAACP's criticisms dovetailed with the unpopularity of his policies among many white residents. Many white Fayettevillians are critical of local government, seeing it as a mixture of nepotism and incompetence that is to blame for the policies that have left the downtown in shambles and the rest a tangled mess. As I showed in chapter 1, conspiracy theories shifted public attention away from these policy conflicts and focused the public's attention on the rise of a racial threat to the social order. Rumors of the "Manning conspiracy" displaced concern about the city manager's role in the racial controversy with an image of him holding up community values.

This chapter turns to how civic leaders used public rituals of protest to make the conspiracy tales come to life. Using city council meetings, demonstrations, and petition drives, civic leaders dramatized the biracial coalition as a threat to order and stability. By presenting the newly empowered black council members as impulsive, oversensitive, and spiteful, civic leaders mobilized perceptions of crisis. Much like during the slave insurrection panics and Wilmington race riot (without the overtly racist rhetoric), civic leaders warned of the calamities that would result from black control of city council— a threat that, if not averted, could destroy order and civility and perhaps return the city to the shameful conditions that gave it notoriety as Fayettenam. From this new position as the city council minority, powerful civic and business leaders cried foul and warned about the dangers and uncertainty that would follow disfranchising "the majority." With these public displays, they performed crisis as they replaced the vague rumors described in chapter 1 with concrete actions that embodied the danger and harm represented by the new majority.

Conspiracy before Our Eyes . . .

Performances of crisis stemmed from conspiracy theories that told scandalous tales of Tom Manning and Sam Johnson carrying out backroom deals between a white faction in the courthouse and black leaders. Overnight, these two white council members became objects of hatred. Strangers harassed them from dawn to dusk. They were called everything from race traitors and nigger lovers to scoundrels. Some residents honked at them in traffic, yelled slurs at them from car windows, and filled their answering machines with hateful messages and a few death threats. Sam Johnson was even shunned by his church congregation. The chorus of disapproval overwhelmed the two men as fear gave way to paranoia and they began believing all whites hated them and were seeking to harm them. I came to understand their fretfulness when they stopped talking to me because they suspected that I was the police department's mole in the cover of an anthropologist. As I will discuss below, many Fayettevillians believed the authorities were actively using surveillance throughout the ordeal.

Even though both Sam and Tom suffered, civic leaders understood their involvement in the schism on city council in different ways. Supporters of city management focused the full force of their anger upon Tom Manning and his brother Billy. With great resentment, civic and political leaders presented the Manning brothers in a less-forgivable way than they did the men's brother-in-law Sam. Reminiscent of the pattern of racial conspiracies that emerged after the Civil War, rumors portrayed the Manning brothers as outsiders; carpetbaggers who sought to exploit African Americans at the expense of the majority.

Originally from Jackson, Michigan, the outsider label stuck to the Manning brothers. They had moved to Fayetteville when their father, an administrator at Kelly-Springfield Tire Company, was transferred to its new plant in the north of the city. After college, Billy Manning returned to Fayetteville and rose quickly through the courthouse ranks. Starting as a deputy district attorney, he was on the fast track as he became a judge in his early thirties and embarked on a well-publicized campaign for district attorney. With his brother and brother-in-law on council, civic leaders envisioned Billy Manning's newfound interest in the black community as part of his attempt to become district attorney. Joanne Billings, a prominent real estate agent, wrote a letter to the editor arguing that the "Manning Family's main priority" was gaining power. She asked when their concern for the black community began: "I have never seen them attend any multicultural events put on by the Arts Council. I have never seen them volunteering at the Care Clinic. I did not see them at the recent Women's Center's celebration of women, where a group of young black girls were honored for completing the Survival Skills training to help guide them to a better future. I have never seen them at any of the Fayetteville State University's functions, or volunteering there."[1] Instead of being concerned with African Americans, citizens imagined that the Mannings were preying on the black community for self-serving reasons.

For his part, Sam Johnson gained infamy as the brother-in-law of Tom and Billy. Rumors were kinder to him. Conspiracy rumors presented him as a haphazard victim of the plot devised by his brothers-in-law. Most everyone I talked with viewed Sam as a nice, albeit simple, guy who had been bamboozled into a role similar to that of the scalawags—white southerners who betrayed their race to conspire with northern intruders and black rebels.[2] Building on this narrative, supporters of the police chief mercilessly exploited Sam's marital connection to Tom and Billy to call into question his motives for supporting the NAACP. They presented him as the hapless enabler of this devious plot.

Undeniably, Sam had little in common with his brothers-in-law. Growing up on the north side of Fayetteville, Sam fondly remembered his district when it was covered in farms, before it became swallowed up by wealthy subdivisions and northern children like the Mannings. Moreover, his political aspirations were humble. The former football star from Reid Ross High School and Fayetteville State University wanted little more than to represent the district in which he was born and raised.

With such close family connections, the ordeal was far more difficult for Johnson. He not only knew but also respected many of the people who turned against him. Consequently, civic and business leaders saw him as the weak link and tried to flip him. Being tugged in one direction by one faction and suspected of losing his resolve by the new majority, Sam became deeply anguished. Attempting to appease everyone, he tried his hand at being the conciliator on council. During many of the heated fights, as racial accusations were flying in every direction, Sam tried to validate everyone's opinions by formulating a middle ground, with the hopes of bringing both sides into compromise. He believed that the factions had become too entrenched and were unwilling to see the ocean of gray area. He repeatedly tried to create plans that would pull both sides together.

Mr. Johnson's hope for reconciliation vanished when black council member Frederick Walker introduced a motion to hire an "outside investigator." As Johnson was trying to bring both sides together during a heated council meeting, Walker presented a 1,700-word document, in which he proposed that the city hire a retired African American police chief to investigate the police department.[3] Exasperated, Mayor J. G. Dawson waited five minutes as Walker read through the tangle of legal language and then deadpanned: "Thank you, Fred, can you repeat that?" Laughter following the mayor's one-liner couldn't veil his anger. He ruled the motion out of order and, as he did before, summoned alarm about violating the "council-manager form of government."[4]

Frustration partly stemmed from the way council member Walker's proposal had put the mayor where he did not want to be: in the middle of conflict. As the self-described ambassador of Fayetteville, the mayor doggedly evaded controversy and often underplayed conflict with charm. For more than two decades, he had been a fixture in Fayetteville politics as his supporters celebrated his affability by proclaiming him "mayor for life."[5] He championed efforts to beautify the city and clean up its image as he became the mouthpiece for a wide variety of civic and business interests. In a rare moment of candidness, the mayor told a *Fayetteville Observer* reporter that Walker's call for an outside investigation "added credence to rumors that certain council members were ready to fire the city manager and the police chief." Though it is the job of city council to hire and fire the city manager, he argued that Walker's motion was illegal and would set a "dangerous" precedent in allowing any employee to question the authority of the city manager, which, he reminded residents, could ultimately destroy the council-manager form of government.[6]

Following this logic, civic leaders used the outside investigation as a symbol that the conspiracy was real. Most importantly, the sense of a dangerous precedent emphasized the negative effects of council members Tom Manning and Sam Johnson's voting with their black colleagues: they had recklessly awakened and stirred the black community into a threatening force. Council member Frederick Walker came to symbolize these anxieties. After all, no racial conspiracy theory would be complete without having a "dangerous Negro" as the coconspirator and supporter of the misdeeds of white schemers. In such a way, civic leaders developed Walker's public persona into the character of the agitator who was directing his black colleagues like puppets and producing anxiety and resentment among African Americas.

In his late forties, Frederick Walker dressed the part of an up-and-coming black leader. He spoke in a formal fashion and chose his words carefully. Many whites took him to be officious and believed he represented the black upper crust. Indeed, he grew up in Fayetteville's most prestigious black neighborhood, Broadell Heights, where his father pastored College Heights Presbyterian. As an alumnus from E. E. Smith High School and Fayetteville State, he formed part of Fayetteville's black middle class, not exactly dangerous or militant, as I will discuss later.

Although many whites felt that Walker was self-important and long-winded, they assumed he was much more intelligent than his two black colleagues, Edna Harrington and Larry Allison. Most whites liked Allison and hated Harrington. Mr. Allison was respectful to white officials and performed the rituals of racial deference. Ms. Harrington, on the other hand, actively antagonized the city's most powerful politicians and business leaders, often calling them racists in public meetings as well as in the newspaper. Though she was a retired army major and a registered nurse, many whites smeared her as ignorant and in private company called her a dumb nigger. She cared little about how whites portrayed her and met criticism by increasing her doggedness in pursuing the forbidden topics of racism and class inequality. For example, in a pitched battle over redistricting city council, she once dismissed the six white council members who voted against single-member districts as "racists" and pointed out how the plan gave inordinate power to wealthy citizens. In other cases, she often explained her unpopular positions as coming from God. Her opponents used her pyrotechnics to dismiss her as a crackpot.

In contrast to these images of Allison and Harrington as feeble-minded, Frederick Walker became the "ringleader." An example of this characterization was expressed by Janet, a member of the Fayetteville Partnership and a proponent of the Marvin Plan. When I interviewed her at the height of the city council conflict, she described Frederick Walker as if he were a one-man wrecking crew who was actively turning the black community against the revitalization project. Her enthusiasm about the Marvin Plan had turned to grief as she explained that it was "up in the air." As she and her allies were supporting the city manager and the police chief against the accusations of the NAACP, she believed that Frederick Walker was bent on seeking revenge. As the "ringleader," she argued, he was actively stirring hatred among blacks and leading them against the city's best interest. In fact, Janet pointed out that both council members Frederick Walker and Larry Allison had supported the Marvin Plan and served on its committee.

By demonizing Walker, white civic leaders imagined a picture of healthy race relations that existed before the dispute. Civic and business leaders spoke graciously about the many prominent black leaders they knew and often collaborated with. Like many white civic and political leaders, Janet took the collaboration of a few African Americans as proof that African Americans were content. Each white civic leader who opposed the NAACP and the outside investigation denied the charge of racism by referring to his or her friendship with prominent African Americans. From these various responses, I developed something of a who's who roster of black leaders according to white civic and business leaders. With Walker's sudden shift against the city manager, he served as a sharp contrast to the prominent African American leaders whom the *Fayetteville Observer* and the Chamber of Commerce glorified as "pioneers of the civil rights."

Taking these relations between black and white leaders as the result of years of building trust and respect between the "races," supporters of the city manager accused Walker of destroying interracial good will. Hoping to save the city from such peril, many powerful whites begged prominent black leaders to speak out against the new council majority and Frederick Walker. Several white civic leaders complained that many African American leaders agreed with them privately about the damage being done yet would not publicly speak out against the city council majority. As one of the more prominent black leaders told me, each side pleaded with him. His relations were complicated. On the one hand, he was disappointed that many of his old friends in the white community had devolved back to the "old forms of politics" that sought unity around racial issues. Yet he was focused on several capital projects to improve the black community and Fayetteville State. He knew that supporting the NAACP could threaten it. He had no place to go. Like many of the most powerful black leaders, he hid as well as he could.

Emergency

Fears about Frederick Walker's call for an outside investigation exploded into a fury of alarms. Leading the way, the Chamber of Commerce described the outside investigation as a crisis and announced an emergency meeting.

Its board of directors formulated a plan of action, which the president revealed to the public in a letter to the editor:

The City Council appears to be on the verge of taking an action at its Monday evening meeting that jeopardizes the council-manager form of government. This action is described in a six-page motion that calls for overtly illegal action. The North Carolina General Statutes are clear in defining the role of the City Council and the city managers . . . a mechanism is in place to handle the allegations of three city police officers. The council must be encouraged to comply with the letter and spirit of the law and follow these prescribed actions rather than acting impulsively, bypassing due process. The Fayetteville Chamber of Commerce has issued a Call to Action to its more than 1,450 members, urging them to contact members of the City Council to express their opinion about this matter.[7]

Equating Frederick Walker's motion with a crime, the letter raises concerns about thwarting due process and trampling over the proper mechanisms to handle race-based complaints in terms of the broader interests of the majority.

Walker and his colleagues had two weeks to revise their proposal after the mayor ruled it out of order. It was not going to be easy. As the sense of alarm spread, supporters of city management raised the stakes by spreading the rumor that council was going to fire the city manager at the next meeting. As it turned out, the rumor started with the city manager when he sent a memo warning city council members that if they were "compelled to take such drastic action" as an outside investigation, then the "appropriate" course of action would be to "terminate" the manager and "replace him with a manager" they could have "confidence" in. He ended with an ultimatum: "I cannot and will not participate in this intrusion into city administration for what I perceive to be purely political reasons."[8]

City management's pressure behind the scenes was supported by the *Fayetteville Observer*'s editorial, which warned council to "cool off" and "not force a confrontation over City Manager Jim Thompson's employment." Further, it argued that firing him before the investigation

would confirm what many already suspect: that at least some of the five embarked on this venture prepared to accept only one outcome. Worse, if Thompson is fired it will appear to be only a means to an end—that one dedicated professional is being ousted in order to get at another: Proctor, whose own record stands in stark and pleasing contrast to his predecessor's. . . . In clogging all over the principles that underpin the council-manager form of government, they will have disserved Fayetteville . . . leaving it looking less like a metropolis

than a not-ready-for- prime-time burg appended to two military bases,
too steeped in grudges, ambition and spite to see where its own
interests lie. We've come too far to let that happen.[9]

The editorial connects the conspiracy theories to the city's history of good ole
boy-ism and Fayettenam, conflating the military with the nepotism and networks of power that preceded Fort Bragg. It challenges those who are interested in uprooting racism to appeal to the professional institutions and the
principles of government that guard the public, including the black community, from the factional politics of spite and ambition.

Business and political leaders used the rhetoric of crisis to great effect.
More than merely a description, civic leaders used ideas of crisis to frame the
dispute as a dangerous turning point that required decisive intervention to
keep the city from descending into chaos (Hay 1996). Illustrating this sense of
crisis, two white residents, Catherine Mitchell and Christine Rutherford,
responded to the Chamber of Commerce's emergency by forming a "social
movement" called the "Committee of 100." They envisioned a broad wave of
citizens stopping the city council from firing the city manager and restoring
"good government." Moreover, they used the ideals of the civil rights movement to mobilize citizens so as to regain popular control of government.
Indeed, Cathy Mitchell equated her call to action with protests: "We should
march like we did for the Equal Rights Amendment."

By invoking the civil rights movement, the Committee of 100 deployed
color-blind language to mobilize racial fear (Bonilla-Silva 2003). Instead of
overtly calling attention to race, both Mitchell and Rutherford focused on
civic problems that presumed a white majority based on shared interests.
Indeed, both had participated in many of the most progressive issues
downtown—from raising money for the Arts Council to building the new
library. Cathy Mitchell's community activism dates back to 1976, when she
and her husband moved to Fayetteville for his stint at Fort Bragg as an army
doctor. Shortly after their arrival, Ms. Mitchell helped found Fayetteville's
chapter of the National Organization of Women (NOW). When Dr. Mitchell
left the military, he and Catherine remained in Fayetteville, and together they
built a thriving medical practice. She became increasingly active in civic
causes and the Fayetteville Medical Society, not to mention the efforts to
clean up the city's image and to improve its services.

Responding to rumors that the council was going to fire the city manager,
the Committee of 100 led a protest in front of city council. The *Fayetteville
Observer* interviewed Mitchell and Rutherford about their "grass roots effort,"
and they situated their activity in the spirit of the civil rights movement. Also,
Mitchell's husband wrote a letter to the editor warning his fellow concerned

citizens about a conspiracy: "Make no mistake; the issue is not discrimination. It is about power and control. It is about the unwillingness of the city manager and the chief of police to compromise their responsibilities to this community in order to pacify a few powerful people with private agendas. Perhaps if all my fellow dazed citizens who are wandering around thinking, 'I can't believe that they are really going to do this evil act,' pack the City Council Chambers to show our displeasure, they won't. Evil often has trouble surviving a watchful eye."[10]

Before the meeting, members from the Committee of 100 marched in front of city hall. Catherine Mitchell led forty citizens in a circle as they carried signs denouncing the "Gang of Five" and its "Kangaroo Court." The march followed the rituals of public protest, reminiscent of the civil rights movement. One of the demonstrators invoked the movement, in fact, claiming that direct-action protest was the last resort to stop the witch hunt of the city manager and police chief. As the demonstrator put it, "We tried everything. We wrote letters to the editor, called into WFNC, called city council members. The only thing left was to take to the streets to protest and really show that we the people are angry at what they were doing to us." Following the protest, citizens filled the council chambers, and the fire chief opened the auxiliary room so the rest of the crowd could watch the meeting on cable TV. Besides the three hundred citizens who attended these meetings, even more watched the televised footage.[11]

Accentuating the image of a racial divide, white citizens supporting the Committee of 100 occupied the left side of the aisle and the NAACP's supporters sat on the right side. Members of the Committee of 100 wore yellow ribbons to symbolize their solidarity with the city manager and chief of police. They borrowed the idea from the 1979 Iran hostage crisis, when many Americans wore yellow ribbons to represent solidarity with the hostages during their internment. The supporters of the city manager wore yellow ribbons because, as one protester explained, "we feel like the city of Fayetteville is being held hostage by a minority that does not have legitimacy with the majority of us voters." Many powerful white citizens in the audience, as well white council members Milo McRae and Kurt Jepsen, also wore yellow ribbons.

In the face of the scare, city council did not fire the city manager. Instead, officials from the Chamber of Commerce had brokered a compromise between city council and the city manager. For his part, the city manager accepted the investigation as long as it was conducted under his authority. Extending an olive branch, he began the meeting by clarifying that his memo to city council was not a threat, nor did it mean he was opposed the review of FPD personnel practices. As he put it, "All I want to do is ensure that this thing is done in an appropriate manner by an appropriate person, with the right kind of expertise."[12] City council voted unanimously to support the compromise, and it was agreed that each council member would submit names of potential investigators at the next meeting.

Within the first few minutes of the next meeting, the spirit of compromise vanished underneath the city manager's torrid attack on Frederick Walker's nominee, the African American chief of police from Tallahassee mentioned earlier.[13] Over the previous two weeks, city management had investigated Chief Tanner, and Thompson used the resulting report to demolish his credibility. The city manager pointed out that Chief Tanner had been reprimanded by the Florida Commission on Human Relations for violating the rights of a female employee, resulting in the ruling that "the Tallahassee Police Department had a hostile environment with regard to female employees." He dismissed Tanner by arguing: "Quite frankly, I think if you review my record and if you review the record of Chief Proctor, the two of us have been involved in municipal administration for, I guess combining it, over fifty years. I have never been found liable in court. I have never been found by any state or federal agency to violate anybody's civil rights and neither has Mr. Proctor. So I think whoever investigates Mr. Proctor and myself at least ought to have the same qualifications."[14]

Edna Harrington, Frederick Walker, and Larry Allison interpreted the well-researched report as a hatchet job and a sign that the city manager was loath to cooperate. This was the last straw, and city council retreated to the back offices for a closed meeting. Residents in the council chambers were left wondering about the city manager's fate, as many speculated the meeting was about his future. About thirty minutes later, council member Milo McRae returned to the chamber and shouted to the audience, "[The] city manager will be [back] here after the elections." Supporters flush in yellow ribbons understood that the city manager was finished. Once seated, Mayor Dawson thanked Thompson for his twenty years of service, and council member Jepsen, clad in a yellow ribbon, eulogized him, as he surely envisioned an apocalypse for Fayetteville:

> When I got on council back in 1986, looking at the needs of
> Fayetteville and looking at the vacant buildings downtown, looking at
> the urban decay, looking at the non-direction that our city was poised
> in. . . . The citizens of our community, be it black or white, do not
> know what they are losing this evening. The long-range repercussions
> are going to be devastating on [sic] the citizens of Fayetteville. There
> are some people here that are gleaming from this idea, but I want all
> of the citizens to know what's taking place and what it's going to take
> for us to recover from this, if we do.[15]

The Voters' Recall Movement

Supporters would continue to foster the belief that losing the city manager would invite uncertainty and crisis to the city. Apart from this rhetoric, the sense of crisis represented by his ouster gave the coalition of business and civic leaders a stronger point of reference to prove the conspiracy was real in ways that would compel a wider constituency of white voters. Seeking to magnify the sense of disaster, one resident wrote a stirring letter to the editor that equated the ouster of the city manager with the death and destruction that followed Sherman's March.

> March 12–14, 1865 made an indelible mark on Fayetteville, when General William Tecumseh Sherman and his renegade Yankee army destroyed the *Fayetteville Observer*, The Fayetteville Arsenal, several cotton mills and extensive private property. On February 17, 1997, Fayetteville witnessed another tragic holocaust. Five City Council members torched due process; fired an excellent city manager before proper investigations have taken place; and, in effect, have burned down the City Hall! Fayetteville is aghast at such boorish, brutish, unethical behavior and such waste of taxpayers' money! We are fighting back with petitions to the General Assembly of North Carolina, and with ballots in November or perhaps earlier. Council members Frederick Walker, Larry Allison, Tom Manning, Sam Johnson and Edna Harrington: The handwriting is on the wall. You are weighed in the balances and found wanting. May God Have mercy on your souls and on our beloved City![16]

Most supporters of the city manager preferred the language of civil rights over this writer's openly racial language, which is associated with defending slavery. Yet he captured the sense of panic that pervaded even the most moderate and liberal members of the dominant business and civic coalition. Openly racist residents came together with white liberals in support of their economic interests in the city manager's economic policy.

Building on the sense of uncertainty and crisis, the Committee of 100 expanded its objective to "retake control of government." Members of the group believed damage was mounting and that resolving the crisis could not wait until the November elections. Instead, the committee launched a petition drive to change the city's governing charter to allow voters the right to recall malfeasant city council members who abused their power and the public's sacred trust. Seeking to soften their image regarding race, the Committee of 100 enlisted white council member Gerald Hodges. He was the mayor pro-tem, an honor given to the at-large member with the most votes. Hodges's success stemmed partly from his relations with the black community; he had cultivated a broad following of black voters and often sided with his black colleagues on many issues.

In this situation, he found himself in an adversarial relation against many of his black allies. In supporting the right to recall, Hodges reiterated his strong support for the NAACP's commitment to "equal opportunity." He presented it in terms of the city's recent progress, stating: "We have gone too far in this city to go backwards. Through our inability as a Council to resolve these issues in a timely manner, I believe we've failed the city." He argued that recall would provide the citizens the power to resolve the issue in a way that would not impede the city's advancement: "I'm very concerned also that we're getting ready to float a multi-million dollar bond project in this City for the PWC [Public Works Commission]. Bond counsel advised me that when things are shaky in a city, they get concerned whether to do business. Lack of confidence in the people that are in charge may spell disaster for this city. There are long-term effects that this division can cause. . . . A change in leadership will cost the taxpayers money."[17] He believed that recall would allow citizens to restore stability to government so they could address serious issues.

Councilwoman Janet Chaney seconded his motion, assuring the public that citizens were working on a "recall project." She then asked one of the committee's leaders, Christine Rutherford, to inform the public as well as the city council "about their progress."[18] Mrs. Rutherford sought to "clear up" misunderstandings as she emphasized that "recall is not directed at any particular council members," nor is it motivated by "race." Instead, recall was about citizens preserving integrity in government. She pleaded with council members to understand the issue from the "citizens' point of view" as she concluded that it was not her group's intention to disagree with the way the council members vote, but "to deal with willful misuse of power and public trust."[19]

True to form, by a 5–4 vote the council majority rejected Hodges's motion for city council to give citizens the power to recall board members; however, these well-choreographed moves between the Committee of 100 and city council's four dissenting members helped publicize voter recall. More importantly, the group had already delivered their recall bill to the members of Cumberland County's legislative delegation. Ex-mayor Ed Shambley and his Republican colleague Kathy Thomas introduced the recall bill to the North Carolina House of Representatives.[20] The powerful Senator Frank Edwards was chair of the Senate Rules Committee, the second most powerful position in the Senate, and he sailed the recall bill through the Senate without any debate on the floor. Part of the reason the bill passed so smoothly was that Edwards did not tell his colleagues about the racial aspect of the dispute.

Moreover, his black colleague from Cumberland County, Neil Sweeney, kept quiet and supported the bill.

The recall bill's passage through the House of Representatives would not be as smooth. Two African American representatives from Fayetteville, Karen McMillan and Ed Hopkins, enlisted the Black Caucus and put up a challenge, an issue I will discuss in more detail in the next chapter.

While the recall bill was working its way through the General Assembly, the Committee of 100 held a rally at the library in Fayetteville. One of the Committee's leaders, surgeon Larry Ehlers, began by declaring, "We're meeting now because the citizens of Fayetteville have had enough." He urged the two hundred residents on hand to call their legislators and ask them to support House Bill 339. The committee would keep citizens updated on the progress of the legislation in Raleigh. By that time, committee members had collected signatures for a petition to recall city council members Sam Johnson and Tom Manning. If the bill passed both the House and Senate, the committee would already have enough signatures to hold a recall election for the two men.[21]

Performing Recall

It took more than three weeks for HB 339 finally to pass the House Rules Committee and reach the floor. Anticipating the bill's successful passage, the Committee of 100 held a meeting for volunteers on a Sunday afternoon at the Prince Charles Hotel. Christine Rutherford announced over the radio that members had already collected seven thousand signatures and should begin organizing for the recall election. The bill would require the Cumberland County Board of Elections to hold a recall election within sixty days of certifying the signature totals; they desperately wanted enough signatures so they could present the petitions immediately to the Board of Elections and quickly remove white council members Tom Manning and Sam Johnson.

About 140 people attended. All were white and most were middle-aged and middle-class. Sitting at tables according to voting districts, one of the organizers, cardiologist Larry Ehlers, welcomed the residents as six young men came in and sat down at one of the tables in the back, which happened to be right next to where I was sitting. I was taken aback to see that the late-arriving group included, of all people, "the Manning Boys" and their brother-in-law Sam Johnson. Equally surprised, an elderly man stood up, interrupting Dr. Ehlers, and asked if the meeting was public or private. After learning it was public, he yelled, in a thick Fayetteville accent, "Well, I see three stragglers who just walked in and I want to know who invited the Manning Boys?"

Ehlers met the man's hostility by welcoming the Mannings and assuring them that they were welcome to participate. He presented such openness to the visitors as an example of his group's commitment to "democratic philosophy" and to have an "open and frank discussion." In reference to the firing of the city manager in a closed meeting, he outlined that the goals of recall were to make politics transparent and chided the guests that "these things should not be done behind closed doors." Several other speakers joined him as they presented the Committee of 100 and its recall legislation as a "catalyst for change." Against voter apathy, Ehlers asserted that recall would allow the citizens to regain control of government and provide the mechanisms for citizens to hold officials accountable. He concluded, "We have no interest in race, color, or religion . . . we are interested in the law that represents the majority, the values that reside within the bell-shaped curve of common values. There are no privileged groups, no entitlements."

The meeting followed these themes of accountability and popular democratic participation, with Ehlers and three others telling the history of the Committee of 100:

> Our movement began to germinate during the late fall when rumor about the potential firing of City Manager Jim Thompson and Police Chief Dan Proctor began to circulate. The NAACP presented the City Council with the information that there were allegations of racism in city hall; all of a sudden the council waved its micromanagement prerogatives to do macro level management. City Council started an outside search for an investigator. . . . Jim Thompson was fired before he could choose an investigator. . . . There is a perception of conspiracy out there. . . . I wish "the Five" would do something that would clarify what they are doing and how they are thinking to make the process transparent.

After discussing the logistics of recall, Joe Pasquale, a downtown real estate agent, joined Ehlers in leading the group in holding a mock recall election. Ehlers called out, "Okay, the floor is open." One man stood up, and this exchange ensued:

> JD: My name is Jerry Downing, from District 1. I voted for Sam Johnson and I want to recall him.
>
> EHLERS: Okay. Who is for the recall of Sam Johnson? [The whole room raises their hands except for Johnson, the Mannings, and their three friends.] Who is against recall of Sam Johnson? [The Mannings, Johnson, and their three friends raise their hands, followed by laughter.] Okay, it is 97 for recall and 6 against.

Social History and Political Action

The Committee of 100's protest, and their subsequent activities, did not merely reinforce the symbolism that pitted the community's values against imputed special interests and ulterior motives. Such performances added a new dimension to the emerging political event, creating a perception of a popular uprising. In this way, their rituals endowed the formal structures of local government, and its bureaucratic logic, with an aura of sacredness.

In such public performances, the Committee of 100 presented Fayetteville's history as a tale of progress, featuring decades of struggle to transcend its image as a southern military town. Yet it told the story in a way that presented the military as a part of the progress that had replaced the days of the good ole boys. The committee contrasted the city's cultural improvements over the past twenty years to the good ole boy past, when nepotism, favoritism, and factionalism impeded the city's development. Many residents explained the controversy in apocryphal stories of a notorious figure in Cumberland County politics, the late Sheriff Jim Williams. Williams was a legendary figure in Cumberland County's politics, and most residents remembered him as the last of the South's good ole boy-style politicians, before professional government and modern governance gradually replaced patronage systems. Such stories presented Sheriff Williams as a political heavyweight who had total control over the county's and city's politics, relating tales of domination ranging from the rigging of elections and ridding the county of the Republican Party to imprisoning his political enemies. Williams died in office in 1986, yet his image as local kingmaker left an indelible mark on many Fayettevillians.

Currently, the most powerful figure in Cumberland County politics is State Senator Frank Edwards. Fayettevillians view Senator Edwards as the contemporary equivalent of Jim Williams. Unlike Sheriff Williams, civic and business leaders view Edwards as a legitimate, although powerful, force that positively contributes to the city's progress. Originally from Wade, North Carolina, Edwards made his way as a trial lawyer to the state legislature, aided by close connections to important figures in the courthouse crowd. Since the mid-1980s, when he was first elected to the General Assembly, Edwards has dominated Cumberland County politics and has used his influence in Raleigh politics as well to become what friends and foes call "the godfather of Fayetteville." Many political observers still believe Edwards is the most powerful individual in Cumberland County but distinguish him from Jim Williams in that he is more honest. Whenever civic leaders in Fayetteville need state resources to fund such efforts as the Care Clinic, the Juvenile Assessment Center, the Fayetteville State Arts Center, or downtown development, they make a point of discussing the issue with Edwards before sending a bill to the legislature.

Jim Williams's and Frank Edwards's perceived power structured the Manning conspiracy theory, whereby Attorney Manning and his kin members used the black community to take control of the Fayetteville City Council. The Committee of 100's protest movement invoked this social history by equating Billy Manning's ambitions with powerful people, as many thought he wanted to be the next Jim Williams, returning the city and county to the old days. In particular, the committee contrasted this retrogressive image of Manning with that of city manager Jim Thompson and police chief Dan Proctor, professional and dedicated public servants who put the public's best interest above factionalism and self-interest.

Conclusion

Civic and business leaders invested in Jim Thompson's administration used rituals of protest to create a sense of crisis. Focusing on the procedures to launch the investigation of the police department, leaders used each move to show that the council majority was acting out the conspiracy. Such rituals became embodied in the Committee of 100's protest and its eventual launch of its recall movement. Private citizens used the protest rituals outlined in the story of progress, whereby the city emerged from its good ole boy days of Fayettenam to its new phase as a modern and progressive government. They retold the social history of backroom deals and old-style power brokers to cast the Mannings and their allies as scoundrels who were intent on taking the city back to the bad ole days. Taken together, these political rites made an elaborate argument about the power that makes Fayetteville's urban regime tangible and effective. The Committee of 100 gave this network a public face and transformed the dispute into a call to action. They took the event as having an unintended consequence: awakening the silent majority. The newly inspired and agitated public was interpreted as being a part of the long-term civic projects to beautify the city and develop its economy. Civic leaders successfully coordinated their actions in terms of populist control of government.

Chapter 5

Threatening Images
of Black Power

THE COMMITTEE OF 100's staging of protests and the recall movement did more than continue the alarm bells of conspiracy. It elaborated the argument about how nefarious white politicians had dangerously empowered the black community and conjured the idea that black council members had an inordinate amount of power, reminiscent of the old fear of "Negro domination." These stories of black power fashioned Frederick Walker as benefiting from this arrangement and interpreted his actions as spiteful and dangerous. Such performances definitely exaggerated the power of not only Walker but also the black masses that were presumed to be lining up and mobilizing behind him. Ironically, the Committee of 100's fear-mongering dovetailed with romantic recollections of the civil rights movement that often mythologize the "black church," as the supporters of the city manager envisioned an empowered black leadership, emboldened by a vast network of black preachers, to rally whites against the power shift.

This chapter goes beneath white fantasies of a forceful and unified black community to examine some of the conflicts among African Americans. I will begin with the way ordinary African Americans understood and experienced the hysteria emanating from city council. In fact, many African Americans ignored the dispute entirely, especially the poor, who held little hope in either black or white politicians. Many of the black residents who did follow the event thought the anxiety and fear of whites was ludicrous. Rather than taking the shift of power as a sign of progress, black residents debated the significance and meaning of "the Fantastic Five"; they used the event to debate racial changes following integration. This chapter will examine how these conflicts shaped the event.

Views from "the Grass Roots"

Shortly after arriving in Fayetteville, I began attending city council meetings. The events were both exciting and troubling spectacles of racial animosity. At first, the bimonthly clashes resonated with stereotypic images of racism in the South. The whites who filled the council chambers were openly anxious and fearful about how the changes on city council had shifted the balance of power in favor of the black community. Terse exchanges and bitter commentaries between black and white board members were often met with a cacophony of cheers and catcalls from the audience. Members of the audience joined the officials in publicly thrashing out their most fervent beliefs about racial issues that were normally hidden by conventions of politeness.

In addition to helping me get to know residents and political officials, the city council meetings gave me a chance to meet city employees—the staff who carried out many of the bureaucratic details the board members debated about. Contrasting the loose talk of the city council partisans, members of city staff were careful and circumspect about their opinions and blinked at the mention of anything close to the controversy. Nevertheless, many staff members enjoyed talking to me about the policies they carried out—from annexation to programs to expand the city's affordable housing. Yet, my access to many staff members was limited. Straightaway I learned to avoid the second floor of city hall, where the executive and mayor offices were located. The dispute and heightened scrutiny of city management raised the anxiety level of the executive officials and they never were comfortable having a stranger like myself in their midst. Although no one was rude or threatening, they were aloof and I figured that my research's success would require me to be as unobtrusive as possible.

In contrast, the top floor of city hall was open to my curiosities. As it turned out, the third floor was devoted to "minority issues" and housed Human Relations, Community Development, and other programs that focused on poverty in black neighborhoods. Staff from these departments embraced me and openly shared information about how the city sought to confront problems of crime and affordable housing and developed programs to extend city services in black neighborhoods. Most importantly, I learned about the ways the planners in this division implemented various strategies to connect the city's policy agenda with many federal initiatives, such as HUD, and made sure that city government complied with civil rights legislation by working with activists and community leaders.

During my second visit to the third floor, Harold James, the director of Human Relations, invited me into his office. Having recognized me from the

Monday night showdowns, he showed curiosity about my presence. After explaining my interests in racial politics, he shared some of his views about racial policies. As it turned out, Mr. James began working for the city as part of the negotiations that halted the student protests at Fayetteville State University (FSU) during the 1960s. As a participant in the civil rights struggles in Fayetteville, he was hired as part of the city's first attempt to integrate city government. Drawing on his experiences, Mr. James launched into a spirited lecture about racism almost on cue. Proudly displaying FSU memorabilia on his office wall, he told me in a casual manner: "Things are better than when I was a boy." He leaned forward, and in a passionate and angered voice, he looked me in the eye and said: "It is the lack of services [in the black community] that really pisses me off."

With more than thirty years of experience in government, he told me that his views and opinions about race were based in what he called "realism." Many of the problems in black neighborhoods result, he stated bluntly, from how the rich and powerful have attained expertise in urban planning, not to mention civil rights laws. He believed that this arena of power required African Americans—by whom he meant working classes—to learn about the planning process so they could "be strategic." He shared few illusions with me. In reference to city government and its policies regarding the black community, he said, "the city is doing what is respectable," by which he meant complying with civil rights laws as stipulated by the Justice Department. However, in the end, he asserted that racial issues boil down to "power and money." To make his point, he described the way that Wal-Mart and other multinational corporations leverage money against the city to get their way. Pointing to the skirmishes on city council, Mr. James said it was overblown. After all, he pointed out to me, "it is a fixed environment . . . the outcome has already been determined. All we are doing [blacks and whites] is jockeying for position . . . all we are doing is fighting for position," what he compared to "fighting a prick," the best one can do is not get hurt within a very narrow set of possible encouraging outcomes.

As he winded down his discussion, Mr. James warned me to get to know "the grass roots." Like many black residents who used this term, he referred to poor and working-class blacks, those people who he said "are in the trenches" and were directly involved in the day-to-day struggles. In this vein, he told me that council meetings had limited value to my research and he encouraged me to be skeptical of African Americans who go to city council meetings and those who were using the council dispute to "jockey for position." He insisted that middle-class blacks did not fully understand the realities of most African Americans. He then scribbled the phone number of a man named Reverend

Troy Jones, who had been working in the poor neighborhoods. With little explanation, he implored me to call the reverend.

When Reverend Jones answered the phone, he was uneasy with me. He confronted me with frank questions about my interests and what I wanted *from* the black community. Dropping Harold James's name did not help, as he seemed unimpressed by my new acquaintance. After I explained my general interests in racial politics and civil rights policies, he relented and commanded that I meet with him the following morning at 7:00 A.M. for breakfast at the K&W Cafeteria.

When I arrived at the restaurant, it took only one glance at Reverend Jones to gather a clear idea about what Harold meant by the term "grass roots." He wore a Vietnam War veteran's hat and a black athletic suit. He had an imposing presence. Looking like an aging heavyweight boxer, he began jabbing me with questions. Inquisitively, he began the conversation by asking about my family background and was particularly interested to know what my parents did for a living. As I began telling him about my father's work on the shipyards of Hunter's Point in San Francisco and my mother's career with the Teamsters, I could see he was readjusting his plan for discussion. He seemed to be pleasantly surprised that I grew up in a working-class family. As we talked, he would refer to my parents' "rough life" (and my privilege) to highlight distinctions among African Americans. In reference to working-class blacks, he used the terms "real" and "authentic" to refer to working-class blacks, whom he contrasted with those who wore neckties and held positions of power. Though he viewed Harold Jones as one of "the middle-class African Americans," the two shared the concern that talking to black politicians and bureaucrats would lead me to wrong conclusions about the black community. He described black politicians and professionals as "one-dimensional" and unaware of the happenings "in the valley," where the poor blacks live.

Even though Reverend Jones was an associate pastor at a powerful church, one would never confuse him with what many black Fayettevillians referred to as "the black bourgeoisie." Moreover, he was proud that he came from Campbell Terrace, Fayetteville's first public housing project. And he was well known for his reputed past as a criminal known as "Boo-Boo." Most people did not know what exactly he had done, but that did not keep them from freely talking to me about his alleged misdeeds. Prominent black politicians were especially mistrustful and kept him at arm's length. As one of his longtime friends explained to me, the "bourgeois blacks don't like Boo-Boo because he was a thug. While Jesus may forgive you, man will always remind." Despite the controversy and rumors about his past, the reverend had supporters who recognized his service in an artillery division during

Vietnam. After years in Chicago, the U.S. Army finally recognized his disabilities from combat and awarded him a settlement. With this relatively large amount of money, he returned to Fayetteville and became active in black neighborhoods.

After finishing the last bite of his bacon-and-egg sandwich, he snapped his fingers and ordered: "Follow me." Having no idea where we were going, I followed him as he drove downtown to a run-down shoeshine shop. Sitting among several unoccupied storefronts, a beauty salon, and the Market House, the shoeshine shop was cluttered with secondhand merchandise, including clothes, shoes, and compact discs. As we walked past a row of chairs along the wall, we greeted Cornell, who was shining a pair of shoes. Reverend Jones asked: "Where's Clay? I have got here an ANTHRO-pol-o-gist." He told Cornell that I needed to meet some "sho' nuff" black folk. Cornell continued shining shoes as he muttered, "Yeah, uh-huh, uh-huh, yeah." He was not really paying attention but told us that Clay was out for the day.

Reverend Jones insisted that I meet Clay, because "he knows more than anyone" about Fayetteville. Indeed, Clay had lived most of his life on the streets of Fayetteville and he enjoyed philosophizing about "the White Man" as well as the many issues that made black people complicated. His understanding of whites was monolithic, while his discussions of African Americans were complex, textured, and emphasized social, political, and class differences. His charm and humor attracted a large cast of characters who frequently visited his shop to hang out and talk about everything from sports and religion to politics and racism. During the early evenings the shop became a political forum as well as an arena for the playing of the dozens.[1]

The following day, I returned to the shoeshine shop. Clay greeted me at the door, mistaking me for a delivery driver bringing in a load of shoes or other merchandise. Clearing up the misunderstanding, I dropped Reverend Jones's name, and Clay responded, "Boo-Boo?" He hadn't expected me. Neither Cornell nor Boo-Boo had told him I was coming. Presuming, as he told me later, "I was a well-meaning white boy," he began glowing about Boo-Boo's rise from being a "zero to a hero" as he unfurled a black version of the Horatio Alger fairy tale. He didn't stop there. Clay gloried about black progress and improving race relations in Fayetteville. He seemed to be parroting the type of stories black officials would often feed me. Intrigued by his narrative, which contradicted the reasons why Reverend Jones had introduced me, I asked him how these ideas of progress related to Grove View Terrace or the many other poor black neighborhoods. I suggested his story sounded more relevant to the people who live in Broadell, one of the wealthier black neighborhoods. Smiling, he said, "Shit, you already know something."

Over the next months, Clay and the many middle-aged men who fre-
quented his shop used the "Five–Four" dispute to discuss class relationships
within and outside of the black community. Clay and his friends often argued
about class conflict and political struggles among African Americans. In contrast to the stories of progress often proffered by black officials, their accounts
emphasized racial decline and what they often called "the failures of integration." During one of my earliest rap sessions at the shoeshine shop, I commented on the way their descriptions of black politics resembled those of the
black talk show host Reverend Tony Jefferson. Suddenly, Clay went silent.
He looked down at his shoes and continued shining them and didn't respond.
I was puzzled and made the situation worse when I mentioned that Clay's
relentless attack on middle-class blacks reminded me of Jefferson's daily radio
show called *Powertalk*. Like Clay and his friends, Jefferson did not view the
dispute on council as a crisis; instead, he viewed it as a "wake-up call for
Afro-Americans."

By the time I met Reverend Jones and Clay, I had already become a regu-
lar listener of *Powertalk*, and I rarely missed the daily broadcast at 11:00 A.M.
Jefferson's discussions were ethnographically rich as he drew from his experiences with local politics—from his childhood in a tobacco town north of
Fayetteville, in the final days of Jim Crow, to the struggle for civil rights after
the movement. After serving as a deputy in the narcotics division of the
Cumberland County Sheriff's Department for more than a decade, Jefferson
began working for a substance abuse and HIV outreach program. His show
drew on these experiences with poor African Americans to emphasize the
unfulfilled promises of the civil rights movement and talked about the worsening conditions in Fayetteville's black neighborhoods. He talked about drugs,
violence, and rising inequality.

Jefferson liked to call himself "the minister of information," as he distinguished himself as one of the few black people in Fayetteville who would
discuss controversial features of racism.[2] He often invoked such figures as
Malcolm X, Cornel West, Jack Johnson, and Louis Farrakhan to criticize
how Fayetteville's elite, whom African Americans often called "the Hill,"
remained racist and indifferent to blacks. Despite his criticism of the
Haymount, he uncompromisingly criticized those he called the "Wazees" (the
black bourgeoisie),[3] on whom he laid as much blame for black suffering as
"the Hill." Jefferson's critique of what he called Fayetteville's "so-called black
leaders" exposed cleavages, factions, and struggles among African Americans
(see Cohen 1999; Gregory 1998; Jackson 2001, 2005, 2008). Jefferson loved
offending black leaders. He had many black enemies, especially black politicians, who disliked how he highlighted conflicts among high-profile politicians,
public officials, attorneys, and the clergy within the black community.

During the dispute, the phone lines at *Powertalk* lit up with callers. He and his audience hammered away at the Hill, and its "mouthpiece," the *Fayetteville Observer*, which he and many of his listeners called the "Fayetteville Disturber," for misreporting the facts, fanning the flames of racial hatred, and protecting the police chief. Jefferson saw his job as correcting the misrepresentations promoted on the other talk radio shows. Jefferson studiously listened to *Top of the Morning* and read the *Fayetteville Observer* to discredit and challenge the assertions of both. He criticized the newspaper and the white talk radio show for putting emphasis on procedure to mask what he considered to be the real issue: the FPD's systemic discrimination against black police officers. Also, Jefferson reinforced the NAACP's claims with accounts of his own experiences with discrimination while he worked in law enforcement; indeed, he knew some of the officers in question and encouraged his listeners to march down to city hall in support of the NAACP as it faced increasing hostility from the white media.

Despite their shared views about how black leaders collaborate with Haymount Hill, Clay did not like Tony Jefferson. And the feelings were mutual. After I brought up Tony Jefferson's name, and his show *Powertalk*, Clay became concerned. He cocked his head, raised his eyebrows, and challenged: "You know he's a Republican?" He was worried that I might be "duped" by *Powertalk* and wanted to set me straight. Like many African Americans, he dismissed the relevance of *Powertalk* because he thought Jefferson's observations were too steeped in personal vendettas. Clay told me that Jefferson's evolution into being an outspoken critic of black leaders, and a Republican, was a result of his failed campaign for county sheriff. As a deputy sheriff, Jefferson had become disillusioned by management in the department. A few black politicians encouraged him to challenge the powerful sheriff, reasoning that he could pick up the black vote and unite the black community. As Jefferson began his bid, he encountered daunting problems, which included an investigation by the State Bureau of Investigation. Democratic officials, as the story went, made a concerted effort to keep him off the ballot. As his opposition mounted, black leaders retreated. Clay felt that this experience of betrayal had taught Jefferson that there were not "any authentic or 'big' blacks in Fayetteville" and gave him the idea that he was just as big as any of the black leaders and "was bold enough to speak."

Black Moses and a Nigger Lover

During discussions at the shoeshine shop, many of Clay's friends and clients expressed a sense of pride, sometimes to the point of gloating, about how three black city council members were holding the Hill's feet to the fire regarding racial discrimination in the FPD. They celebrated the conflict as "the first time" in Fayetteville's history that African Americans controlled politics.

Along with their delight about the ongoing challenge to powerful whites, many African Americans expressed amusement at the hysteria and fear-mongering over Frederick Walker and the NAACP. Many of the shoeshine shop's visitors dismissed Walker as a "Broadell Boy." They assumed that, having grown up in the wealthiest black neighborhood, he had had a sheltered upbringing. They thought it was laughable that anyone could interpret him as a threat to anyone except maybe himself. To be sure, Walker grew up in Broadell Heights and held a professorship at the community college. But he was by no means wealthy or powerful. However, from the perspective of the shoeshine shop he had enough privileges to keep him from being "hard."

When it came to African Americans who were ready to fight the white power structure, working-class blacks looked to Edna Harrington. White civic and business leaders disliked Harrington and often discounted her as a fool, presuming she was merely taking her cues from Frederick Walker. However, ordinary African American saw the relationship the other way around; they believed Harrington was the real ringleader. They pointed out that Walker had rarely taken risky positions on controversial issues and that he avoided conflict because of his larger political ambitions. Harrington was retired and had few ambitions in the political realm. She viewed herself as a biblical character, acting and speaking for God. Instead of making political calculations and alliances, she spoke defiantly against Fayetteville's wealthy. She embraced controversy and rarely dodged a fight. Many whites believed she was dumb and made a mockery of the political process. The same stunts and games that made whites think she was a buffoon won her admiration from many blacks. Rather than being confused and stupid, people who knew her well understood her games and performances as filibustering, creating confusion, and derailing business as usual. Moreover, many blacks appreciated her for "speaking her mind," forcing whites to confront the forbidden topic of racism and to hear what "real" blacks were thinking. Many conceded she was not the best speaker and that she was eccentric, but as one supporter explained, "She gets her point across."

Harrington did much to solidify her reputation as a fighter for the poor and a nightmare for the city's wealthy. As many African American residents told me, if you have a problem with the city and something is not right, "Edna will be like a dog on a bone" in her pursuit of resolving the problem. Countless people, including whites living in her district, told me that if they called Edna about an issue related to poverty or the city disrespecting the rights of citizens, it was guaranteed to be on city council's agenda. Most famously, she helped a group of activists fight the city and move several poor people whose homes had become besieged by stench and vermin from the city's garbage dump.

With a strong track record as a fighter, she was seen by many African Americans as having a central role in the controversy; they laughed at the idea that Frederick Walker was pulling her strings, as many white residents believed. Many black residents saw it much differently and often assumed it was Ms. Harrington who had to convince Walker to join the struggle. Adding credence to this view, Edna bragged that she was the decisive figure and that she had been waiting all her life for such a moment to turn the tables on wealthy whites. She told me that when she heard that there were white council members who were with the NAACP, she was ready to go.

Many African Americans appreciated how the three black council members had forced the issue of discrimination into the public arena. Nevertheless, they also understood that such expression of black political power would have been inconceivable without sympathetic (if not crazy) whites. Many of the guys at the shoeshine shop liked Tom Manning and Sam Johnson as much as Edna. They appreciated their concern about blacks who suffered racial discrimination, and they imagined the horrors the two men faced when they were branded "nigger lovers." Tom Manning gave some African Americans hope about racial change in terms of white attitudes. A retired army officer named Brian recognized Tom Manning as "an outsider," the type of person who had contributed to Fayetteville's progress:

> Cumberland County was a dry, racist, and Baptist town. People
> migrated in, bringing with them new visions and experiences. This is
> a very conservative place, would be more so without the outsiders.
> Imagine a dry county and the type of segregation that would be here if
> it weren't for [Fort] Bragg. People here are becoming more progressive
> as Fayetteville grows. People in leadership, a short time ago, were not
> progressive; they were good ole boys. See, Fayetteville should be like
> Raleigh, but all those years with status quo people, they are just
> getting around to building a beltway. Now, you have some progressive
> people who have made a difference. We need a city manager that can
> think big. Tom Manning, now he is a progressive!

Many black residents, like Brian, did not interpret the Mannings' alliance as a scandal. To them, Manning symbolized the arrival of a new generation of white politicians who were willing to subordinate the South's racist traditions to the city's development as a metropolitan center.

House Negroes and Other Enemies

African Americans in Fayetteville understood the Committee of 100's and Chamber of Commerce's cries of conspiracy and apocalypse to be paranoid reactions that overstated the power of Frederick Walker, the NAACP, and other black officials.[4] Rather than focusing on the event as evidence of black political power, many working-class blacks used the dispute to discuss how racial integration served as a tool for controlling blacks. Illustrating this aspect of racial reform, many African Americans came to know the political dispute much differently than the conspiracy theories that exaggerated the power of black council members would suggest. Instead they came to know the event through conspiracy theories that told about Haymount Hill and the police chief using blacks to crack down on African Americans who challenged the white police chief.

The most familiar story of the chief's misdeeds emphasized how Chief Proctor had used high-ranking African American officers to help him control black line officers. Such accounts spread among African Americans through stories about how the FPD's highest-ranking black officers—Major George Moses and Captain Robert Chambliss—served as "house Negroes" or "yes men" who helped the chief retaliate. After all, the controversy began when Proctor ordered these two men to interview all sixty-eight black officers about their opinions about the FPD's racial policies. In one popular version of the story, which circulated in barbershops, shoeshine shops, churches, and the black media, several African American officers met Moses and Chambliss at a prominent Baptist church and aired their views. After discussing their issues, the two high-ranking black officers turned over the information to the chief. Behind the dramatic action were Haymount Hill's elite and their control of Fayetteville. Such a criticism simply reduced the chief to Haymount Hill's proxy, merely carrying out the founding fathers' racist policies, which nevertheless depended on house Negroes and Uncle Toms to keep the "field Negroes" in line—and, as it turns out, divided.

Promotion of African Americans to upper management in the police department resonated with the ways in which many blacks believed integration weakened black politics. One man who was deeply involved in the process was a barber named John. He moved to Fayetteville in the 1950s to escape rural poverty. Several years later, John joined the struggle for civil rights and helped organize the protests at Fayetteville State. Because he was neither a student nor a local, authorities branded him an "outside agitator," and when the city began negotiating with black leaders and student protesters, he was left out and returned to cutting hair.

Despite his disappointments, John was proud of his participation in the civil rights movement and he boasted that "in the 1960s the door swung open" for African Americans. Significantly, he pointed out that African Americans could vote, hold office, and go to college. After pausing, he continued on a sober note as he pointed to the ways racism continues through more sophisticated forms: "Put it this way, we were allowed to move forward to a certain extent. At one point they let us know, 'You are getting out of hand.'" Looking for an example, he pointed at me: "Like when Frederick Walker spoke. He wasn't supposed to say what he said. He was supposed to behave. And now the Hill is going to make him and the Manning boys pay!" Though John didn't know Walker, he worried about his well-being; he presumed his job at the community college could be jeopardized.

John's assessment of how white politicians control politics, and the type of dilemmas it creates for people like Frederick Walker, highlights a crucial dimension of black politics, not to mention a challenge. Black politicians must represent African Americans against discrimination yet cannot be too adversarial to powerful whites. The problem resonates with how sociologist Oliver Cox described the dilemma: black leaders "must be specialists in the art of antagonistic co-operation," as their success requires that they cultivate friendships with powerful whites at the same time that they project an image to blacks that they are "aggressive and uncompromising" in their struggle for black interests. They have to be selective in whom they identify as the enemy because they do not want to push powerful decision makers into a "hostile camp." He took this to result in a "baffling problem for the Negro leader" in that he must "befriend the enemy while championing the interests of blacks. He must not be so aggressive as to incur the consummate ill will of whites; hence, no small part of his function is engaged in understanding the subtleties of reaction to the manipulations of the whites of his community. No contemporary Negro leader of major significance, then, can be totally void of at least a modicum of the spirit of 'Uncle Tom'; ingratiation, compromise, and appeasement must be his specialties" (Cox 1949, 592).

Cox's insights resonate with the ways many working-class African Americans understand racial reforms. As described earlier, many of my informants believe that powerful whites use prized positions and jobs to control African Americans. Racism, however, remains in more "sophisticated" and "subtle" forms. Instead of using overt racial exclusion, white civic leaders now carefully choose which blacks they will deal with. According to this view, if someone wants to enter politics, it is more important for him or her to gain the support of powerful whites than grassroots support from African Americans. When there is a racial problem or when a major project needs voter support, white leaders rely upon a set of black officials and clergy to either quiet protest or to bring black leadership within the prevailing policy agenda. By calling attention to what they viewed as collusion between black officials and powerful whites in Fayetteville during the "Five–Four," many working-class blacks ridiculed the black leaders who were most celebrated and revered among whites. Rather than seeing these men and women as "leaders" or representatives of the black community, many black residents suspected these men of colluding with "the Hill."

Pitfalls of Arrogance

The clash between the city manager and the NAACP brings us to the way working-class blacks described the conflicts that shaped the event, causing it to become public. Many whites presumed that the NAACP took an adversarial role and started the fight with the local government. Such an assumption misses the key feature of postsegregation racial politics—the ways in which organizations that grew from protest have been readapted to governance. Indeed, Thompson had a long history with the local chapter of the NAACP. He sought their help for everything from complaints about racial discrimination to major public image issues like the recent Burmeister killings. Notoriously, many black activists remember the Fayetteville NAACP's role in the redistricting. The Justice Department ordered the city to comply with the 1982 Civil Rights Act and represent African Americans in city council according to their population in the city, which was roughly 40 percent. Black activists lobbied for the city to meet the Justice Department's condition by creating nine single-member districts, which would result in five white districts and four black districts. Like many cities throughout the South, the administration devised a "mixed" voting plan that diluted black representation by combing six single-member districts (half of them black) with three at-large seats. The at-large voting districts worked to dilute the power of black representatives and resulted in 6–3 votes on controversial matters. Many African Americans blame the NAACP for helping city management finesse the mixed plan. One activist who organized the campaign for single-member districts laid the entire blame on the NAACP. He referred to the ways "those necktie-wearing niggers and satin-dressed Sallies believed Fayetteville did not have enough educated blacks for single-member districts. They cut a deal with the city management." And then afterward the city sent out their human relations person to "gather up all the niggers and tell them it was a good compromise."

Having a similar dislike for the Fayetteville NAACP, Frank Norris sought to intervene in the police department controversy. Even though Norris was a resident of Fayetteville and a teacher at a city high school, he boycotted the Fayetteville chapter of the NAACP and chose to work with the more radical group in nearby Robeson County. After several black officers called the Robeson County NAACP, Frank called the city manager and attempted to seek a resolution. Thompson refused to speak to Norris, telling him that he would work with "our own NAACP."

At this point, city management attempted to resolve the matter with the help of the Fayetteville NAACP, as described earlier. It appears that the city manager felt overly confident in his ability to control the issue and did not take into account that the NAACP was not acting in a vacuum. With several officers becoming unhappy with the progress of these talks, and with the Robeson County NAACP looking over its shoulder, the leaders of the Fayetteville NAACP began to feel pressure from many quarters. It never became clear how effective Norris was or to what degree he precipitated the conflict. However, the Fayetteville NAACP did change its approach and eventually challenged the city manager. On another level, several black police officers appealed directly to city council members. In a chance meeting in a grocery store parking lot, two black officers informed council member Frederick Walker about how the police department's management had used interrogations and demotions to punish black officers. Fearing negative publicity, Walker encouraged the officers to exhaust all avenues. He told them to see the city's personnel department and file a complaint and assured the officers he would watch the progress of the grievance procedure, making sure city management acted quickly on their complaints.

Not mindful to the implications of these internal conflicts among African Americans, Thompson felt confident that he would be able to control the Fayetteville NAACP. His plan was dashed when his dependable partners challenged his authority, as described in chapter 1. After city management failed to respond to the NAACP leadership's demands—that the chief apologize to the aggrieved officers, set up an Equal Employment Opportunity committee in the police department, and rescind all punishment—the NAACP decided to take the conflict to the city manager's superiors, city council, and insist that they intervene. It was not until Thompson learned that the NAACP officially put its complaint on the city council agenda that he began to worry about the NAACP. One member of the NAACP explained that he "sent one of his 'boys' to talk to us, thinking that we would change our mind. He didn't realize how serious we were, but also, he was not willing to take action. . . . He wanted to continue to talk, and we were damned tired of talking."[5]

Thompson's failure to fully understand the political situation led the NAACP to take the embarrassing issue of racism into the public. As members of the NAACP changed their tack, Thompson's position hardened. He became invested in the idea that the NAACP's insistence signaled a threat to his authority, and that his authority represented the will of the people. As one black politician (who knew about the behind-the-scenes negotiations) came to believe, the city manager did not see how the gathering of these forces had actually pushed the NAACP leadership to change its approach. Instead, the city manager appeared to have taken the shift in tactics as a "betrayal" of his trust and authority. Feeling insulted, he became increasingly intransigent. One city council member explained that the problem stemmed from how political and business leaders were accustomed to controlling black leaders. He explained, "The Hill never saw us [blacks] in a stressful situation." He believed that the city manager had sorely miscalculated, as they "did not know we could handle it. They wanted to be good ole boys and forced us [the three black council members] into this arena—one I've never been before."

African Americans understood the hysteria following the NAACP's call for an outside investigation to be a strategy to shift the focus from Thompson's managerial mistakes to "misbehaving" and "marauding" blacks. As one activist put it, when the police department controversy emerged, "the Hill" became alarmed because the NAACP and city were running amok. He said, "This is classic, you know, *Birth of a Nation?* The black politician didn't understand the democratic process. He makes the most that he can out of the goodness of his heart, but he doesn't understand the process. But we [the black community] did understand! The chief had violated Title VII of the Civil Rights Act, and the city manager was doing everything he could to whitewash his retaliatory tactics as good management techniques."

A Historical Moment

Amid the many voices and disagreements among African Americans about racism in the FPD, black leaders jockeyed for position, as Harold James discussed above, and sought to portray the shift on city council as a progressive development in black politics. With the city manager's mishandling of the event, certain black politicians entered the breach and attempted to portray the event as an example of the black community's increased power. Representing this perspective was an elected leader, named Frank, who had become inspired by the prospects for the black community. He called the "Five–Four" a "historical moment" that resulted from the victories of the civil rights movement, victories that had given the "black community" the power and leverage to "make a move." Similarly, Frank, a member of the local chapter of the NAACP, proclaimed that with the firing of the city manager, "we sent the political establishment a message: the Hill could no longer abuse African Americans arbitrarily." He stated, when "the system abuses its membership and the safeguards fail, then we [elected officials] become the safeguard." He reasoned that the city manager and police chief had worked with the consent of the more powerful political and business leaders because retaliation had been going on for quite a long time. But, finally, "all the pieces in the puzzle came together" and the city manager could no longer hide the issue from the public.

Similarly, Karen McMillan, an African American member of the North Carolina State House of Representatives, stood up against Fayetteville's most powerful white leaders when she challenged the recall legislation described in the previous chapter. As discussed earlier, the Committee of 100's recall efforts were coordinated with Fayetteville's powerful senator Frank Edwards. Allies of the city manager and white civic leaders were confident in the imminent passage of recall because of Edwards's legendary status as a high-stakes power broker in the North Carolina General Assembly. However, out of nowhere, Representative McMillan blindsided Senator Edwards and put a chink in his figure as the all-powerful godfather of Fayetteville. She derailed the recall legislation by mobilizing the House of Representatives' Black Caucus and revealing to her colleagues in the General Assembly the racial nature of the recall legislation. She described it as "the most divisive" and "unnecessary request the city had seen in years" and revealed that it was a reaction to a shift in power on city council. She concluded: "The majority of the City Council voted for an investigation. The majority of the City Council voted to fire the city manager, and the majority of the City Council voted against sending this request up here."[6] Her plea both mobilized the North Carolina Black Caucus and alerted white colleagues to the racial polarization, leading to a defeat of the recall by a resounding 77–35 vote.

In addition to defeating recall, McMillan organized a "town hall meeting" at Mount Sinai Baptist Church to "inform" and "mobilize" the black community. Over three hundred African Americans—largely comprised of politicians, clergy, and middle class—participated. NAACP attorney William Wilson told the crowd about how the chief of police's routine retaliation against African American officers was part of a broader pattern whereby city management was turning back gains in civil rights. He explained that not only had the FPD failed to fulfill the 1974 Superior Court decree for minority representation, but the city manager was disbanding the decree because it represented "racial preferences."[7] In light of this trend, many attendees urged "the community" to participate in the political process: stop the rescission of the court decree, attend city council meetings, and, most importantly, support

Tom Manning and Sam Johnson. One minister denounced the Committee of 100 as a "hate group" that sought to punish whites who dared to question racism in city government. He argued that in defining the two men as race-traitors, the recall movement was an "electoral lynching" designed to strike fear into other politicians who dared cross the color line and to break up "the Five."

Following this meeting, McMillan instituted the "town hall" meeting as a monthly event whereby black leaders and representatives would keep "the community" informed and mobilized for the elections. From the beginning, it appeared that the meetings would be a vehicle whereby black leaders and residents would mobilize their support for the aggrieved police officers, their supporters on council, and especially the white council members who had risked their political lives. In this way, McMillan succeeded in projecting a powerful image of a groundswell of political momentum in the black community.

Conclusion

Amid the confluence of ideas of racial progress and the backlash from the middle-class whites who protested the city council majority, many working-class African Americans used the "Five–Four" to criticize the effects of integration. Challenging the ideal of racial progress, working-class blacks criticized how city officials integrated African Americans. Including African Americans in government and affluent white neighborhoods had coincided with worsening social conditions for most blacks. Failing to see that the NAACP's shifting approach resulted from internal struggles among African Americans, city manager Jim Thompson mishandled the dispute between black officers and the police chief, and, as a result, the embarrassing issue of racism became public. Amid these internal fissures, certain black leaders succeeded in using the event to project their power and in this way became complicit with the Committee of 100's calls about crisis.

Chapter 6

Power Shift

Though the idea of a crisis framed the conflict on city council, many whites were skeptical about these narratives. Many white opponents of the urban regime believed that the intense reaction to the NAACP's alliance with whites was an example of the backwardness of local authorities. This view was especially strong among residents who self-identified as "the military." Increasingly, military retirees have become vocal critics of the downtown coalition, and they revamped the local Republican Party to challenge what they called the "one-party rule" of the city and county. John Duncan was just such a person. After retiring as an enlisted member of the Special Forces, which included tours to Vietnam, he stayed in Fayetteville. He owned a home, worked as a real estate agent, and became active in civic life. As Duncan shifted from military life, he became ever more frustrated with what he per-ceived as the local elite and its "good ole boy" system of patronage and nepo-tism. Like many in the military, he felt that the locals exploited military personnel economically and closed ranks against them politically. Most prob-lematic for Duncan was the way these well-connected business and political leaders controlled both the city manager and city council.

For many residents who shared Duncan's views, the "Five–Four" conflict was not a crisis for the majority of residents, it was a crisis for "the old guard." Accordingly many white residents watched the drama with amusement; they thought it was comical to see black council members in a position of power and the Haymount crying foul. More importantly, many critics of local government looked at the racial drama with considerable optimism. They interpreted the hysteria on council as a sign that the dominant coalition of business and political leaders was losing control, and thought that perhaps the backlash against the NAACP and the new council majority was its last gasp.

This chapter focuses on the way in which citizens and politicians representing the military attempted to use the downtown debacle to take control of city council.

Taxpayers' Revolt

Karen McMillan's defeat of Frank Edwards's "recall bill" sent a powerful message to Fayetteville's urban regime: putting a stop to the council majority's investigation was not going to be simple. White civic and business leaders had to rethink how they would contend with the power and authority of black leaders. The threat of black elected officials came to the fore as controversy grew about the $28 million plan to regenerate downtown. After learning that city council, with the exception of Edna Harrington, agreed to give $500,000 of public money to the project, retired general Frank Roberts became angry. Rather than representing the wider public's interest in economic development, he saw the intricate design of lakes, parks, and a waterfall as a "cash cow" for the wealthiest developers and home builders, not to mention the "slumlords" who owned the "decrepit buildings downtown." He feared that city council's approval would start a hemorrhage of public money into the coffers of the "downtown elite." Taking umbrage with what he termed "the arrogance" of city council in passing out the public's tax money, he fired off a letter to the editor, as he often did, urging citizens to demand a public referendum before another cent was provisioned.

General Roberts's commentary inspired Terrence Puckett, also a retired army officer and a well-respected medical doctor, to launch a petition drive to bring the plan before a public referendum. Excited about finding a like mind, Dr. Puckett wrote the general to invite him to help start a movement to raise awareness about the misuse of tax money. He and his wife, Joanne, had already studied the issue and learned about two North Carolina statutes—160a-103 and 160b-104—that granted citizens the right to demand a referendum for large public projects. Putting the Marvin Plan up for referendum would require five thousand signatures. Puckett reassured the general that he had many friends who shared his "outrage and frustration" and he supposed it would be "easy" to mobilize these people to "bring sane government to our city and county." In closing, Doctor Puckett told the general, "Perhaps the time is right for a viable challenge to the status quo."[1]

General Roberts and his wife, Hilda, joined the Pucketts in forming Fayetteville Taxpayers for Financial Responsibility (FTFR). In a short time, the two couples enlisted almost a dozen friends and started its referendum campaign.

During my first month of fieldwork, I met Mrs. Puckett at the Cumberland County Democratic Party convention when I spotted her makeshift exhibit for FTFR's petition drive for a public referendum on the Marvin Plan. After reading several articles, I introduced myself as a graduate student working on my Ph.D. dissertation. Puckett gave me an earful. Not only did she have a wealth of information about local politics—including genealogies that linked powerful Fayetteville families—but she was willing to talk. She explained what she viewed as the political machinations behind the cover of a "public-private partnership" (the Fayetteville Partnership). While she explained these issues, a politician was on stage trumpeting the Cumberland County Democrats as "the party of change and progress." She stopped. "Did you hear that? Party of change?" Though she had been a lifelong Democrat, Puckett believed the Cumberland County Democratic leadership not only "resisted change" but was behind what she called "the racial stuff on city council." She connected the reaction against the "Five–Four" to the protection of the economic benefits of public money; land developers, the Chamber of Commerce, and the *Fayetteville Observer* together formed an elite, which she called "the Haymount."

Puckett's passionate critique of the Marvin Plan provided me my first glimpse of how many middle-class military understood local politics. Feeling enlightened, I asked if we could meet again for a lengthier interview. Unexpectedly, Puckett's talkativeness vanished as she began eyeing me with a bit of suspicion. After a long pause, Puckett asked if she could verify my credentials. I gave her my business card and the phone numbers of my academic advisers, whom she in fact called. Much like the way Tom Manning suspected me of being a spy, I started to see a pattern of how residents feared local authorities' covert means of collecting information about their enemies. Many residents felt unease and distrust, and this would not be the last time a resident would suspect me of being a spy.

After confirming I was a graduate student, Mrs. Puckett invited me to her home to meet the members of FTFR. When I arrived at 7 P.M., the Pucketts' living room was packed with eight of their colleagues. Before I could pull out my notebook, General Roberts, whom I was familiar with through his letter to the editor, launched into a lecture about the "Fayetteville elite." Beginning with the standard stories about how locals abuse the military and only appreciate soldiers on payday, he placed downtown revitalization in the city's history of land development since the arrival of Fort Bragg. Much like the P. J. Middleton narrative discussed earlier, Roberts told how Fayetteville's developers became rich and powerful by building cheap houses for soldiers. He argued that they skirted regulations and scoffed at urban planning, which left the city a mess. Other members of the group added to the discussion as they collectively told a story of plunder whereby land developers and homebuilders exploited the military, left the town in shambles, and reduced downtown to an embarrassing skid row, riddled with decrepit buildings. And now, one member asked, "they want the taxpayers to bail them out and raise their property values?"

FTFR countered the downtown business leaders' argument that the Marvin Plan would help create a "new" Fayetteville. Instead, they viewed the Marvin Plan as part of an old tradition of insider deals that allowed land developers and home builders to swindle the military. They feared that this type of access to city government allowed developers to streamline their development project by excluding the public from debating or voting on it. For the members of FTFR, the "public-private" partnership was a new and sophisticated way to keep the majority of residents, especially the military and the black community, from shaping political decisions.

General Roberts and his colleagues envisioned a public referendum as a foil to this "old" style of patronage politics. Looking beyond this issue, they hoped opening up debate about the Marvin Plan could inaugurate a new era of local politics that would seek to include military residents. Against the icon of the downtown coalition as an insular southern elite, members of FTFR held the military as valuable members of the community who were excluded from decision-making and policy. Like many military, they were self-critical and believed that part of the problem stemmed from the military residents' apathy. Although most members of the military were skeptical and critical of local politics, this did not translate into political power. FTFR hoped to energize the large, and mostly silent, majority of military people.

After listening to Kelly, Puckett, and their collaborators, connecting their exclusion to that of African Americans, I asked if they had worked with the black council member Edna Harrington. After all, she was the bane of the downtown coalition and the sole council member who opposed public support of the Marvin Plan. Curious about their relationship with black leaders, I said, "Harrington is against revitalization, too." Catching me off guard, General Roberts rebuked me: "Wait a second! Edna Harrington is not against revitalizing downtown. She is opposed to using public funds to do it." Like many people involved in political battles downtown, he made certain to "straighten me out," fearing that I may be accepting the downtown coalition's perspective. Roberts had two points. First, he responded to the way the downtown business leaders often ridiculed Edna. Though he thought she could be "a little crazy," Roberts pointed out that she was a military nurse, a retired major, and a conscientious protector of her constituents, and she was not to be dismissed as a "dummy." Second, he clarified her point to make his: "The long and the short of it is we are about participatory government." For FTFR, such participation and inclusion would begin with bringing the voters into the conversation with a referendum about how public officials should use tax money.

Geography of Exclusion

Feelings of being exploited economically and excluded politically transcended the concerns of the middle-class retirees who formed FTFR. When land developers transformed the rural landscape into an urban environment, they created military enclaves. These military communities stood outside the city in unincorporated areas on the western side of the county. Living with closer connections to Fort Bragg's institutions and services, military personnel and retirees came to view themselves as separate from the city and as having completely different interests from those expressed by city government. Such alienation was enhanced by the dearth of urban amenities. Most of these areas had septic tanks instead of a sewer system. They also lacked sidewalks, libraries, and recreation facilities. Poorly built roads, ill-connected to the main thoroughfares, enhanced the sense of isolation.

An absence of urban services has encouraged active-duty soldiers and retirees to view Fayetteville as a southern backwater. Often coming from places where sidewalks and sewer systems were taken for granted, many in the military see the city as a dump and believe the poorly performing schools, bad roads, and lack of entertainment resulted from corrupt and ineffective political leaders. Indeed, Cumberland County schools were poorly performing and had become infamous for the makeshift huts and leaky roofs that plagued the system. In this sense, FTFR drew on the substantive concerns military families had about crime and education. For struggling military families, revitalizing downtown seemed like a luxury and an impractical attempt to recapture the city's bygone traditions of the old South.

Feeling like they had taken the brunt of local leaders' inability to deal with the city's growth, the military resented how business and political leaders framed the city's problems in terms of "the military." Indeed, city manager Jim Thompson and his allies had refashioned government and created a policy agenda around downtown revitalization in ways that reinforced the stereotypes that scapegoated the military as the cause of the city's problems. Their political projects and programs, from annexation to revitalization, presumed that Fayetteville's troubles stemmed from Fort Bragg. City leaders sought to expand the city's infrastructure as a way to rid the city of its military image. With parks, roads, and a revitalized downtown, leaders envisioned a "new" and metropolitan Fayetteville that would transcend its shortcomings as a military town. For example, the MetroVisions project viewed the subdivisions and the military communities as representing fragmentation and the main obstacle to progress. MetroVisions and the Chamber of Commerce sought new urban plans that would "build bridges" to the military and encourage the military to transcend their myopic view of their individual neighborhoods and understand the "bigger picture."

Military retirees often become infuriated by the view that the military caused the city's urban problems. After all, most of the military believe that Fort Bragg rescued Fayetteville from rural poverty by attracting money, government resources, and scores of skilled and educated people. From this perspective, the city's problems did not come from "the military." Instead, the disarray was caused by how land developers, real estate agents, retailers, and the political establishment chose to deal with these opportunities. They spurned long-term urban plans and failed to build the proper political and administrative institutions necessary for handling the massive growth that accompanied Fort Bragg after World War II. In this sense, many in the military believed that the city's problems were representative of local customs and not the military. From the ugliness of the town to the lack of entertainment, they pointed to a miserly elite who did not have a civic vision and made Fayetteville a laughingstock of North Carolina.

MetroVisions and the Chamber of Commerce understood these grievances. Some business leaders even agreed with the idea that local developers and civic leaders were to blame for the city's appearing backward. In fact, civic leaders designed MetroVisions and pursued annexation as a way to fix many of the problems that grew from how previous generations of leaders had neglected urban planning. As part of this new outlook, they sought to create a more inclusive government and policy agenda by targeting military personnel and retirees living in the subdivisions. They hoped to include their opinions and wants into the city's expanding policy agenda.

Despite its rhetoric of inclusion, city government's efforts to modernize its urban institutions increased conflict with the military, which finally exploded when the city began its annexation project in the late 1980s. Through several phases, the city added 60,000 new residents. Most of the new citizens of Fayetteville were unhappy about how much they had to pay to retrofit the water and sewage system, roads, and other services to these sprawling neighborhoods. In addition, they had to begin paying city taxes. Harboring hard feelings from their experiences of being preyed on by local entrepreneurs, the military residents felt the costs of annexation added insult to injury. Such animosity was displayed in city council meetings, as neighborhood organizations, often organized by military retirees, faced off against city council. They used the rhetoric of an invasion and hostile takeover, as many of the military associated the city's expansion with the Haymount elite.

Rebellion of the Military

The confluence of public rage associated with annexation, racism in the FPD, and the Marvin Plan led FTFR to believe the time was right for a serious challenge to the status quo. By developing their movement in the shape of a tax revolt, FTFR hoped to mobilize the anger of recently annexed citizens, the many military residents who normally did not participate, as well what they saw as a disaffected black community into a political force. They believed they had more to offer African Americans. Moreover, they thought the demographic changes created by Fort Bragg had reached a critical mass and were finally eroding the power of the local elite. According to this view, annexation represented the tipping point. Now city government would have to directly contend with thousands of new citizens who were angry about being forcibly annexed. As one member of FTFR put it, "The people being annexed into the community are going to have a *long* memory when it comes time to vote. Because they are already experiencing problems, people who thought they were going to get sewers are not getting their sewers. It's poor planning and when it comes time to vote they will remember all this."

Struggles between the military and city government called attention to the potential of military retirees to become a political force. Belying the connotations of being elderly and inactive, military personnel retire young: from the late thirties to early fifties. Therefore, military retirees enter Fayetteville's civilian life with an eye to creating a new career. Moreover, they bring many resources and privileges that locals do not have: pensions, national and international work experience, and modest amounts of wealth. Drawing my attention to this dynamic, one retired lieutenant colonel bragged about his ability to thwart the local power structure because of his economic independence. He summed up his point pithily: "I'm not rich. But I do have enough money that they [the Haymount] can't fuck with me."

Other retirees described the friction between the military and local authorities more politely. A wife of a retired officer described how working on civic projects led to frustration because her opinions were not accepted by what she felt was a tight-knit group of people who control civic groups. She believed that the military populations have trouble because of their experiences living in other cities and countries. As she put it: "We have experience. We know things can be done differently." In this capacity, she saw herself as part of a larger military community that carried a variety of cosmopolitan ideas and visions that were remaking Fayetteville. Yet this cosmopolitanism, no matter how positive, she believed, would result in conflict until a new and more progressive political coalition came to power.

Building on this motif of change and shifting political patterns, FTFR sought to mobilize the military. They looked to the way military retirees had revamped the Cumberland County Republican Party to provide the military an alternative to the Democratic Party. Indeed, Joanne Puckett's new friend General Frank Roberts had worked for many years with a lieutenant colonel named Bill Gunderson. After retiring, Gunderson stayed in Fayetteville and set up a business managing properties. Becoming active in civilian life, he was frustrated by how he perceived the local political establishment had excluded and exploited the military. He eyed the Republican Party, largely defunct since Reconstruction, as an alternative for the military.

Brash and confident, Gunderson wanted to cripple the local establishment. He began at the top of what he saw as Fayetteville's vast patronage system, the congressional seat of Jimmy Kelly. Born and raised in Fayetteville, Kelly held his seat in the U.S. Congress for more than twenty years. In 1991, Gunderson was an upstart and ran a spirited campaign against the long- time congressman. He accused the congressman of being a poor public servant, beholden to elite interests, and an enemy of the military. Two elections later, in what became a perennial event, Gunderson nearly succeeded in ousting Representative Kelly. Although Gunderson claims he won the race, Kelly officially edged Gunderson by less than one percentage point. Gunderson sued, accusing Kelly of voter fraud. Nevertheless, it was Representative Kelly's last election, and Gunderson claims credit for running him out of politics and for making a crack in the good ole boy system.

After running for, and losing, many elected offices, Gunderson never gained credibility with the most powerful political groups. He is notorious for his belligerent, no-holds-barred style of politics. Gunderson publicly attacked many powerful business and political figures. He harangued his opponents with nasty direct mailings. Despite becoming a pariah among powerful whites, Gunderson motivated enough ex-military, especially working-class retirees, to revamp the Cumberland County Republican Party. One retiree who became active in the Republican Party told me how Gunderson had inspired him: "He forced issues onto the agenda . . . we never had upstarts. Seeing him challenge Jimmy Kelly got me motivated. Back then, I thought: Wow! The military is finally standing up. I had hoped they [the military] would wake up."

Indeed, there were signs of the military becoming politically engaged during the election that brought Tom Manning and Sam Johnson to city council. Though city council is nonpartisan, Gunderson organized a slate of Republicans to run for almost every city council seat and the mayor's office. Naming his line-up of candidates "Team 2000," he hoped to undo what he viewed as the Democratic Party's stranglehold. He believed that the nonpartisan rules had made city council in effect Democratic. Although each member of Team 2000 lost, the effort raised the Republican Party's profile by representing the first time Republicans had a candidate for each office. In addition, the Republican Party sent its first representative from Cumberland County to the North Carolina House of Representatives since Reconstruction, a woman named Kathy Thomas, the wife of an officer in the 82nd Airborne.

Confronting a Partnership

Embodying the military community's contempt for Fayetteville's politics, FTFR fashioned its campaign against downtown revitalization in terms of social movement against a feckless and out-of-touch elite. One of the leaders of FTFR explained that she and her collaborators had envisioned themselves as collectively serving as "the larger community's point man" by standing up to and challenging the local elite. Placing the issues of education and public safety as top priorities, FTFR belittled downtown revitalization and its heralded "Marvin Plan" as irrelevant by publicizing the plan's centerpiece: a forty-foot dirt mound with a cascading waterfall. Critics of the Fayetteville Partnership had already succeeded in calling the project the "Bubba Mound," a name inspired by another dubious public project, the construction of a coliseum known as the "Bubba Dome."

In addition to the Bubba Mound, FTFR mercilessly attacked the Fayetteville Partnership, the group in charge of leading revitalization, and its director, Peggy Cartwright. For many, even supporters of the Marvin Plan, Ms. Cartwright epitomized the insular network of powerful Haymount families. Fitting the stereotype of "the Haymount," Cartwright hailed from one of Fayetteville's oldest and most prestigious families. Moreover, she ran in exclusive circles, spoke with an elegant southern accent, and waxed about Fayetteville's wonderful history as a southern city. FTFR argued that she lacked expertise in urban planning and economic development and tagged her as merely a cheerleader who ran the Fayetteville Partnership like it was a private association. Most problematic, Ms. Cartwright's major achievement was leading the efforts to refurbish the Market House. Built in 1831, the Market House was admired by many of the more elite locals. However, African Americans and the military saw it as a shrine to the city's ignoble past of slavery. Widely called the "slave house," many criticized the Fayetteville

Partnership and the city for adopting the Market House as the symbol of downtown's renaissance. Even worse, the Fayetteville Partnership leased the Market House from the city and used it as its headquarters.

FTFR pointed out that what the Fayetteville Partnership lacked in expertise it made up for in connections and publicized how developers "fast-tracked" the Marvin Plan, which displayed their "lock" on city government. FTFR pointed out how city government and its allies in business created a private group, called the "Once and for All Committee," to avoid sunshine laws by posing as a separate citizens' group. Working closely with government officials, Joanne Puckett argued, the revitalization groups had created "a drift of public money into these private organizations, where the money is not accountable for." She was concerned that the many groups promoting economic development with the city had questionable links to the city. She saw them as "secret groups" that were "carefully selected to create a homogenous group as opposed to a group with varied perspectives and insights . . . they are the 'go-along to get-along' crowd."

It Is About Power and Money

It was from the context of struggle over the Marvin Plan that members of FTFR understood theories about the Manning conspiracy. They were skeptical about the coincidence of the "crisis" in government at the moment the downtown coalition was trying to push the public project through without a debate or referendum. Rather than seeing the shift on council as a threat to the principle of professional government, members of FTFR argued that the racial animosity illustrated a lack of leadership. One member of FTFR tried to shift the terms of debate when she wrote a letter to the editor. She argued that the "circus atmosphere" revolving around the "Five–Four" highlights an "essential issue . . . our city has outgrown the council-manager form of government." She asserted that it was time to "retire the present system" and implement a "metropolitan" government and "elect a mayor, with appropriate compensation, whose mandate is to provide leadership to both a cabinet and the people of Fayetteville. Rather than a recall, etc., why not a referendum to give our city both the leadership and management it deserves? It's time for something better than this embarrassment we currently face daily."[2]

Seeing the circus atmosphere of city council meetings as an opportunity, FTFR took a page from the playbook of the Committee of 100 and held a rally downtown to launch the petition drive to put the Marvin Plan on the November ballot. Overturning the ideal of "professional government," FTFR's members criticized city government for carrying out the will of the "good ole boys" and seeking to avoid public debate by pushing the project through the backdoor with "certificates of participation." They warned citizens about the dangers of funding the Marvin Plan without a bond. Because they had a taxing mandate whereby the government promised the given lending agency that it would raise taxes if necessary to pay off the bond, bonds required voter approval. Without a bond referendum, FTFR argued, the City of Fayetteville would instead use certificates of participation (COPs) to pay for the Marvin Plan's $28 million price tag. In allowing city government to enact projects faster, COPs are not counted as legal debts against governments. Without the promise of a taxing mandate, which comes from a bond, their interest rates are much higher. FTFR warned citizens that city council would use this "sneaky trick" to "backdoor" the Marvin Plan.

In addition to the referendum, FTFR fought the Fayetteville Public Works Commission's (PWC) commitment to the Marvin Plan. With the positive momentum that surrounded the developers' and city government's support for the Marvin Plan, the PWC pledged $10 million over a five-year period, which it would draw from electricity revenues. Half of the donation would pay for the construction of an amphitheater, and the remainder would pay for utility relocation and park construction. FTFR argued that the PWC was a public corporation and its charter was to provide citizens with inexpensive utilities. In order for the PWC to make such a large contribution, FTFR argued, it would have to impose drastic rate increases to generate the profits necessary. Dr. Puckett compared the PWC's actions to those of King George III as he summed up the situation: "Taxation without representation is alive and well in Fayetteville in 1996. The PWC board unilaterally decided to give $10 million to support the Marvin Plan."[3]

FTFR's attack on downtown business leaders gave Tom Manning a glimmer of hope to save his political life. Desperately searching for ways to escape the vilifying conspiracy theories, he envisioned FTFR's protest as an opportunity to define his agenda as fiscal responsibility and a commitment to economic development. Trying to turn the conspiracy theory on the downtown coalition, he expressed this view in a lengthy commentary to the *Fayetteville Observer*. He stated baldly that his decision to support an investigation of the police department stemmed from the chief's "Gestapo tactics" that made the city vulnerable to lawsuits. Responding to the cries of how much tax money would be spent on an investigation, he wrote that the city had already spent more than $30,000 in legal fees to defend the chief. Manning asserted: "The real conspiracy has been formed between the local press and the ancient political powers in this community . . . as they work tirelessly to form committees to promote recall efforts. These groups consisted of well-meaning citizens, most of whom had no day-to-day contact with the department and who had no real information concerning the allegations forwarded to the EEOC." He urged citizens to "not be hoodwinked by the subtle lies floated by the press and the political machine who push a private agenda associated with a multimillion-dollar downtown revitalization plan. They are not willing to seriously address this crime crisis for fear it might endanger the sacred downtown money pit into which more tax money will surely fall."[4]

Manning took this message and joined FTFR at their protest. He promised to be their voice on city council and to support their cause there. At the rally, he reminded the crowd that their petition for a referendum had been his position since he joined council, and he promised to put the Marvin Plan up for a referendum. Going even further, he took aim at the Fayetteville Partnership and its maligned director, Peggy Cartright. He criticized the city for its misuse of funds; he argued that after spending $1 million dollars to restore the Market House, they irresponsibly rented it out to the Fayetteville Partnership for a token $1 annually. He was going to change that.

Although members of FTFR agreed with Manning about the way downtown business leaders were benefiting from the fits of anxiety created by conspiracy theories, they believed he was toxic and were not thrilled about his being their voice on city council. FTFR was friendly with him, but they did not see any upside to connecting with him. This illustrates the power of crisis language; it produces a situation of limited options. There was no middle ground.

Seeking a safe distance from Manning and conspiracy theories, FTFR turned to black representative Karen McMillan to help them guide their legislation through the North Carolina General Assembly. Members of FTFR and their sympathizers were duly impressed by the way she stopped the seemingly all-powerful Senator Frank Edwards. With his extensive power in Raleigh, it was no small feat to stop recall. They disliked Edwards, but their dislike added to his legendary status as the godfather. They viewed him as the linchpin to the local regime. However, in McMillan's victory they saw his inability to end the crisis as a clear sign of the regime's declining power. Moreover, they believed that by teaming up with McMillan they could expand their coalition to include the black community.

McMillan submitted FTFR's legislation seeking a referendum on the Marvin Plan and signaled a threatening image of the type of biracial alliance that started the crisis in the first place. Indeed, McMillan's support of FTFR's referendum caught the downtown revitalization coalition by surprise. Having been blindsided by FTFR at a moment when they counted on white solidarity, civic leaders became increasingly anxious about regaining control of city hall.

For FTFR, the city council struggle demonstrated something that Fayetteville's authorities have long known: the black community could hold the balance of power in forging a new coalition. As one member of FTFR explained:

> The Haymount is not dumb. The racial divisions in Fayetteville are not clear; they are syrupy and paternalistic. You have certain blacks that the Haymount has anointed. But this stuff on city council is larger. Fort Bragg and Kelly Springfield represent "outside" people who have an interest in this structure. The Five–Four is symptomatic of this shift. Blacks are supposed to stay in place. Your have two iconoclastic whites who hooked up with the blacks. Players are not behaving the way they are supposed to behave. They have focused on the marital thing. They are missing it! The marital thing keeps Manning and Johnson tight, but it is not the source of rebellion. The old guard is losing its grip. On top of that they have FTFR; FTFR has been a tremendous surprise. The Haymount is not used to having so many people who do not go along with their program.

He placed FTFR in the same category of being iconoclastic and not following proper racial customs. Most importantly, this behavior encouraged blacks to defy the status quo and not stay in their place. In this sense, members of FTFR sought to provide African Americans an alternative to the Democratic Party and further loosen the ties that kept the Haymount in control.

Meritocracy and Southern Racism

"The military" is a broad category that Fayettevillians use to describe both active-duty and retired members. Retirees and soldiers appeal to the term to distinguish themselves from locals and to formulate a common ground in broader national values that are at odds with what they believe to be the antiquated traditions of the South represented by the ruling Haymount. An important aspect of the military's sense of distinction from local whites is the relationship between meritocracy and race. Although most military whites do not identify as "liberal," and some have been persuaded to support the national Republican Party's attack on civil rights protections, they view local whites as racist. Such claims stem from the fact that whites in the military have worked with African Americans and, respecting the "chain of command," have taken orders from blacks as well as from members of other minority groups. Many military described the racial relations and politics as representative of a "plantation mentality" and criticized the inability of residents to see that their interests transcend race. They thought blacks suffered from this myopia and failed to see that their interests were closer in line with the military.

Many military saw the city council dispute as a sign of this contrast. They drew attention to how the hysteria about blacks taking over and becoming out of control stemmed from leaders of the Democratic Party. Members of FTFR and its Republican allies believed that the Haymount control, ironically, depended on black support for the Democratic Party. In many fundamental votes for bond referendums and large projects, the black vote was absolutely necessary as the majority of whites often voted against these programs. Thus, FTFR and the Republicans believed that this moment of racist reaction against the NAACP would provide the opportunity to make an appeal to the black community. Believing themselves to be open to working with African Americans and believing that they understood blacks' plight better than the white Democratic leaders, FTFR thought an alliance between military residents of all races and African Americans was not only possible but a much better opportunity for black advancement.

The idea of uniting the military with the black community was not entirely new. When Bill Gunderson became the de facto leader of the Republican Party and focused his attention on the military community, he viewed the black community as allies. In fact, the controversy about *Powertalk* radio host Tony Jefferson derived from Gunderson's attempts to expand the Republican Party. As mentioned earlier, Clay at the shoeshine shop dismissed Tony Jefferson and his show *Powertalk* as merely a vendetta following his failure to get black politicians to support his bid for the sheriff's office. However, Clay knew only part of the story. It is true, as Clay described, several black leaders had encouraged Tony Jefferson in what turned out to be a foolhardy attempt to run for county sheriff. Once Jefferson officially declared his candidature, he sent shockwaves through the establishment; clearly he threatened them because he would have access to the black vote. Democratic officials and allies of the sheriff encircled Jefferson and squashed his attempt. The end result was that they used a technicality to keep Jefferson off the ballot.

After learning that the Cumberland County Board of Elections had ruled him ineligible to run in the Democratic primary, he bumped into Gunderson. After telling Gunderson how black leaders had "hung [him] out to dry," Gunderson challenged him to not take this abuse sitting down. He suggested that the battle was not over and explained to Jefferson that he could wage a campaign as a write-in candidate. Both knew that it would be impossible to win. However, it would provide an opportunity to publicize his issues and get name recognition.

The experience left Jefferson dumbfounded, not knowing where to start, when Gunderson said, "Let's go." Jefferson followed Gunderson to the law office of one of his friends and strategists during his wars with Congressman

Kelly. Having been wary of white people all his life, Jefferson was shocked that Gunderson and several of his white friends not only helped him but gave him quite a bit of support, working feverishly to make sure his showing was respectable. And it was.

From this positive experience with Gunderson, Jefferson started to believe the biggest problem and obstacle for African Americans was that black leaders had a cozy relationship with the Haymount. He began to see that the military and the Republican Party offered opportunities to African Americans and had fewer hang-ups about racism. He and a few other activists started to promote the idea that blacks should be equally active in both parties. With no viable black presence in the Republican Party, he and many white Republicans argued, the Democratic Party took the black community for granted. This is how his infamy as a "Black Republican" began.

Despite his collaboration with local Republicans, Jefferson was at odds with the national Republican Party and especially its move against many of the civil rights provisions—including the way the city manager was trying to dissolve the consent decree. Most importantly, Jefferson's participation in the Republican Party, much like that of many white retirees, stemmed from his disdain for the Cumberland County Democratic Party and its relationship with the dominant downtown growth coalition. As discussed earlier, rather than espousing Republican ideology, Jefferson's *Powertalk* used certain points like accountability to trash the "Democratic good ole boys" and their "bourgeois black" accomplices.

In an attempt to fuse the police department dispute and the Marvin Plan, Tony Jefferson invited FTFR to *Powertalk*. He thought it was important for the black community to learn about the ways that the Marvin Plan would cost taxpayers. The two speakers told the audience that the use of public money would bypass the black community and support the absentee landlords downtown. Moreover, they also pointed out that architect Robert Marvin had planned to raze Grove View Terrace—a downtown housing project—and move 258 African American families there into double-wide trailers.[5] Reminiscent of urban renewal of the 1950s and 1960s, they argued that the plan sought to "redistribute" the poor black residents into trailer parks throughout the city and county.

With the help of McMillan, FTFR and the Republicans saw the black community as a viable coalition. These interactions between black electoral power and white dissent toward the local establishment illustrate how the real threat was the possibility of a biracial alliance. FTFR succeeded on this front, and over the next several months, its campaign presented the Marvin Plan as the Haymount's entitlement to acquire public funds in order to benefit the few

landowners and real estate agents involved with downtown property specula-
tion. Many black Democrats considered the possibility. As Ben, a longtime
Democrat, explained: "In annexing 50,000 citizens from the county, city management has introduced new political interests, many of which were either
hostile or indifferent to downtown interests." These new residents, he argued,
shared African Americans' resentment: "With annexation, the downtown
crowd has to peddle their wares to 50,000 new citizens who are not happy with
downtown politics. The Mannings' alliance with the black community is just
the tip of the iceberg. The Haymount smoked this event up to use racial fear
to draw these people in. If they [the newly annexed citizens] go with the old
power structure in the November elections, they are going to get fucked. We,
all citizens who are not of the Haymount crowd, have a chance here to change
things."

Conclusion

Many whites who opposed downtown development plans and the city's
annexation program saw the "Five–Four" and its shift in power not as a threat
but as an inspiration. The military believed this to be a sign that the
Haymount was on its last legs and would be vulnerable. They, like some black
politicians, viewed this as a historic moment and thought they could provide
the black community a new alternative in building a controlling coalition.
They looked to the black community to forge a workable alliance and take
control of the city. FTFR used the crisis to attack downtown revitalization,
which they saw as the real issue behind the hysteria about the council-
manager form of government.

Chapter 7

Outsiders and Special Interests

BLACK REPRESENTATIVE Karen McMillan's defeat of recall and the Fayetteville Taxpayers for Financial Responsibility's (FTFR) powerful criticism of downtown revitalization shined a new light on the city council turmoil. Highlighting weaknesses in the downtown coalition, they believed that the old power structure was on its last legs. These critics envisioned grandiose scenarios that would result in dethroning the Haymount and cleaning government of its nepotism and racism. Hopes of an insurgency, however, were built on naive understandings of political power. To be sure, the power shift on city council and FTFR's successes in discrediting the Marvin Plan distressed city management and its regime partners. However, such criticism was not fatal. Instead, it provided city management opportunities to revise and strengthen its policy agenda by repairing the flaws being exposed by its opponents.

Taking up the issue of city management's role in multiple political battles, this chapter will focus on how the downtown coalition engaged the political struggles with FTFR and the black community on two levels. Members of the coalition used the Committee of 100, the *Fayetteville Observer*, WFNC Radio, and the Chamber of Commerce to produce the sense of a mobilized citizenry defending the city manager from city council's attack. On another level, city management modified the downtown revitalization plan and coordinated these changes with public protests. This chapter focuses on the connections between public rituals of popular protest and the bureaucratic power of city government in producing and maintaining the urban regime.[1] Specifically, this chapter will focus on the ways private citizens and civic leaders used the outside investigation of the police department to build city management's authority and readjust both racial policies and revitalization plans in ways to answer critics, on one hand, and provide an example of city management's capacity to represent the will of the people on the other.

Counterattack

FTFR's successes in fomenting vocal opposition to downtown revitalization, and the ever deepening conflict on city council, led many critics to believe that the end of the "Haymount's rule" was near. FTFR promoted the idea that the military was mobilized and poised to make a serious challenge for control of government in the upcoming elections. Moreover, FTFR's alliance with Representative Karen McMillan, an African American, drew attention to the way the military communities, if organized, could form a dominant political coalition with black politicians.

With the escalation of conflict from both sides of the racial divide, white civic leaders and supporters of city management turned the public's attention to the dangers of the outside investigation. The city manager was fired because he resisted city council's efforts to hire an outside investigation of the police department. During the struggle, city council accepted the applications of numerous experts. Shortly after firing the city manager, city council settled on Susan Gannett, an African American attorney from Cincinnati, Ohio, to investigate the police department. Once again, the Committee of 100 presented the hiring of Gannett as a dangerous intrusion of an outsider into local government. The Fayetteville Police Department (FPD) complemented these public performances by opening up an investigation of Gannett. In a repeat performance of the act that led to the city manager's firing, the police department ran a background check on Gannett and used the information to write a damning account of her character and qualifications. Focusing on the attorney's race, the report detailed Gannett's purported history of preferentially treating blacks and being biased against law enforcement.[2]

News about the FPD digging up dirt on attorney Gannett embarrassed some supporters of the police chief. For example, a *Fayetteville Observer* editorial rebuked the police chief for what appeared to be unseemly behavior. Other allies also thought that shadowing the attorney was inappropriate and only damaged the cause. Despite these criticisms, the interim city manager, Roger Reynolds, in his acting role as the chief's department head, upheld the background check as "routine" for a government to protect itself against "an outsider." He raised concern about the dangers of an interloper combing through confidential materials and personnel files and justified measures to safeguard the city's best interests.[3]

Regardless of the disagreements about the background check, rumors about attorney Gannett spread as supporters of the police chief speculated on the attorney's motives. Stories vacillated between her being either a malicious force or her lacking the expertise required for the job. In these stories, politicians and citizens often repeated the key tag lines from the FPD's background check that claimed she was prejudiced against police and whites. These tales dovetailed with broader stories of conspiracy that envisioned the black community expanding its power and increasing its influence of city government. Many whites began imagining personal and political connections between Gannett, leaders of the NAACP, and Frederick Walker. One rumor told that council member Walker was feeding Gannett information and directing her investigation, leading some white residents to envision a vast network of African Americans stretching from Fayetteville to Cincinnati and beyond. Often, white supporters of the police chief presumed that Gannett was going to merely write up her foregone conclusion. Treating her as if she were a member of Fayetteville's black community, they expected that she would provide a report that was convenient for the majority in their presumed quest to fire the police chief.

Amid suspicions that attorney Gannett was Frederick Walker's coconspirator, she began her investigation uneventfully. On her first visit, she spent one week reviewing public records, examining previous lawsuits against the FPD, and interviewing both line officers and managers in the FPD. In an interview with the *Fayetteville Observer*, she showed no signs of animosity. She spoke well of residents, politicians, and officers, whom she said had treated her with respect. Likewise, many civic and political leaders complimented her. They seemed surprised that she was "articulate," "well spoken," and "polite." Some civic leaders, especially those uncomfortable with the racial overtones of the dispute, became optimistic that her report could be beneficial.

Goodwill toward Gannett turned to be ephemeral. When she missed her deadline and requested an extension, white council member Milo McRae retracted the olive branches and attacked her character. Continuing to play the role of the hard-liner against the investigation, McRae accused the attorney of theft when he complained about her "taking our $50,000" and not delivering on her part of the bargain. He demanded that Gannett turn in an executive summary immediately so that city council could begin its review and make its final judgment. Council member Walker discredited McRae's demand as a thinly veiled attempt to attack and belittle the executive summary and moved to give attorney Gannett an extension.

Though Walker's motion carried, his opponents used the delay as another example of his coalition's incompetence and to further raise suspicions about a conspiracy. The following morning, callers on the white talk radio show hammered Gannett and her supporters. Host Scott Simpson led the discussion by shaming council for rejecting McRae's request. Simpson cried out, "Council has forgotten on whose behalf they are serving: The People!" Holding McRae as the voice of the people, Simpson chastised "the Five" for having let "emotion" take over, as he asserted they were "too embroiled in politics," that they had "lost perspective. . . . It is insulting, Councilman Frederick Walker, to suggest that Gannett's report could be subject to interpretation."

Several weeks passed and anticipation of Gannett's report continued to build. Nearly nine months after the NAACP raised the issue of an outside investigation, Gannett was finally scheduled to present her findings. On the day of her presentation, anxiety and tension spiked. Callers to both talk radio shows speculated on the outcome. By early afternoon, citizens were poised for the verdict. Adding to the sense of excitement, trucks from the major news networks in North Carolina lined Hay Street with their massive antennas. Local news outlets were even more enthused, and the *Fayetteville Observer* dispatched a team of five reporters to cover the event. Anxious residents followed suit, and the council chambers filled up quickly.

Excitement soon gave way to confusion. By the start of the meeting, with the chambers jammed beyond capacity, attorney Gannett had not shown up. Fretfully, the mayor told the crowd that Gannett's whereabouts were unknown. Citizens remained in the chambers as the partisans milled around and speculated anew about this most unpredictable twist in the ordeal. Supporters of the police chief conjectured that Gannett was either too incompetent to finish the report or that she could not find the necessary information to fire the police chief. On the other side of the aisle, the NAACP's supporters interpreted her disappearance in terms of her safety. Many believed that by coming into the community, with the resentment of white political leaders, her life was in danger. Conjecture about her safety resonated with the fact that many of the council members who voted to bring her to town had received death threats.

Eventually the mayor announced that attorney Gannett had arrived at Raleigh-Durham Airport and would appear by 9 P.M. Two hours stretched into three, and Gannett did not arrive until after 10 P.M. Disheveled and embarrassed, attorney Gannett apologized to city council and revealed that she did not have the report because her husband had packed the wrong document in her travel bag. Amid the rancor of the anxious crowd, city council adjourned the meeting until 5 P.M. the following day.

Gannett's blunder created an emergency for black supporters of the investigation, as I will discuss in the following chapter. However, for the Committee of 100, each misstep increased their confidence. Gannett's gaffe validated the protest against the investigation as jokes about attorney Gannett's "henpecked" husband combined with their doubts of her competency. It appeared as if "the Five" could not do anything right and their position vis-à-vis the police chief continued to weaken. This commanding sense of failure increased when the city manager released the report to news outlets three hours before the meeting. Soon thereafter, WFNC preempted the broadcast of the conservative *Dr. Laura Show.* Hastily reading through the report, Scott Simpson announced to his listeners that the report "is a sham." He ridiculed the report for being merely sixteen pages and rife with typos and grammatical errors, leading him to declare, "We've been fleeced!" He continued to scan the document. Then, all of a sudden, Simpson paused. When he recovered his voice, he read a line that credited the police chief with "running a tight ship." Having a eureka moment, he announced with joy: "The report exonerates the chief!" He read further and told his listeners that Gannett assured the city that they should be proud of Chief Proctor.[4]

Amid the delight from his epiphany, Simpson interviewed white council members Milo McRae and Kurt Jepsen about the report. McRae and Jepsen began to shift their perspective and endorsed Gannett in what they took to be vindicating the chief. McRae told the audience with laughter that "Gannett did a good job. For our side!" Further, he mentioned that, despite her positive take on the police department, the previous and interim city managers had already begun making the changes suggested in the report. Moreover, Jepsen and McRae denounced the entire proceeding as a waste of money that had damaged the lives of the previous city manager and the police chief: "We have a first-rate police chief who is a far cry from his predecessor. Nonetheless, we spent $50,000 of the taxpayers' hard-earned money to learn what we already knew."[5]

News that the report vindicated the police chief spread quickly. Members of the Committee of 100 abruptly changed their outlook and appeared at the meeting with a decidedly less confrontational view toward Gannett. Feelings of victory and redemption calmed the crowd. Moreover, the supporters of the committee made a point of sitting on the other side of the aisle, with African American residents. So complete was the sense of triumph that even supporters of the investigation started to believe the report was favorable to the police chief.

Unaware of the shift in the mood of white civic leaders, attorney Gannett was on edge. She knew full well that her report did not exonerate the police chief and accordingly began her talk from a defensive position. Gannett clarified that her report was not part of a "pretext to 'get rid of the police chief.'" Instead of bashing the chief, she was respectful of his accomplishments and credited him with reforming and modernizing the department. She duly noted that his reforms led to the FPD's gaining national accreditation for the first time in its history. Gannett continued to heap praise upon the chief, in ways that resembled the way the Chamber of Commerce had about Proctor's impeccable credentials, hard work, and well-respected leadership.

Gannett then honed in on the fundamental question regarding discrimination. She explained that, regardless of his past successes, there was plenty of evidence that proved the FPD's management had violated Title VII of the 1964 Civil Rights Act. For that reason, she agreed with the NAACP that the three officers were victims of retaliation. Complicating the picture, she deemed the officers' original complaints "groundless" and furthered the idea that the complaining officers were troublemakers. Nevertheless, she pointed out that the department's interrogation of its black officers opened the city up to lawsuits. Gannett summed up her findings by noting: "The city of Fayetteville can be proud of its police department under its current leadership." However, in the final analysis, she blamed both the FPD leadership and the NAACP for making mistakes "that snowballed into this community crisis." She concluded: "The chief should not have ordered his two highest ranking African Americans employees to interview all the blacks to see if they felt there was racism in the department. . . . Notwithstanding the chief ordering the interview, it was not a hostile racist act. It is the subsequent follow-up hearings, interviews and interrogations by Lt. Boynton and the Office of Professional Standards that exposed the city to liability."[6]

The disjunction between the damning report and the sense of jubilation among the police chief's supporters produced a sense of the surreal. The feelings of euphoria about the chief's exculpation, however, did not last. On the following morning, I picked up the newspaper from my porch and read the headline: "Report Criticizes Police Actions: Risks of Lawsuit Cited in Gannett's Report." Staff writer Maura Singer reported that "civil rights lawyer Susan Gannett said, despite its good intentions, the FPD created a racially hostile environment."[7] The article captured the report's nuance in ways that mirrored my field notes. Singer did not confuse Gannett's contextualization of the chief as a "reformer" with her subsequent confirmation that he violated civil rights protections and retaliated against officers who criticized his administration. From Singer's article, one could conclude that Gannett's report did exactly what the NAACP and its five supporters on council had hoped. Singer's reporting pointed out the legal problems the FPD would be facing down the road.

By the time I turned on WFNC's morning show, Singer's article had already ignited a firestorm. WFNC had been swamped by calls that assailed the *Fayetteville Observer* for distorting the facts about Gannett's presentation. Callers complained that they had heard Gannett state that "the city of Fayetteville should be proud of its Police Department," but then the newspaper asserted "Report Criticizes Police Actions." One caller asked, "What happened? I went to bed, living in one town, with a great police chief, and woke up, in another, with a police chief who discriminated against blacks." Complaining callers inundated the phone banks at the *Fayetteville Observer* as well.

Anger about the headline spread through the city manager's office and the police department. Soon, city manager Roger Reynolds and Police Chief Dan Proctor paid James Tully, the publisher of the *Fayetteville Observer*, a visit. I never found out what went on in that meeting. However, the next morning, publisher James Tully printed a full-length article entitled: "Our Report Missed the Big Picture." He told his readers of the many complaints he received, one which he shared: "I was watching TV, and your report is 180 degrees from what I saw." Tully told the readers it was important he respond to this wave of criticism because "with a story of such importance to our community—I wanted to take a step back before moving ahead." He continued: "We did OK on a point-by-point basis, I think, but we failed to acknowledge the bigger picture. Although Gannett's report cited problems, it also contained statements such as: 'the city of Fayetteville can be proud of its police department under its current leadership.'"[8] He concluded that the report was positive, and he helped alleviate the fear that it could be either the basis for a lawsuit or a validation of the outside investigation.

Making Recall a Reality

Tully's commentary underlies the importance of the *Fayetteville Observer* to the urban regime in managing the event. Though Tully's embarrassing retraction of the headline was a quick response to criticisms from his allies, such framing of the event had begun several weeks before Gannett's visit. The Committee of 100 had already planned, well before Gannett's fiasco, to use her visit to launch its campaign to take back city council in the election that was now just a few months away.

In connecting attorney Gannett's upcoming visit to the crisis in government, the Committee of 100 sent out a flyer to the seven thousand citizens on its mailing list, declaring: "It's time for RECALL to become reality!" The call to action criticized "our State Legislators" for their failure to grant the citizens recall. In light of the shortcomings of politicians, the flyer summoned the ideals of self-government and implored "the citizens" to end the crisis with their vote. The flyer announced that election day will be "our recall" and "the Committee of 100 is planning its alternative course," adding, "With your help, we can win." The flyer avoided racial terms and clarified the Committee of 100's goal: to elect responsible leaders who were concerned about the community and prepared to make intelligent decisions. Emphasizing "growth and development," the group began to expand its message beyond the conflict and included the importance of passing the Marvin Plan, as an example of good government and the city's best interest. However, the flyer closed by returning to the crisis and pronounced election day to be an opportunity so that "we" can "bring an end to the tyranny of 'the Five.'"

Following the plan, as soon as attorney Gannett finished her presentation, members of the Committee of 100 directed residents across the street to the Prince Charles Hotel. Joining a handful of members, I rode a packed elevator to the twelfth floor. We were welcomed by cofounder Christine Rutherford as she shouted, "The chief has been exonerated!" As the meeting hall filled, Rutherford explained, "We are here to make sure that the citizens don't forget what *they* ["the Five"] did to *us*." She stopped her speech when council members Milo McRae and Kurt Jepsen, wearing yellow ribbons, joined the meeting. Greeted with a standing ovation, council member Jepsen grabbed the microphone and reminded the audience that the city manager's firing was "totally unjustified." He dismissed the report "as damage control" and condemned "the five council members" for dividing the city and firing a "very good and visionary city manager." He continued: "What our citizens have gone through overshadows this [Gannett's positive report] and we must keep the community focused on what happened to us. . . . . We need everyone involved. Without your help the same thing will happen again. We have to tell them, 'No. You can't do this; we are Fayetteville, not some little town.'"

Although McRae ceded the spotlight to Jepsen, he would remain the most vocal opponent of the "Fantastic Five." McRae's campaign certainly would keep the public focused on the fallen city manager. In many ways, he used the dispute to jumpstart his flagging political career, spending the previous eight months in the limelight as he routinely denounced the NAACP and attacked Tom Manning. In the previous election, McRae barely squeaked by his challenger, an African American guidance counselor at Fayetteville Tech Community College, winning the third and final at-large position by a mere 200 votes, more than 2,500 votes behind newcomer Tom Manning. Now, as the vocal leader of "the Committee of 100's" resistance, he revived his political career. As a southern Democrat, he based his campaign on the slogan "Your conservative voice."

After the enthusiasm about council members McRae and Jepsen subsided, Catherine Mitchell moved the meeting to the technical and legal aspects of the group's campaign to rid the council of Tom Manning, Sam Johnson, and Edna Harrington. She assured her supporters that the Committee of 100 would continue mobilizing citizens but that it could not raise funds for candidates. Similarly, she reported that the Chamber of Commerce supported the efforts but, as a public group, it could not openly support the campaigns of specific candidates. To comply with these laws, Mitchell announced the creation of a political action committee called "Good Government Now" (GGN). She told the crowd that GGN would focus on raising money for the four council members and mayor who supported the city manager. It would also seek candidates who would support city management.

Comprised of prominent civic leaders, professionals, and business owners, GGN was smaller and more exclusive than the Committee of 100. GGN grew from a small group of residents who lived on Haymount Hill. I came to know the chair, named Charles, who comes from one of the most prominent families in Fayetteville. He explained how he and many of his friends formed GGN out of a sense of urgency from what he called a "scandal." Though he had lived most of his whole life in Fayetteville, he had never been involved in politics. He voted but had never seen the need to get involved with city council because he thought that city council members generally "did the right thing." He explained that "firing the city manager was the major turning point." Charles conceded that many residents became too enthralled by the "racial issue." He believed the problem was deeper. He pinpointed the moment in which he became active: when Tom Manning joined FTFR in attacking downtown revitalization and the Fayetteville Partnership. Manning may have created good will with some military retirees, but Charles saw it differently: "I came to realize that they ['the Five'] were not stopping with the outside investigation." He was particularly enraged when the council "attacked Peggy Cartwright [of the Fayetteville Partnership]. After all the work she had done— really, the past seven years with all these local, state, and federal agencies to refurbish the Market House—Manning announced at the meeting that he was going to motion for the city to renegotiate the contract for the Fayetteville Partnership. I started to realize that it's true, that they have a different agenda than my agenda. They want to change Fayetteville for the worse."

In reaction to Tom Manning's agenda, Charles helped form the group that would evolve into GGN. The members of GGN met informally many times in an attempt to develop a list of possible candidates by studying voting districts, learning about the new changes to districts, and deciding which incumbents to support and which to try to remove. GGN offered their information to individuals whom they believed would make strong candidates. Many of their attempts to enlist candidates failed. As another member of the group told me, most people they wanted to run, successful people, were too busy being successful to be on council.

As the election grew near, GGN converted its recruitment efforts into a political action committee (PAC). By registering as a PAC, the group could actively support candidates who would oppose the city council members who investigated the police department. After announcing the new PAC, members of GGN held formal interviews with city council candidates. The interviews combined the crisis on city council with the downtown revitalization efforts and the school bond. The interviews focused on four questions: 1) Would you have voted for an outside investigation of the police department? 2) Would you have voted to fire the city manager? 3) Do you support downtown revitalization? 4) Do you support the school bond?

Though GGN held the Marvin Plan as an embodiment of the city's best interest in that it transcended the racial and factional squabbles that produced the "Five–Four," it broadcast to the public that the most important issue was to end the crisis on city council. In the middle of its campaign, GGN released an editorial in the newspaper presenting its central issue:

> A few months ago, a group of people stopped wringing their hands and started asking "what can we do about the City Council?"
> We formed a political action committee, Good Government Now.
> We realized that as individuals with four votes each, we would have little effect on the majority stranglehold of the council. So we set out to find and encourage seven or eight reasonable people in their campaigns. . . . We found more good prospects than we hoped. Since we are a diverse group ourselves, various candidates and viewpoints appeal to us. There are obvious choices. Janet Chaney, Kurt Jepsen, and Milo McRae have repeatedly stood up to the severe and still-unexplained actions of their five colleagues. We stand with these three and against the other five incumbents.[9]

Rationality of Power

City management complemented these protests and demonstrations by working behind the scenes in ways that would solidify the urban regime's control of power. To be sure, the city council majority, the NAACP, and FTFR informed the residents about a wide array of embarrassing problems in city government. As described earlier, these relative successes in discrediting city management led some dissenting groups to believe that the downtown leadership was wounded and that the exhortations of the Committee of 100 and Milo McRae represented desperate attempts by the old elite to retain their grip on power. These predictions of demise failed to consider how modern political institutions, in the liberal tradition of the Enlightenment, productively use criticism to build and expand their power.[10] Rather than weakening the regime, public criticism provided city planners and administrators crucial information that allowed them to strengthen the city's authority by reforming city policies.

To understand the ways in which city management worked within, and helped constitute, the crisis, we have to go back to the moment city council fired city manager Jim Thompson. With his ousting, the Chamber of Commerce lobbied city council to hire Roger Reynolds, the deputy city manager, on an interim basis. Business and civic leaders rallied around Reynolds when he took office, and they presented him as having the expertise and experience to retain continuity as the dispute raged. Civic leaders championed his seventeen years of experience in local government and his experience in overseeing the administration's two largest capital projects, annexation and downtown revitalization, and argued he would help stabilize government.

Interim city manager Reynolds had no honeymoon. With his eye to keeping the broader political and economic coalition together, he coordinated city policy with the public campaigns of the Committee of 100, the Chamber of Commerce, and the Fayetteville Partnership. However, he primarily labored behind the scenes in ways that sought to ease concerns about the administration's racial problems. No matter how hysterically the civic leaders had reacted to the NAACP's call for an investigation, he worked to alleviate the issues of racism so as to minimize the city's vulnerability to lawsuit in the face of the Justice Department's ongoing investigation. In this regard, he drew on his experience in human relations, spoke about "healing wounds" in the black community, and worked with the Human Relations Commission and the NAACP to develop a framework to allow black employees to raise issues of racism without threats of retaliation. His actions resulted in a new personnel policy review and an employee relations team that was set up to specifically address the type of race-based complaints that led to the city council dispute.

Paradoxically, city leaders held Jim Thompson as a martyr while they championed Roger Reynolds as representing a "paradigm shift" in improved race relations. In this sense, the urban regime began reforming itself through the works of Reynolds. In many ways, they found him to be an improvement in this political environment while at the same time he represented continuity with the previous administrator. Even Council members Frederick Walker and Tom Manning heralded Reynolds's creation of community forums to get whites and blacks to speak about race as having helped to "heal" the city's wounds. Attorney Wilson, representing the NAACP, lauded his efforts as well. In this sense, he helped short-circuit criticism of the city's administration.

Racism was not the only public relations problem that Reynolds encountered. He was part of the administrative team that had made downtown revitalization and the Marvin Plan the centerpiece of the city's policy agenda. And as we saw earlier, FTFR discredited many aspects of the plan and forced questions about how and why city government had endorsed the Marvin Plan. Most damning, FTFR publicized that the project would use public money to benefit downtown slumlords at the expense of poor blacks who lived in the impoverished neighborhoods near downtown.

Rather than delivering a deadly blow to the urban regime, FTFR's criticisms clarified weaknesses in the project. As will be discussed in the next chapter, city management reassessed revitalization plans regarding the black community. Though many supporters of downtown revitalization despised FTFR, city management took its criticisms seriously. City manager Reynolds engaged Dr. Puckett and General Roberts in dialogue about rebuilding downtown. He accepted the group's proposed referendum and announced that city government would not spend more public money until it could hold a bond referendum. Second, he responded to FTFR's most damning criticism about slumlords who were holding on to downtown property. He established appearance standards and levied fines of up to $100 a day against property owners who neglected their buildings.[11]

Most significant, however, was Reynolds's elimination of the "Bubba Mound" from the design. As noted earlier, critics of revitalization struck a nerve among city residents when it connected Marvin's dirt mound with the unpopular arena that had become known infamously as the Bubba Dome. Downtown boosters had scrambled for nine months trying to replace the label, to no avail. As the notoriety of the Bubba Mound grew, the president of the Chamber of Commerce and city management looked to the military establishment for help. Fort Bragg's commanding general was in the process of planning an Airborne and Special Operations Museum. Reynolds and the president of the Chamber of Commerce negotiated a deal with Fort Bragg's leadership that would move the $12 million project downtown; the Special Forces and Airborne Museum would take the place of the notorious Bubba Mound. After the agreement, Fort Bragg officials joined Reynolds and the Chamber of Commerce in heralding the museum as revitalization's spark plug, promising thousands of visitors to city restaurants and hotels. Also, Senator Frank Edwards secured money from the North Carolina General Assembly, further bolstering the image of downtown revitalization.

Roger Reynolds's changes in the revitalization plan had strategic implications for the downtown coalition as well as for the elections. First, they presented the Marvin Plan as a "vision" that was not written in stone.

The repackaged plan was a "flexible" guideline that would be adapted to contingencies as they arose. By agreeing with FTFR that further infusions of public monies to the Marvin Plan would require a referendum, the interim city manager stole the group's thunder. Most importantly, by adding the military to the mix, FTFR could no longer denounce their opponents as being simply "the Haymount." Second, Reynolds acquired the military museum at the same moment city council was entering the final stages of its search for the next city manager. Reynolds was a finalist for the position and was pitted against Dan Robins from Sentinel County, Florida. The Chamber of Commerce, Good Government Now, and the Committee of 100 lobbied city council to hire Reynolds. They heralded the progress he made to the city's racial policies and the acquisition of the museum as momentous changes.

Despite the full-court press, city council voted 5–4 to hire Dan Robins, meaning Reynolds would return to his previous post as the deputy city manager. Civic leaders, the Committee of 100, and Milo McRae cried foul when "the Five" decided to hire "outsider" Dan Robins as the permanent city manager, and McRae promised that if his side were victorious in the upcoming election he would motion to fire Robins at the city council's first meeting. Two days later, a member of the Committee of 100 published a letter to the *Fayetteville Observer*'s editor echoing McRae's message:

> Why this unseemly rush to hire a city manager so soon before a City
> Council election? Clearly this is the last opportunity for the majority of
> five to enact their original scheme. . . . The issue is not about the city
> manager. It never was. As you will recall, the issue has been our chief
> of police. The alleged scenario has always been that a group of trial
> attorneys dependent upon making deals that benefit their clients would
> prefer a chief of police more willing to compromise the law and less
> willing to rail against the low rate of DWI convictions in our courts.
> To cobble together a majority to effect this change, Billy Manning's
> brother and brother-in-law, both members of the city council, pledged
> to our three black council members that once the firings began, either
> the new city manager will pledge to replace the chief of police or the
> new chief would be the candidate preferred by Walker, Allison, and
> Harrington. I read of the disastrous fire of 1831 that started in the
> kitchen of the Kyle home and almost destroyed Fayetteville. This
> second great disaster in Fayetteville apparently started in the
> Manning's kitchen. I hope it will prove less destructive than the fire.[12]

With this fire burning, GGN and the Committee of 100 replaced former city manager Jim Thompson with a new martyr: Roger Reynolds. Milo McRae led a slate of twelve candidates, who had secured support from GGN, to take a pledge to fire the new city manager and rehire Reynolds at the first council meeting. Despite McRae's incendiary rhetoric, supporters of Reynolds reached out to middle-class and business interests who were committed to the urban regime's policy agenda. Using various messages, they appealed to civic and business groups who were committed to such things as public education, the arts, museums, and libraries. In fact, many citizens involved with the Chamber of Commerce, the Arts Council, and the school board disapproved of the Committee of 100's racial undertones. One informant who worked to get Tom Manning out of office was embarrassed by "the Committee" because it was "knee-jerk." More importantly, many of these middle-class interests believed they had no choice because the alternatives—the Mannings, "the Five," and FTFR—were not viable. Civic improvements would require coalitions with powerful groups like the Chamber of Commerce.

Staging a Coup

As described earlier, FTFR and many of the leaders of the Cumberland County Republican Party viewed the disarray on city council as an opportunity for political change. They envisioned many residents who could see past the conspiracy theories and Milo McRae's fanning of racial flames. Moreover, they feared that the downtown coalition was using race to close ranks on city council as a way to slip the Marvin Plan beneath the noses of the public. To keep the city from getting saddled with the expensive downtown revitalization project, Joanne Puckett, cofounder of FTFR, ran for the most coveted council seat, district 9, which included the Haymount and the equally wealthy neighborhood of Vanstory. Building on the successes of FTFR, Puckett hoped to create an alliance between military retirees, other middle classes, and the black community.

Puckett's campaign for city council picked up where FTFR left off. She attacked city government's alliance with powerful developers and a policy agenda that was compliant with Haymount and its "country club mind-set." She carried FTFR's self-described "populist" platform and she sought to expand her constituency by seeking to "protect the taxpayers" from waste in government. Believing that the downtown business and civic leadership was using the alarm about blacks taking over city council to push the Marvin Plan, Puckett refused to discuss the issue of firing the city manager. Moreover, she argued that the new council should not fire the new city manager, Dan Robins. In her mind, the previous city manager, Jim Thompson, was a failure, as evidenced by his acceptance of the flawed Marvin Plan. He facilitated the type of insider deals that made Fayetteville appear backward. In contrast, she believed that Robins was worth keeping as he brought an "outside" perspective yet to be tainted by the local good ole boys.

Puckett was unsuccessful in taking the debate beyond the "Five–Four" and the city council dispute. Her opponent, Hal Johnson, focused on the firing of the city manager: "I was born and raised in this town and had a love affair with Fayetteville that has lasted forty-one years. . . . Last spring I watched city council fire Jim Thompson and thumb their nose at recall and spend $50,000 on the Gannett Report that was absolutely unnecessary. I watched them hire an out-of-town city manager weeks before an election. . . . I support downtown revitalization, annexation, and commonsense leadership." Born and raised on Haymount Hill, Johnson embraced Milo McRae's call to undo the damage of "the Five." During his campaign, he stressed his local roots and drew on his father's legacy as a popular civics teacher and member of the powerful Kiwanis Club. He connected his bid to rid the council of "the Five" to the broader project of improving Fayetteville: downtown revitalization and annexation.

GGN, the Chamber of Commerce, the Fayetteville Partnership, the school board, and the Arts Council campaigned against Puckett, and she responded in an aggressive manner. She sought to expose Johnson as a member of the "Haymount crowd" and his political philosophy as an example of a small, insular group of people who thought they could ignore the public. She hammered him for his connection to GGN, the Chamber of Commerce, and downtown revitalization; she argued that GGN's main purpose was to find candidates who would support the Marvin Plan without a bond referendum. In this way, she chastised the city's most powerful residents, from the owners of the *Fayetteville Observer* to developers and real estate interests.

Ultimately Puckett's strategy failed. Hal Johnson and Good Government Now presented her as a mean-spirited and divisive person. They argued that in light of the "Five–Four," city council needed someone who was a team player and could subordinate his or her personal agenda to the city's greater good. Moreover, her enemies connected her with the Cumberland County Republican Party, which was notorious for being a bunch of divisive ex-military residents who were "anti-everything" and were led by Bill Gunderson, the urban regime's biggest enemy. Puckett's fate was sealed when a member of the Committee of 100 wrote a letter that connected Puckett to the infamous Gunderson and his associates:

> Voters in the 9th district should be aware of Joanne Puckett and her cronies. Her largest contributor, campaign manager Mike Harper is a former lawyer who was also Bill Gunderson's campaign manager. Harper was disbarred by the North Carolina Bar in 1995 for acts of

"dishonesty and providing false information under oath." He also campaigned against the school bonds. In their campaign against Hal Johnson they have resurrected one of their former tactics for a losing attempt in a congressional race. . . . It's called negative campaigning. They know they can't win on the issues, so they chose the negative route.[13]

Although Puckett was not friendly with Gunderson, she became tarred with his name. Puckett's candidacy mirrored the failures of Manning's in that it was not able to pull powerful factions and groups away from the downtown coalition. To be sure, many powerful middle-class and business interests believed that their interests were better served by the dominant business and political coalition.

In contrast to the Committee of 100's performances, the city's military community was not inspired by FTFR's conspiracy theories about the downtown elite using race to pass their development projects without a bond. Rather than threatening the regime, FTFR emboldened it; the regime incorporated its criticism and altered the revitalization plan. Moreover, FTFR's inability to threaten the urban regime, or take it over, resulted from its inability to provide a viable opportunity to regime partners who were willing to try change. These weaknesses in FTFR would have important ramifications for how the black community's leadership would align itself in the election, as we will discuss in the next chapter.

Conclusion

Having lost control of city hall and failed to pass the recall bill, Fayetteville's dominant coalition used attorney Susan Gannett's visit to Fayetteville to discredit her report and "the Five" who hired her. Taking advantage of Gannett's blunders, the Committee of 100 and Good Government Now produced powerful images of private citizens resisting the illegal actions of city council. City management complemented these public performances by fixing the problems exposed by the NAACP and FTFR. In this way, public rituals complemented city government, as city management readjusted its policies in ways that answered its critics, on one hand, and provided an example of city management's capacity to represent the will of the people, on the other. Local political power turned out to be more expansive and complicated than the members of FTFR imagined. By adjusting to criticism, city management and the Chamber of Commerce expanded its project to include key players representing the military. City management's institutional power allowed it to incorporate middle-class and business interests in ways that made its power and authority strong and durable.

Chapter 8

Single Shot

The Committee of 100 actively created fear about how the controversy on city council had dangerously empowered the black community. Fear-mongering exaggerated the power of black leaders and helped create the image of a mobilized and united black community, poised to maintain the power shift on city council. Such presentations of black political power concealed the many debates and conflicts that divide black Fayettevillians. Further, public performances of white anxiety and crisis distorted the manner in which formalized black politics supports and legitimizes the dominant business and political coalition. Forming an important part of the urban regime, the city's most prominent black leaders and representatives disappeared from the struggle. In the vacuum, Karen McMillan, Frederick Walker, and the leaders from the NAACP came to be viewed as symbols of a mobilized black community.

This chapter examines the way the image of a singular and unified black community gave way to bitter disagreements and struggles among African Americans as the electoral campaigns heated up. Indeed, many of the debates among African Americans about the role of black leadership described earlier became sharpened as the Committee of 100 and Good Government Now pursued their goal of driving white council members Tom Manning and Sam Johnson from politics. Many ordinary African Americans valued the sacrifices of these two white council members to support the aggrieved black officers. Empathizing with their suffering, scores of African Americans felt a sense of obligation to, and in some cases admiration for, both Manning and Johnson. However, many of the most powerful and prominent black leaders actively worked against Manning and Johnson, which led to a nasty disagreement among African Americans. This disjunction between black leadership and ordinary black residents became a divisive issue that ripped through the black community and shaped the political outcome in surprising ways.

Images of Black Politics

As the local media and powerful political leaders sounded the alarm siren about what they viewed as dangerous and unlawful actions of city council, white business and civic leaders became compelled by the idea the NAACP was wreaking havoc on the community by unfairly using the hard-won civil rights protections in ways that had spun out of control. Such emotion was represented in a letter to the editor, which described the NAACP's investigation as being akin to accidentally setting a house on fire:

> It was as if the NAACP officials were trying to get the fireplace
> started and have succeeded in setting the entire structure ablaze.
> The rights of the police officers associated with this controversy
> cannot be minimized, but neither can the rights of Jim Thompson and
> Chief Dan Proctor. It would seem that these two men are caught up
> in private feuds and individual agendas. . . . At the core of the
> NAACP's mission is the elimination of unfairness and injustice to
> any person, regardless of race. It would be a sad day in Fayetteville and
> Cumberland County, for that matter, if the actions of the Fayetteville
> chapter produced an opposite outcome. The community is on fire and
> damage is mounting. Let the greater good of Fayetteville be served by
> getting this fire put out and local government refocused on issues that
> heal and promote our city.[1]

Many whites believed that putting the fire out amounted to the citizens of Fayetteville using their collective power to return the NAACP and the black council members to their position as minority representatives and relinquishing control of government to the white majority. In efforts to mobilize whites, supporters of the city manager overstated the power of "the black church." In this way, the hysteria about the NAACP's burning down the city dovetailed with mythologies of racial progress that often exaggerate the power and rights African Americans have attained from civil rights reforms. Referring back to Representative Karen McMillan's successes in mobilizing black residents at Mount Sinai Church, many whites told me stories about how "the black church" was using church meetings to organize the black community to maintain its control of city council. At a city council meeting, an elderly white woman told me fantastic tales about the black church and its power to mobilize; she insisted that my research would benefit from seeing "the other side." Pointing to the left side of the city council chambers, which was packed with black residents, she envisioned politicized preachers behind the masses, charismatic preachers working with the NAACP, Frederick Walker, and Edna Harrington.

Shortly after hearing dramatic portrayals of the black church, Tony Jefferson announced on *Powertalk* the upcoming "town hall meeting" at Evans African Methodist Episcopal Zion. He urged "the community" to attend the meeting, and his enthusiastic support of the meeting gave me the impression that there would be a large turnout. I was not prepared for what I was to see. Not only did I not see the masses behind the "the black church," but the pews were practically empty, with the exception of an elderly couple patiently waiting up in the front. Off to the side stood a small group of black elected officials huddled in a tight circle as they talked and caught up with each other.

Serving as a stark contrast to the vibrant images of black rebelliousness that supporters of the city council had painted for me, the meeting was quite passive and barely touched the issues of racism in the FPD or the city council dispute. Clearly something had changed since the meeting at Mount Sinai regarding how the dominant black officials were dealing with the controversy. In fact, most of the prominent black leaders were absent. Instead of fiery speeches about racism and discrimination, elected officials gave "progress reports" about policy issues revolving around the school bond and downtown revitalization. Contrasting the Fayetteville Taxpayers for Financial Responsibility's (FTFR) torrid criticism of these public projects, these black officials endorsed the projects and legitimized them by insisting on their positive contributions to the black community in terms of jobs and minority set-asides for African American businesses. As the meeting continued, I became puzzled about the sense of crisis and racial animosity that many whites feared. Certainly this building was not on fire.

It became clear that black officials had a publicly prominent role in the urban regime, as they sanctioned the city manager's broader policy agenda. Moreover, it became clear that the black city council members were marginal to the urban regime. These meetings gave a sense of the powerlessness of the three black city council members. As it turned out, Frederick Walker was the sole representative of city council who attended these meetings. And at that, he played a minor part. Further shattering the image of an elaborate conspiracy, the Manning family and its courthouse friends were nowhere to be found.

The most telling aspect of this picture was the way that Frederick Walker's colleagues on council, Larry Allison and Edna Harrington, boycotted these meetings. Both council members believed the town hall meetings were duplicitous because their organizer, Karen McMillan, was an ally of the controversial preacher of Mount Sinai Baptist Church—William Jackson.

Reverend Jackson had become infamous among many African Americans for being a Republican. Even worse, after serving on city council, he became known as a friend of Milo McRae. Having warred with Reverend Jackson over many issues—Jackson opposed the renaming of Murchison Road after Dr. Martin Luther King—Allison and Harrington believed the meetings were a subterfuge for forces that sought to harm the black community. Council member Harrington even told many of her supporters that the meetings were designed to "misdirect" the black community.

As I got to know Edna Harrington, I came to see that she was disconnected from most black officials. One day, she took me on a car ride through her district, which contained both the poorest urban neighborhoods and the most rural ones in the entire city. She drove me from its northernmost stretch to across the river, taking me on what seemed like a horror show, as she showed me brownfields, the neighborhood overtaken by the dump site, and sinkholes eating up backyards. Everywhere we went, the elderly council member was greeted by residents as she slumped out of her minivan with the aid of a walker. Her popularity stemmed from the way she thumbed her nose at powerful political leaders. In the middle of meetings, she derailed discussions by raising issues of poverty. She was equally critical of black leaders whom she openly called "crooks," and whom she called out by name. These attributes that made her popular with residents were extremely frustrating for her colleagues on city council and many black officials, which led many civic leaders to dismiss her as dumb, out of touch, and crazy. But people who watched her closely knew better. As one observer of city council meetings told me, "Edna is as dumb as a fox."

With prominent black politicians retreating, less prominent black leaders jockeyed for position as they sought to project their power in both speaking for and leading the black community. In this regard, Representative Karen McMillan was a big winner. She had used the town hall meetings to present herself as a powerful mobilizing force. Part of this success resulted from the way she delivered by defeating recall and its seemingly all-powerful patron, Senator Edwards. Despite the low turnout and seeming uninterest in the monthly meetings among ordinary as well as prominent blacks, McMillan continued to use the town hall meetings to present the image of a unified black community. McMillan presented the monthly meetings as if they were the outcome of mobilizing in the black community. Crucial to understanding the events, as the Committee of 100 raised the temperature in its mobilization, the town hall meetings became increasingly disengaged from the struggle. Unknown to most whites, the black political meetings actually legitimized the broader coalition of interests that revolve around the city manager's office.

For me, these meetings put to rest the idea that Frederick Walker and Tom Manning had hatched a grand scheme to take power. Instead, a grand scheme was being hatched to mobilize black leaders and voters away from them, which I will return to below.

We Have No Leaders

As the Committee of 100 and GGN raised the conflict to a crescendo with the election campaigns, ordinary African Americans who were following the controversy on city council became increasingly disheartened. The sense of despair was heightened by attorney Gannett's debacle. Many black residents blasted her and blamed her for worsening the situation. Taking this frustration as a point of departure, Tony Jefferson devoted an entire show to what he called the bankruptcy of black politics. He clarified to his listeners that Gannett's report indeed showed that the police department discriminated against black officers. Notwithstanding, Jefferson felt that supporters of the aggrieved black officers lost the battle of public perception, and in this regard he concluded that the report was a failure. He conceded that powerful whites, whom he referred to as "the Hill," and their "groups" won the battle and discredited her: "She is an African American. You know how it is with us. If one black does something, then it has something to do with the rest of us. That's the way they see it: We hired her and she's incompetent, so that's a reflection on us." Moreover, he pointed out that she had a hand in this outcome because she was not prepared and ultimately produced a sloppy report that was easily manipulated.

Jefferson's use of Gannett as part of the broader problem in black politics gave way to weeks of debate on *Powertalk* about accountability. A frequent caller named Simon—who was a Muslim imam—was pleased that Jefferson focused on accountability. In this vein, he pleaded with the audience to "search for a deeper principle" to guide politics rather than simply expecting people with black skin to do the right thing. Rather than worry about what the white community thought, he asserted that "we need a healthier concept of ourselves" and we need to "hold our leaders accountable." It was from this perspective that Simon and Tony believed it was important to speak out against Gannett and her "mediocrity." Simon asserted "we can't accept mediocrity . . . we need to establish more independent people who don't need jobs or are worried about how Caucasians perceive us." Moreover, both Jefferson and Simon pointed out that successes for the majority of blacks will require creating alliances with factions in the white community.

Instead of despair about Gannett's poor showing, Jefferson encouraged his listeners to envision ways for "grass roots" African Americans to step into the breach left open by prominent black people. Representing this hope, Shanna, a frequent caller, reiterated that Gannett's presentation was a "letdown," as she emphasized, "We have to start thinking proactively. We have to start getting organized and not get defeated, feeling like we just can't win." William Wilson, the NAACP's lawyer, was a guest and he used Shanna's plea to urge citizens to "make the town hall meetings our agenda." Jefferson agreed that participation was needed. However, he pointed out that the Committee of 100 had already been meeting and organizing for the elections: "It's amazing. These folk have their act together. They are coming up with a strategy, and our folk? Well that's another story."

Despite his pessimism, Jefferson enthusiastically advertised the next town hall meeting and urged his listeners to attend and begin to mobilize to support the embattled coalition of "the Five." He hoped the Gannett debacle could "finally" serve as the "black community's wake-up call and galvanize black voters." Without either a political organization in place or a voter registration drive, black citizens—even those as critical as Jefferson—would continue to speak about the election as if there was something magical within the black community and its churches which could suddenly draw black voters *en masse* to ensure the Five would return to their seats.

Tom Manning and the Single Shot

Such hopes that the town hall meetings would be the catalyst for grassroots mobilization was quickly wiped out. At the next town hall meeting, attendance was a little higher than usual—however the church was nowhere near full. Instead of an organizing meeting for the grass roots, most politicians were in attendance, including white politicians. Two members of the ministerial alliance led the meeting, and they framed the forum in terms of how the Chamber of Commerce's two signature projects—downtown revitalization and the school bond—would benefit the black community. By side-stepping difficult questions about Gannett's report and racial discrimination, debate gave way to sound bites as each of the more than twenty candidates for city hall tried to capture their positions vis-à-vis the many struggles that enveloped city council.

Following the meeting, Simon called in to *Powertalk* and returned Tony Jefferson's attention to the issue of accountability. Powerless to hide his contempt for the two preachers who officiated the meeting, he asked rhetorically: "What was that meeting about? Were they [the two preachers] there just to show the white people they have influence?" Jefferson responded: "HNIC brother!" Simon agreed with Jefferson's quip that the event was about a few people jockeying to portray themselves as being the proverbial "head Negro in charge" of the purported black community. However, he was arguing that African Americans have to look beyond skin color and look to actions. In contrast to the words of "the community," he focused attention on people like white council members Tom Manning and Sam Johnson as holding hope.

Simon's open support of the white council members dovetailed with the way many of my black informants admired the way these two men put their livelihoods—and perhaps their lives—in jeopardy. To people who shared this appreciation, it was clear: without the "Manning boys," black council members would not been able to "make a move" and force the issue of racial discrimination into the public's view. As the Committee of 100 and Good Government Now raised the heat on the renegade council members, Tony Jefferson responded by reminding his listeners of the way that Haymount Hill vilified them as "nigger lovers." For this sacrifice, there was a sense of responsibility to support white candidates who put themselves on the line. It was, as the argument went, people like Tom Manning—liberal, open-minded whites—who offered black politicians and activists the power to challenge the status quo. This argument made it clear that the threat to Haymount Hill was neither Frederick Walker nor the NAACP; it was whites who were willing to break ranks with the city's powerful.

When it came to practical ways in which black residents could show their support for their embattled allies, there was little black voters could do for Sam Johnson. He represented a white district with several affluent subdivisions.

In Tom Manning's case, it was quite a different story. Everyone—blacks and whites alike—knew that African Americans could play a decisive role in the at-large race and potentially held the power to reelect Manning by using the "single shot" strategy. Single-shot voting refers to the tactic black voters in the South have used to elect black candidates in citywide elections. When African Americans gradually gained suffrage rights, southern politicians switched from single-member voting districts to at-large elections. In this way, authorities were able to dilute African American electoral strength by requiring them to gain a majority of white votes.[2] In response to at-large election schemes, African Americans have employed the "single shot" to win seats. This method calls for each black voter to vote for a single designated candidate and forgo using his or her other votes (see Black and Black 1987). By collectively placing their electoral strength on that single candidate, they are often able to "single-shoot" the candidate to the board. With the Committee of 100 and Good Government Now seeking to destroy the coalition and aiming directly at Tom Manning, many people presumed the black community would use the single shot.

Black Leaders and the Urban Regime

Manning's single shot gradually become a hot topic among ordinary black residents who followed the city council schism. Though black leaders made an impressive show at Mount Sinai Baptist Church when the conflict was in its early stages, they quickly receded from the glare of publicity. This is most clearly demonstrated with the shift in the town hall meetings. After that first event, the town hall meetings were not well attended and stayed away from direct confrontation with city government and its powerful allies in the business community.

In an important sense, the town hall meetings were not exactly the failure Tony Jefferson and many of his listeners presumed them to be. Instead, the meetings were the result of careful negotiation between city management, the white civic and business leaders who formed the bedrock of the urban regime, and prominent black officials who were subordinate members of the regime. At this particular conjuncture, city management and the Chamber of Commerce found themselves in a thorny predicament. On the one hand, their conflict with the NAACP had helped them consolidate support among many whites who would normally question the city manager's policies, especially when it comes to spending public money. Yet, the success of downtown revitalization and especially the school bond would require significant support from black voters.

Members of the urban regime understood the school bond as part of their broader economic development plans. Public schools were poorly performing and proved to be a liability in recruiting professionals and businesses. Moreover, Cumberland County schools were notorious for their poor condition. Buildings were dilapidated and many classes took place in makeshift bungalows. Business leaders had targeted the school system as a dire economic need. Leaders from the Chamber of Commerce developed a plan that focused on the fact that Cumberland County was a "low-wealth county" and that it had a tax base that resembled a rural area, and therefore the schools did not meet the needs of the city. Leaders at the Chamber saw improving the schools as a key to promoting investment in the city.

Understanding the importance of the black community to the passage of the school bond, the president of the Chamber of Commerce had carefully put together a plan to mobilize black voters. Business and civic leaders feared that the school bond might fail. In an interview with me, the president of the Chamber of Commerce explained that the voters of Cumberland County—many of whom had been annexed and had become reluctant residents of the city—were notorious for voting against referendums. With the specter of angry white voters turning back the school bond, he believed that black voters would be essential to the school bond's success.

By the time the dispute broke loose, the president of the Chamber of Commerce had already enlisted a group of black residents and politicians to the committee for passing the school bond. He recruited a young public health official, Tom Denby, to lead the committee. As the director of public health for Cumberland County, Denby had become increasingly active in the black professional group (the Fayetteville Business and Professional League) as well as the Chamber of Commerce and MetroVisions.

Viewing the school bond as essential to improving the condition of African Americans, he came to see the racial divisions on city council as an obstacle to his work. Because the effort was associated with powerful whites, he believed that the conflict required him to be more careful about whom he would chose to represent the school bond. But in many regards, the committee's recruitment strategy followed the normal patterns of seeking the support of the Fayetteville Business and Professional League, the Cumberland County Ministerial Alliance, black elected officials, and the most prominent black leaders.

Once the "Five–Four" exploded, Denby and other African Americans working with the Chamber of Commerce on the school bond stayed away from the city council schism. Even in his discussions with me he was careful. He showed empathy and respect for Frederick Walker, but he believed that the success of the school bond required that he stay out of the fracas. Like many African American leaders, Denby told me that he was being pulled by both sides. Similarly, black County Commissioner Bob Ellersley, who worked alongside Denby, feared the "Five–Four" would negatively affect the bond issue. After the elections, he rationalized his lack of involvement in the police department controversy: "We said, 'For God's sake let's not confuse the two.' Just like in the case of many people, I myself was one, that you could pass by our yard and see 'Vote Yes' for the school bond but we would not permit any political candidate to put a sign in our yard. I'm not interested in the 'Five–Four.' I don't want to get myself involved in this; I want to work with the school bond. That way we were not going to take sides from the political point of view. Many of us stayed clear." After the eventual success of the school bond, Ellersley took pride the black community's role in passing it: "If we had not participated, it easily could have been defeated. But we set aside our differences on that point. The total community should be indebted to the fact that we did support . . . if you look at the white precincts, it failed."

Clearly black professionals and officials who were members of the urban regime made a choice that cannot be reduced to being "coopted." In short, they chose their battles and felt the political and economic ramifications of not passing the bond would be too great. To be sure, the measure brought $98 million into the city and county coffers. In addition, Senator Frank Edwards used his influence in the General Assembly to have the state government add an additional $78 million to the school fund, under the condition that the bond passed. This influx of public money would come with minority set-asides. Black supporters of these policies were especially sensitive to civic leaders' mantra that though Fayetteville was North Carolina's fourth largest metropolitan area, it remained a low-wealth tax base. The school bond thus provided one of the few opportunities to infuse the city's infrastructure with public money. Moreover, the bond issue forced many Fayettevillians with liberal tendencies, including black officials, to give priority to the school bond, as it represented $176 million in construction contracts.

Members of the urban regime actively lobbied black leaders to support downtown revitalization. The city manager led the charge by redoubling his efforts to gain black support in the aftermath of the successful campaign of the Fayetteville Taxpayers for Financial Responsibility (FTFR). As I described above, FTFR publicized how the Marvin Plan not only called for the city to raze Grove View Terrace, but also excluded the historic black neighborhood of College Heights and the historically black Fayetteville State University (FSU) from the plan.

Rather than issuing a blow to the urban regime's revitalization efforts, FTFR provided the city manager and his partners an opportunity to shore up and expand its connection with African Americans. Recognizing the Marvin Plan's serious oversight regarding the black community, the interim city manager redirected the revitalization project. First, he spelled out that the Grove View Terrace housing projects would not be demolished. Because the city—under the aegis of the Fayetteville Housing Authority—had received over $9 million from the federal Housing and Urban Development office to restore the project, it would not relinquish this valuable chunk of housing for low-income residents. Second, Reynolds ordered the lead architect to revise the revitalization plan so that the boundary of the plan would be extended to include the College Heights neighborhood and FSU. Harold McLean, the chancellor at Fayetteville State University, was already a member of the revitalization committee and actively supported it, even without its inclusion of his institution. With the changes in design, Fayetteville

Partnership increased the visibility of FSU by electing him president of the organization.[3]

Passage of the school bond and the promoting of downtown revitalization reveal the ways African American leaders participated in the urban regime. These interests in the broader policy agenda of the city manager shaped the manner in which the town hall meetings refused to consider the issue of voter mobilization in support of the aggrieved police officers or the NAACP, let alone the biracial city council majority. To a noticeable degree, what Tony Jefferson and William Wilson identified earlier as the black community's lack of organization and indifference was partly the outcome of a well-organized plan to redefine the black community's agenda. Consequently, the town hall meetings did not challenge the city and county's policy agenda. Instead, it ratified this agenda. An important aspect of these negotiations was the ambiguity that surrounded them. Black leaders had an investment in hiding their loyalties from black voters.

A Trojan Horse

Such collaborations between black and white officials burst wide-open during the last week of registration for the election. As the deadline for filing for the city elections neared, a young African American by the name of Michael Pearson registered to run in city council's at-large race. The sudden appearance of the upstart stunned Tom Manning and his black supporters. With Manning already feeling embattled, Pearson's entry seemed to threaten his hopes of being the "single-shot" candidate for the black community.

Although Pearson was well liked by those who knew him, he was largely unheard of in political circles. Being an unknown, his sudden appearance in the city council race took on a mysterious quality. White civic leaders glowed, as they believed he would make it difficult for African Americans to put their entire power behind a white candidate. Their glee was matched by rumors that spread among African Americans that speculated about backroom deals between Pearson and the Haymount. Pearson deflected such hearsay, as he seemed stunned to be in the middle of a heated fight.

Pearson's denials were called into question when Good Government Now (GGN) released its financial report. The chair of the political action committee reported that its largest contributions went to Milo McRae and Michael Pearson. Being paired with McRae, for many African Americans the standard bearer of racist reaction, was difficult for Pearson to live down. News of his alliance with GGN was blasted into the airways when Tony Jefferson asked his listeners: "How could GGN, in its fight against 'the Five,' support a black candidate and Milo?" Immediately the lines were filled, and a well-known, and respected, activist responded to his question: "Hi Tony. This is Martha Jones. It's simple. That's Haymount's game plan to pull votes from Tom Manning. . . . They've made it clear they are opposing the five council members who are really concerned with *our* community. This group [GGN] is only concerned with their own agenda. It's clear for anyone to see that if they are supporting these three [the incumbents] and Pearson, they are fighting against what is best for our city. If they are endorsing Pearson, then we need to hang with Manning. That's the way I see it: Michael is being bought off."

Ms. Jones was known as "a straight shooter" and had been active in local politics since the marches at FSU in the 1960s. She was not part of the black inner circle and would never be accused of being a "bourgeois black." Yet, she had the distinction of being the first African American chair of Cumberland County's Democratic Party.

Over the next several weeks, Martha Jones actively campaigned for Manning and became the symbol of the "Manning single shot." Using her political clout, she continued to denounce Pearson and urged him to withdraw from the race. Following suit, council member Edna Harrington joined Martha's call to action as she issued a warning on *Powertalk* that "if we lose Manning, we lose everything."

Apart from the practical concerns of maintaining the city council bloc, others worried that Pearson's act sent the wrong message to whites who sympathized with African Americans. Supporters of Manning were passionate about the way that voting for Pearson was akin to a slap in the face and would send a sobering message to other whites who would dare to think of supporting the black community. A caller to *Powertalk* named Harry expressed this sentiment as a caution to his fellow citizens:

> HARRY: If we let Mr. Manning get voted out of office we deserve what we get, we don't deserve anybody else standing up for our concerns or fighting our fight.
>
> TONY JEFFERSON: Brother, look, all they [Pearson's supporters] are talking about: "You know he [Manning] had an agenda." I'm serious! There are some supposedly pretty well-educated African Americans, in their circles, I'm hearing them talk, and that's the *first* thing out of their mouth. I'm like: "What does that have to do with anything?"[4]

Over the next several weeks, the lines at *Powertalk* became jammed up with black residents championing Tom Manning and black supporters of Pearson arguing that their view had nothing to do with Manning. Instead,

Pearson's supporters raised the issue of the black community deserving one of "its own" in one of the at-large seats. The debate went on as if there was a mystery that had not been solved. One caller became frustrated by the manner in which a debate about Manning and Pearson persisted. He asked: "Why can't we see the forest for the trees? Something stinks and I'm glad this came out; hopefully this will galvanize us." He made sure his point was not a personal attack: "I like Brother Pearson, but I have already committed to Manning, and he's been there and he supported what was right for the community, not just for the blacks. I would rather see Manning get in there, so I'm going to vote for Manning and hope everybody will support him."

Animosity about Pearson's candidacy became connected with an African American county commissioner, D. B. Shaw. Rumors had spread the story that Shaw recruited Michael Pearson in order to pull votes away from Manning, much as Martha Jones had speculated. Little by little, this accusation stuck. Shaw was an insurance salesman and had had reasonable success in politics. Many believed the story because they thought he was trying to ascend the political hierarchy and would need favors and help from the powerful figures in the Democratic Party. Nobody really knew what he was doing, but it became clear that he did recruit Pearson, and it was hard to deny Pearson's candidacy was creating division among blacks that would contribute to the urban regime's efforts to banish Tom Manning from Fayetteville politics. Both Martha Jones and Edna Harrington openly accused Shaw of working for "the Hill." Black supporters of Manning cursed Commissioner Shaw for "creating confusion" and "dividing" black voters.

After this revelation, Tony Jefferson blamed Shaw for "creating this mess" and challenged him to come on *Powertalk* and explain his actions to the black community. Shaw agreed. He spoke firmly, was not defensive, and used charm to present Michael Pearson in the positive light of black progress. He shared his pride in convincing Mr. Pearson to run, while he denied the accusation he was working for "the Hill" or collaborating with the all-powerful Senator Edwards to keep Tom Manning out of office. Moreover, Commissioner Shaw complimented Tom Manning for being "an advocate" and asserted that "the minority community has supported him." The problem, he argued, derived from Manning's inability to draw votes from whites. With that said, he distanced himself from Haymount Hill and Frank Edwards by focusing on the city's legacy of keeping blacks from winning the at-large slot. In this vein, he insisted, "We have one person of color running for one of those three seats. . . . Since we have gone to this at-large system, we [African Americans] have not been able to win an at-large position." He concluded that "blacks should not turn away from one of your own," as he believed the black community's commitment to Pearson ran deeper than its loyalty to Manning.

Commissioner Shaw's interview on *Powertalk* did little to dampen the belief that he was involved in a plot hatched by Senator Edwards to end to the city council crisis by driving Manning out of politics. Purveyors of this conspiracy theory drew upon previous rumors that speculated about how important black leaders brokered deals with Haymount Hill. This event, after all, had dominated Fayetteville's politics for an entire year, and white and black leaders proved to be ineffectual in controlling the situation. One informant believed that "the Hill" had become very impatient with black leaders during the event. They had failed to get any of the prominent black leaders "to step up." Now, they had the hope D. B. Shaw would step up and "clamp" the crisis down.

In addition to being bothered by the appearance of collusion with powerful whites, many black residents were offended by Shaw's appeal to race. By insisting "we" should back "one of our own," many black residents believed he was no better than Milo McRae and the racial fears he provoked. With the Pearson controversy roiling, council member Frederick Walker finally started to speak out. Before the members of the NAACP, in a subtle way, he took issue with Shaw's appeal to race:

> I came to talk about how people are trying to buy the election, plain and simple. We have two people [Sam Johnson and Tom Manning] who have put themselves on the line to do what was right. It took great fortitude. . . . In the at-large race you have three votes. Whatever your reason for voting is, you need to ask: which candidates have [been there for us]. . . . Because we got one black in this race, many of the people on the Hill don't think blacks have the sophistication to vote for a white candidate. Tom Manning did something that put his political career at risk . . . whether he wins, or loses, people are going to look at the result. Can you imagine what whites are going to think if we don't support him? If you are happy with things on the Hill, fine! It's imperative that you, people that look like you, vote for the individuals that will represent you.

Animosity between black factions over Tom Manning increasingly came to dominate discussions as the elections drew near. As discussed earlier, many African Americans believed that the biggest threat to ordinary African Americans came in the form of black middle classes. Indeed, many African Americans came to know the police department controversy through stories about how the highest-ranking black officers helped punish critics of the police chief. Many Fayettevillians explained with elaborate metaphors

and myths why people like Shaw and other African Americans of higher status would work against African American officers. One dominant metaphor
was a "bucket of crabs": As one crab escapes the bucket, another reaches up
with its claw and drags him back down.[5] Other informants drew on the myth
of Willy Lynch to express what they viewed as a character flaw distinct to
African Americans. They borrowed the Willy Lynch story from Louis
Farrakhan's speech at the 1995 Million Man March, in which he described the
plight of the black man as the result of a Caribbean slaveholder named Willy
Lynch. According to the story, Willy Lynch sold southern slaveowners a fool-
proof plan to keep blacks divided and under control for the next three hundred years. Lynch's plan was to exaggerate differences among blacks—by the
relative darkness of their skin color, the size of the plantation on which they
worked, hair texture, age, and gender—in order to pit slaves against each
other. By making slaves hate each other, Lynch guaranteed slaves would trust
only their owners.

When it became known that D. B. Shaw was responsible for the dispute
over the single shot, an informant named Harold explained that:

> We are still living under the Willy Lynch syndrome. . . . Black
> people have the tendency to destroy the resources that they already
> have. As far as Tom Manning and all the fab-five . . . this is to our
> advantage.
>
> GEORGE: You think that some blacks opposed to the "fab-five"?
> HAROLD: Most definitely. All that goes back to the Willy Lynch
> theory. Unbeknown to them, they are being controlled by what has
> been instilled into our forefathers. They are saying, "Michael
> Pearson would be the first at-large black city council member,"
> not really thinking this through. This is the Willy Lynch
> Syndrome. . . . We divide ourselves and distrust each other. It all
> boils down to that there are no black leaders that you can really
> identify with. The blacks making the decisions are in a higher tax
> bracket and really don't know what the grassroots people are going
> through.

Shall We Overcome?

Allegations that D. B. Shaw revived the spirit of Willy Lynch became a
public relations disaster for black leaders. As the division over the black
community's debt to Tom Manning grew, Karen McMillan called a special
town hall meeting to stop the widening rift so that "the community" could

"decide" on an electoral strategy. On October 26—merely ten days before the election—seventy black residents gathered at John Wesley Baptist Church to resolve what McMillan called "misunderstandings."

Martha Jones and D. B. Shaw sat close to the front, on opposite sides of the aisle. The tension between them was palpable as they avoided eye contact. Many of the members of the audience, including myself, believed that the war of words that had been waged over the airways of *Powertalk* was going to lead to a showdown. Supporters of Manning believed that the meeting was going to reveal to the black community that Commissioner Shaw and others had colluded with powerful white leaders. Pearson's supporters, however, viewed it as an opportunity to make amends with their enemies and come up with a compromise that would benefit the black community.

County Commissioner Bob Ellersley convened the meeting: "We are here to accomplish something because this is an important election. We must bring our community together and we must roll up our sleeves and get out the vote." Before he continued, Frank Bowman, a city council candidate and Martha Jones's ally, stood up to say, "We have a split to where it is causing serious misunderstandings and this is not healthy for the community." Bowman presented the schism in terms of whether the community should single shot Manning. He wanted to put the question on the table right away and was ready to call a vote.

His motion was halted by Representative Karen McMillan. She pardoned herself and explained to Bowman that "we" have to hear from "our elected officials" before we "talk strategy." Following her suggestion, each elected official spoke about his or her board's work. Like at the previous town hall meetings, each official declined to talk about city council. Instead, they talked about the school bond, economic policy, and creating a Martin Luther King Park.

Frustrated by these diffuse discussions, city council member Frederick Walker redirected the debate back to the city council election, warning that there were many people "operating in direct opposition of what they profess to represent." His indirect condemnation of black officials who had abandoned him and his colleagues was directed to the citizens, who seemed to be confused. In this vein, he urged the audience to "think" about what was going on in "our community."

County Commissioner Ellersley understood that he was being assailed by Walker for not supporting city council and for working closely with the Chamber of Commerce on the school bond. Ignoring the substance of Walker's comment, Ellersley opened the floor to audience members to "share their feelings." Michael Pearson raised his hand and walked to the podium.

As his body nervously shook and his voice trembled, Pearson appealed to the crowd:

> I'm beat down . . . I'm a little disappointed in my community. There are conspiracies that Senator Frank Edwards got me to run. Not true! There are conspiracies that I'm running to upset Tom Manning. Not true! I thought I had a chance to serve on city council. I thought my community would embrace me. I got in the race and look what happened. I thought my opposition would come from the other community, but to see the division among African Americans has hurt me. But, the divisions haven't been in our community. It has been with the leadership. I can count on my three fingers those who've helped me. I've never been against Manning. I'm not against Tom . . . I want to be a positive force. This is not about Manning; it's a power struggle in the black community. It's because I didn't go through the right lines, I have no experience. It's been the Afro-American leaders that have turned their backs on me.

Commissioner Ellersley applauded attorney Pearson's speech. He turned to the audience and in disgust he pronounced: "I will not allow us to [pointing toward Martha Jones's side] turn our backs on one of our own."

Understanding that Ellersley was throwing down the gauntlet, Karen McMillan sought a middle ground. Visibly anguished by the tensions in the room, she sympathized with both factions and tried to recast the problem in less combative terms: "We've been here for an hour and a half; we came to talk about strategy, to get input from the community. We had a meeting a week ago; we are here tonight to make very specific recommendations. When we talk about divisiveness, we are talking about the at-large race. Let's face it! We had recall, the firing of the city manager, and Manning and Smith stood up and supported the black community. Then we have Pearson. There are some that say we have to support both. We can live with that? Single shot? Some say we won't get anywhere."

City council member Larry Allison, in a rare appearance to the town hall meetings, stood up and responded to Pearson's plea for help from his community and McMillan's suggestion the black community follow through with the double shot. In displaying his anger and frustration, he shamed the black community for abandoning Tom Manning. He pointed out that he and his black colleagues on city council had known about the problems in the police department for a long time. Knowing they could not get white council members to assist, he said, "we" [the black council members] were powerless. But then he erupted, "Because of the willingness of these two courageous people [Tom Manning and Sam Johnson] I came to the conclusion now was the time! And after this long struggle what do we get? I stand on the threshold of getting kicked in the butt?" He went on:

> I receive faxes and telephone calls twenty-four hours a day cursing
> me for what we have accomplished. We took it with a smile. I was
> brought up in Fayetteville seventy-three years ago to hate nobody.
> My grandfather was sold at the Market House. I have been here!
> I know more about Fayetteville than you, you, and you [pointing to
> Pearson and two other members of audience]. I've been kicked in the
> butt. Edna Harrington has been kicked in the butt . . . and Tom
> Manning has been kicked in the butt. You better think about what's
> happened in Fayetteville, otherwise you will be in for the shock of
> your life. You better vote straight [for "the Five"] and then pray.

Allison intuitively knew that he was going to lose, as were his colleagues. However, he wanted to point out that this discussion about Michael Pearson and the double-shot strategy was going to guarantee the defeat.

Allison's speech raised the ire of an older man, who stood up and yelled, while pointing to Michael Pearson, "This young fellow hasn't done anything. I can't cast but one vote. I will vote for the guy that brought us this far. The white man is the one who stuck with us." It was clear that many of the residents believed that the black community's interests, in this battle, were best served by supporting Tom Manning. Karen McMillan tried to stay quiet and listen. After hearing these two impassioned speeches in support of Manning, a direction she seemed to be going in, she stood up and was ready to call a vote among the residents over which way the black community would go.

Right when she was ready to formulate the vote, State Senator Neil Sweeney stood up and commanded, "This discussion can't go on. I don't think we are ready for the consequences if we take a vote among us to support one or the other. The only thing to do is 'double shot.' If we go out in large numbers, we can get two." Sweeney had remained quiet during the entire struggle. As discussed earlier, he had stood quiet in the North Carolina Senate when Frank Edwards passed the recall bill for the Committee of 100. Everyone knew that Sweeney was close to Edwards and involved in downtown revitalization.

The crowd fell quiet and McMillan stopped in her tracks. Suddenly the silence was broken by Martha Jones. She knew she did not have the pull to upend Sweeney. Nevertheless, she told the crowd, "I have been honest to Pearson and I still think we need to support Manning." She paused, then looked toward Sweeney and Shaw, and said: "I understand what you are doing."

Commissioner Ellersley took the silence as a cue that the meeting was over. He urged his fellow citizens not to give up hope and that "we must get the vote out." Before adjourning the meeting, everyone held hands, forming a circle, and sang "We Shall Overcome."

News of the meeting spread the next morning on *Powertalk* as Tony Jefferson informed his listeners that the black community's officials had met and decided that we will accept two: "We will double shot both Manning and Pearson." His announcement was meant to show he was toeing the party line, but it was apparent he did not agree with the decision. Many callers criticized the decision not only for being a compromise, but for being a faulty plan, as the black community did not vote at a high enough rate to get two across. Off the air, black supporters of Tom Manning argued he was being sacrificed as a concession to a small group of black leaders who were helping the Haymount win the election. After the barrage of calls, Jefferson reassessed: "The double shot is a compromise. Cut out all the whining. This is politics. You are not anti-black if you don't vote for the black candidate."

Conclusion

FROM MILO MCRAE'S PERSPECTIVE, the black community's double-shot strategy was wildly successful. Michael Pearson's candidacy guaranteed Tom Manning's defeat. And, coupled with the work of black politicians to break up single-shot efforts, Good Government Now (GGN) helped drive Sam Johnson, Edna Harrington, and Larry Allison from city council. Frederick Walker remained the sole survivor of the "Fantastic Five." Rejoicing in the council majority's monumental collapse at the polls, the headline from the *Fayetteville Observer* blared: "Voters Crush Fayetteville City Council Bloc." White civic and business leaders celebrated right along with the newspaper, treating the election as a model of self-government and a "referendum" on "the Five's" investigation of city government.

Milo McRae appeared to be the big winner. As the top vote-getter in the at-large election, he became the mayor pro-tem. Reflecting his new position, he congratulated the citizens who responded to his campaign slogan, "Vote for me if you don't like what Tom Manning and the Fabulous Five have done this year," for restoring popular control of government.[1] Behind his pronouncements lay the true accomplishment of the year-long spectacle of crisis: the policy agenda of Fayetteville's dominant coalition would be protected by the new city council. Rationalizing this power, McRae held up city government's policy agenda and its downtown revitalization plan as embodiments of what was best about the city.

Before civility could be restored, however, McRae had to attend to one last bit of unpleasantness. The first meeting of the new council, normally a ceremony to swear in new members, would become the capstone to the year-long spectacle. What is normally a brief formality became a greatly anticipated symbolic event where the victors of the election could put an end to "the

Five's" tyranny. After swearing in the new board members, McRae hastily called the council to order and moved to terminate Dan Robins's contract and rehire Roger Reynolds as the permanent city manager. In sending Robins packing for Florida, McRae and his allies rejoiced in having erased "the last symbol of what 'the Five' did to us."

However, eight months later, on the Fourth of July of 1999, the EEOC issued its ruling and found that the police chief had indeed discriminated against black police officers and violated Title VII of the 1964 Civil Rights Act. Tony Jefferson announced the ruling to his *Powertalk* audience and congratulated the NAACP's representative to the EEOC, Bill Sherman. Sherman expressed that the outcome was both heart-warming and disappointing: "Good people on city council, the fallen comrades, Larry Allison, Sam Johnson, Edna Harrington, and Tom Manning, have been damaged. From the beginning, these courageous people understood there was a problem. And they were opposed, people saying there were hidden agendas, side issues . . . they committed political suicide to hold up what's right."

The emergence of the "Five–Four" schism and its development as a spectacle of "crisis" gives us an occasion to rethink the ways the idea of crisis functions as a framing device in politics. Politicians, ordinary citizens, and academics often use ideas of "crisis" to depict social change in dramatic fashion. Calling a situation a "crisis" is thus not merely a way to describe the situation but a means to augment the perception of dramatic change (Koselleck 2006) in ways that demand political intervention (Blyth 2002; Hay 1996, 1999). In this instance, white civic and business leaders also invoked conspiracy theories about the crisis as a way to connect their interests to those of broader constituencies. These theories depicted the biracial alliance that held a city council majority as dangerously upsetting the balance of power by irresponsibly empowering the black community and thwarting the system of checks and balances that protected the white majority from special interests and factions. This construction of the crisis succeeded because it recruited the anxieties that many whites harbored about Fayetteville's image and its social problems. By treating the conflict over the city council as part of the collective struggles of Fayettevillians to improve the city's negative reputation, civic leaders presented this shift in city council power as a dangerous alteration in normal patterns, one that would drag the city into chaos and disorder and back to the bad ole days of Fayettenam if not brought to a halt.

And much as in earlier racial crises that have rocked Fayetteville—from the Haitian Revolution and the Wilmington race riot to the racial panics of World War II—once the dust had cleared, white business and political leaders appealed to symbols of racial healing and reconciliation. The chair of

Fayetteville's Chamber of Commerce reached out to the president of the NAACP, and the erstwhile foes coorganized a community meeting to "heal the wounds" of the city's "strained race relations." Prominent black and white leaders met at Fayetteville State University to discuss the importance of communicating "between the races." After the meeting, the Chamber of Commerce and the NAACP launched a new group called "Fayetteville United." With the support of city management, they implemented "study circles," a government-backed initiative that brought blacks and whites together to speak to each other about racial problems and concerns.

Civic leaders used these performances not only to underscore proper relations between representatives of the minority and the majority, but as a spectacle that served to enforce the dominant coalition's understanding of governance and race (Goldstein 2004; Handelman 2004; Wedeen 1999). Such projections of power displayed both continuities and changes in contemporary patterns of racism. Even after passage of the landmark Civil Rights Act of 1964 and the repudiation of white supremacy, local authorities continued to use racial ideas to stigmatize African Americans as a minority population that is deeply troubled and must be carefully regulated and kept subordinate to the "majority" values that putatively connected all whites across class lines. Nevertheless, the structure of black politics was transformed as federal agencies and local political leadership incorporated African Americans into mainstream political organizations.

The "Five–Four" spectacle illustrates this double movement. On the one hand, the Committee of 100 led the chorus of protest against the NAACP's call for an outside investigation and mobilized perceptions of crisis and racial fear about the shift on city council. On the other hand, city manager Roger Reynolds worked behind the scenes as he took the charges of racism in the police department seriously and reformed the city's anti-discrimination policies. Most notably, he created an employee relations team to handle discrimination cases and the police chief established an ombudsman employees could approach anonymously to voice concerns about discrimination. Far from harming the regime, the NAACP's criticisms thus provided the city manager opportunities to readjust his racial policies in ways that ultimately strengthened the regime and reaffirmed the city government's links to prominent figures in the black community (Flyvbjerg 1998).

Such relationships between city management, business leaders, and black elected officials highlight the ways civil rights reforms have resulted in a form of black politics that deemphasizes political mobilization of black constituencies or fighting for political needs of poor and working- class blacks (Reed 1999a). The defeat of the city council bloc highlighted this broader pattern in which Fayetteville's white political leaders have regularly used civil rights reforms to gain greater control of black politics through an expanding matrix of boards, commissions, institutions, elected offices, and publicly funded economic projects. In this process, black political leadership has increasingly developed in anti-democratic fashion, for once African Americans were appointed to a board or appeared in a representative capacity they were widely and automatically treated as "black leaders" who were assumed to represent the will and interests of the black community (Gaines 1996; Reed 1999a). Instead of mobilizing voters, the most prominent and powerful among such black leaders used town hall meetings to create the perception of a mobilized and united black community in ways that dovetailed with the racial conspiracy theories about changing political power structures. And yet behind the performances, black leaders maintained productive relations with the city's dominant coalition. By providing strategic resources to black officials and civic leaders, Fayetteville's city management and its political allies were thus able to split black residents in ways that ensured their electoral defeat.

The repression of dissident black voices and the incorporation of mainstream black leaders suggest some of the ways postsegregation racial politics have been shaped by broader fiscal policies known as "neoliberalism" (Harvey 2005). Over the past thirty years, federal funding cuts for public education, social services, transportation, affordable housing, and job creation produced great challenges for city governments throughout the United States (Brenner and Theodore 2002; Davila 2004; Eisinger 1998; Hackworth 2000). In response to these political challenges, Fayetteville's city management and its allies produced a policy agenda that sought to deal with the problems of a dilapidated downtown, sprawling suburbs, racial inequality, imploding schools, and crime. An important part of this agenda has been working to implement racial reforms in ways that support and reinforce the city leaders' broader policy agenda instead of undermining it. It is in this sense that many African Americans who did not support Tom Manning, and lobbied for the school bond and revitalization, acted as what political scientist Clarence Stone calls regime partners (Stone 1989). Indeed, by adopting business-oriented development models that emphasize economic growth, black leadership has often helped rationalize the broader economic policies that have worsened the standard of living for most African Americans. In many ways, contemporary structure of black leadership in the United States embodies neoliberalism.

The "Five–Four" crisis also underscores some of the ways class conflict and struggle among African Americans developed and was deployed after legal segregation was forbidden. After the electoral defeat of Tom Manning and his allies on city council, the conflict and struggle that occurred in private conversations among ordinary black citizens came out into the open. Ordinary black citizens used the event to discuss the failures of the way civil rights reforms have been implemented and to speak to such issues as systemic patterns of racism and the worsening of living conditions for the majority of African Americans (Cohen 1999; Gregory 1998; Pattillo- McCoy 2007).[2] This increased scrutiny of black leadership was exemplified by a middle-class resident who was a faithful member of the Democratic Party and a critic of Tony Jefferson's *Powertalk*:

> It concerns me when we say "black leadership." There is no
> leadership, no strategy, and no agenda. All you have are people
> positioning themselves for self gain. Now, the Haymount has a
> solid majority [on city council] and now we are crying. The black
> leadership put Pearson in the game and caused this problem. With
> the resounding defeat of "the Five" and the landslide victory of Milo
> McRae, race relations in this town have been put back a couple of
> decades. What really bothers me is that the two whites . . . put it on
> the line and we [the black community] didn't support them. You will
> have people talking about this for years, in the back rooms they will
> say: "I will tell you about what happened to Tom Manning when he
> tried to work with African Americans."

Talk show host Tony Jefferson used *Powertalk* to further this sense of crisis of black leadership. In describing the monumental failure of black politics, he urged blacks to make political decisions free from the influence of white power brokers. He proposed a plan that would help develop mechanisms that would allow black residents to voice opinions and build a political agenda. He attacked the NAACP and its new organization, Fayetteville United, as part of the repertoire of techniques that the powerful whites use to talk about race in ways that stymie debate about difficult questions of poverty and inequality. Jefferson therefore promoted a new series of town hall meetings to discuss problems in the black community, meetings that would exclude whites. He argued that such exclusion was necessary for blacks to come together and develop a real agenda of their own—instead of merely rubber-stamping the downtown coalition's development agenda. Jefferson argued that "common sense would say something is wrong, externally and internally," and proclaimed the object of black politics must shift toward "true equal treatment for blacks. . . . It is insane to think that we can continue to do the same thing and get different results. We can't continue to do the same thing. It's madness." Response to Jefferson's call to action was swift. WIDU officials suspended him and cancelled *Powertalk*, as white civic leaders accused him of being racist.

The political uses of racial fear are always about more than controlling and defining black politics and African Americans. As I have shown, in Fayetteville civic leaders used conspiracy theories to regulate relations between white factions and black representatives in ways that illustrate how racial fears interweave with class struggles that divide whites over social and economic policy.

Indeed, racial ideas of "whiteness" underlie the performances of crisis— not to mention the day-to-day processes of implementing the city's policy agenda—and work to help the dominant coalition present its class interests as those of a wider, racially defined majority that transcends class differences among whites. By creating a fearful image of the black community being empowered and excited by a faction of whites, civic leaders attempted to link all other whites in Fayetteville behind a collective image of dominance (Brodkin 1999; Frankenberg 1993; Lipsitz 1998). But such a racial vision is far from self-evident. And in fact many Fayettevillians contested and struggled over the meaning of majority values and of whiteness (Arnesen 2001; Hartigan 1999, 2005). Indeed many white critics challenged the vision of the city's dominant coalition during the "Five–Four" crisis and sought to impose an alternative vision on the city council. Perhaps most importantly, the Fayetteville Taxpayers for Financial Responsibility (FTFR) and other military retirees challenged the narrative of racial crisis and attempted to turn the public's attention instead to the economic policies and interests that supported the use of public money for downtown revitalization. Many residents, especially those who self-identified as "the military," also believed the racial anxiety expressed by the leading political and business figures revealed the backwardness and ineptitude of the city's political leaders.

In this way, "the military" emerged as a threatening force and a critical faction that could form an alliance with black leaders. Yet, at the very moment when FTFR seemed to have discredited the dominant coalition's agenda for downtown revitalization, the leadership at Fort Bragg helped prop up the coalition by moving the military museum downtown. Indeed, in August of 2000, the Airborne and Special Operations Museum opened and gave downtown revitalization a spark. With this major project, the renovation of downtown has continued at a rapid pace. However, revitalization remains controversial. In addition to successes with developing downtown, the urban regime made important gains in terms of its racial image. In 1999, Michael Pearson reemerged in Fayetteville politics and became the first black to win in the at-large race. His successes were the result of support among African Americans as well as powerful white members of the urban regime. His historical achievement was topped in 2001 when Pearson became

Fayetteville's first black mayor by defeating Milo McRae. His success illus-trated the way a significant portion of the urban regime supported him. However, in his second term there developed a protest movement to his attempt to annex an additional 46,000 residents into the city. Though his opponent won the election by mobilizing the anti-annexation sentiment, he would eventually carry forward an even more audacious annexation agenda. By 2008 the city of Fayetteville had incorporated Fort Bragg into its city limits and increased its population to surpass 200,000.

Epilogue

THE COMPLEX PLAYS of political power that constituted the "Five–Four" prompts me to offer some reflections on broader issues of military power and its influence on Fayetteville's political structure. I have shown that neither Fort Bragg nor the more general expansion of federal power into the South have one-sidedly determined Fayetteville's present-day problems of racism, crime, urban sprawl, and inadequate public schools. Fayetteville's particular experience of these national problems stems instead from the ways local power brokers and business leaders used federal policies—from militarization to civil rights—to control local affairs.

Instead of suggesting that democratic reforms are inherently at odds with inequality, my analysis has shown how federal agencies and Fayetteville's local leaders have often used social reforms to legitimize class power and racism. In this way, Fayetteville's development challenges us to rethink modern democracy as a method of power rather than as an instantiation of universal truths or values. I have also sought to provide a nuanced examination of the interplay of civic and military power that challenges the kind of criticisms of the U.S. military that presumes that military power is at odds with American political traditions (see Lutz 2001; Mills 1956). Far from suggesting that military institutions stand as a contradiction to American ideals, Fayetteville's political development shows how military power elaborates and extends national ideals of popular sovereignty, citizenship, and liberty by extending the central state's authority into the realm of economics, health policy, and civil rights.[1]

This account of Fayetteville's history does not treat militarization as a process that descends on Fayetteville from afar. Instead, militarization functions as a site at which many actors have struggled to shape the contemporary political reality of the city. Since World War I, the federal government has actively sought to use military institutions and agencies to reform the nation's economy and its racial laws. Viewing the South as the nation's most backward, impoverished, and unstable region, federal planners had even earlier begun sending federal resources to modernize public institutions, expand transportation links, and grow the southern economy (Grantham 1983; Kryder 2001).[2]

Despite their condescending view of the region, federal planners faced many limits as they attempted to reshape the South. During World War I, after sixty years of conflict with southern political leaders dating back to before the Civil War, federal agencies began to realize that the best way to change and modernize southern society was to use the power of the political leaders of the urban South. Thus the U.S. Armed Forces' officials at Fort Bragg—much like other federal agencies—did not seek unilateral control of the town of Fayetteville. Instead, federal agencies sought to construct productive relationships with local authorities and achieve influence and control not simply through coercion but by delivering funds and authority to local power brokers—as evidenced by the way the commanding general at Fort Bragg moved the museum downtown. The ways southern politicians implemented federal war preparation programs for World War I to support and reinforce white supremacy and their "New South" approach to economic development offer a clear illustration of how this process of negotiation and devolution of power worked.

But as many authors have pointed out, New South-style urbanization collided with the federal intervention involved in the development of the military during and after World War II (Dudziak 2000; Keith 2004; Kryder 2001; Tyson 1999). The growth and development of the military often helped advance social movements and economic endeavors that steadily undermined Jim Crow segregation and white supremacy. In Fayetteville this clash has resulted in a complex social structure comprised of many competing groups that depend on military power. By connecting issues of military power with economic policy, we can see that Fayetteville's contemporary social problems reflect not just the role of the military but broader patterns that many historians of the urban South have described, including sprawling urban development, sparse urban infrastructure, lack of regulation, segregation, and paltry tax bases (see Brownell and Goldfield 1977; Grantham 1983; Hanchett 1998; Kyriakoudes 2003).

Fayetteville's complex relationship with southern politics further suggests that we must avoid simple and abstract formulations that either glorify the military as an embodiment of the American Dream or demonize militarization as corroding the true values of the nation. Such stories trivialize military power and fail to examine the centrality of military power in the development of Western democratic nation-states.

Indeed, if we look beyond our own shores, it is clear that the role of the military in the development of democracy is not only unmistakable in the United States, but has been central to the development of the Western democratic ideals (Geyer 1989; Gillis 1989; Mann 1993). No doubt, the French Revolution inaugurated the era of democratic nationalism, as France used its expanding military power as a symbol of the universality of citizenship (Bell 2007). Throughout Europe, state officials matched the universal symbolism of citizenship with the prolific use of military institutions to expand authority into distant regions (Sewell 2004). The ascendancy of military power came about not simply through coercion but also as a result of its usefulness in reforming social institutions, collecting taxes, and intervening into arenas of public health, economics, education, and civil rights (see Mann 1993; Weber 1976).

Military power thus grew to be intertwined with the institutions that became hallmarks of western Europe's democratic society, and the military came to symbolize national progress and ideals of sovereignty. Indeed, military power has been central to the emergence of modern democracy and its ideals of sovereignty and self-rule,[3] as European and U.S. nation-builders have deftly used military power to expand their nations' institutions into impoverished and stigmatized regions, enlarge the opportunity structure, develop economic markets, and industrialize (Bensel 1990; Brewer 1989; Kryder 2001; Mann 1993; Skowronek 1982).

Much like state power in general, military power fosters productive relationships with many constituencies, institutions, and agencies (Bell 2007; Geyer 1989; Joas 1999; Katznelson and Shefter 2002; Klausen 1998; Mann 1993). The racial reforms that followed World War II offer perhaps the most powerful example of the efficacy of the U.S. military as a social force. With the vast growth of the southern economy and the use of African Americans in the war effort, southern cities were rife with racial conflict. War mobilization spurred economic growth and created many jobs in the civil service, war-related businesses, and the military. Many African Americans, and poor whites, achieved new degrees of economic independence and social status as a result of government jobs or military service. These changes undermined Jim Crow segregation and the ideology and practice of white supremacy.

In response, many white authorities mobilized anti-black hysteria and many black soldiers returned from war to face political violence and persecution. Reacting to this public relations nightmare, the federal government in

1948 issued Executive Order 9981 to desegregate the armed forces. This order helped lay the groundwork for the Supreme Court's 1954 *Brown v. Board of Education* ruling that overturned the legal basis for segregation and prompted the gradual dismantling of the Jim Crow system in the South (Dalfiume 1969). But while such changes opened up opportunities for monumental civil rights victories, they also helped create new ways for political leaders to limit black politics. As I have tried to show, in the process of desegregating southern society, federal agencies also transformed the history of slavery and racism in the United States into a story of progress (Dudziak 2000). And in the post–civil rights era, federal and local governments have worked to limit black politics to the narrow confines defined by the reforms the movement helped create. Indeed, in the wake of the civil rights movement, local governments and city planners often deployed race as an increasingly overt political tool. By incorporating African Americans and groups like the NAACP into formal government processes, some city planners and government officials have effectively presented changes in the racial balance of power as progress even as they contained these changes within the narrow limits of urban economic development schemes.

By focusing on these complex and nuanced relations, *Conjuring Crisis* has scrutinized Fayetteville's municipal politics in an effort to come to understand how liberal capitalism—with its high ideals of freedom, liberty, and civil rights—has been so amenable to a process of militarization that is widely viewed as deeply at odds with those principles (Klausen 1998; Light 2003; Lotchin 2002).

Notes

Introduction

1. See Tom Brokaw (1998) for one of the more popular attempts to lionize the World War II generation. Scholarly books have shown how the federal government has used military spending to build state agencies: see Mark R. Wilson (2006) and Ira Katznelson (2002). See Jennifer E. Brooks (2004) for an analysis of how black and white veterans used their experiences to inspire increased involvement in politics. Despite the importance of these scholarly works, they have not fully examined the mythic elements of this process. They seem to infer that it is primarily an American phenomenon and do not take into account how military power and war experience reproduces the logic of the state.

2. See Jeanette Keith (2004) for an examination of southern politicians who opposed military spending and the expansion of the War Department during the early twentieth century.

3. I thank professors Dorothy Holland, Donald Nonini, and Catherine Lutz for inviting me to work on their project and the National Science Foundation for funding this research (SBR-954912).

4. All names are pseudonyms. I have hidden the identities of everyone involved in this study, including public officials and authors of letters to the editor.

5. This drama for control of the city council provided me the type of event that anthropologist Max Gluckman calls the extended case method (Handelman 2006; Van Velsen 1967; Werbner 1984). Gluckman developed the extended case method from his skepticism with the way anthropologists produced abstract theories about the societies they studied that made daily life appear harmonious and ideal. Instead, he saw human life, cultural patterns, and social structures as messy and deeply involved in conflict and hierarchy. In his classic essay *Analysis of a Social Situation in Modern Zululand* he laid the basis for the extended case method as he carefully described the ceremonial opening of the first bridge built by the Native Affairs Department of the South African government. He used the method of ethnography—the careful description of beliefs, customs, social relations, and history—to describe how European colonists were culturally and socially connected with Zulus into a colonial hierarchy. Eschewing abstract theories, he drew his analysis and ethnographic descriptions from conflicts whereby subjects competed, disputed, and cooperated in battles over political control and social prestige. Most famously, Gluckman summed up the value of the extended case method as a solution to the enduring problem of the "apt illustration," whereby the anthropologists derive their theories from an informant's ideal of norms (Gluckman 1961, 7).

6. Such orchestration of a crisis is illustrated by the way the Bush administration and the national media portrayed events of September 11. They framed the attacks on the World Trade Center and the Pentagon as the sign of general "crisis" that threatened "our way of life." Government agencies and the national media, therefore, created an enemy—in the guise of "militant Islam"—that represented a threat to "our way of life." Against this image, they mobilized Americans by splitting the world into a Manichean division of good and evil, eliminating the middle ground; the sense of crisis demanded solidarity—you are either with us or against us. The federal state's power, therefore, was not revealed in its subsequent response to the attack; instead, its power resided in its ability to define the attack as a crisis for all Americans. Once the attacks were collectively experienced as a crisis to America's sacred principles of liberty, democracy, and, of course, the unstated underlying primacy of free market capitalism, then the state held the key to resolving the problem. Accordingly, the Bush administration created a series of institutions—for example, the Unity and Strengthening America by Providing Appropriate Tools Required to Intercept and Obstruct Terrorism Act (USA PATRIOT Act), the Office of Homeland Security, and the "War on Terrorism"—that responded to this narrative construction of crisis, as opposed to responding to the historical conditions that resulted in the attack.

7. Anthropological research has increasingly attended to the importance of conspiracy as a powerful cultural model and as being valuable to understanding political mobilization (Jackson 2008; Marcus 1999; Silverstein 2002; West and Sanders 2003). As a growing literature points out, conspiracy theories represent a narrative form that constitutes an important aspect of modern life; modern life is full of bureaucracies, agencies, factions, and groups. Political outcomes emerge from opaque and difficult to understand forces. Political actors use conspiracy theories as a mode of cultural knowledge that seeks to reveal and make intelligible the hidden forces and estranging dynamics of modern politics (Boyer 2006; Jackson 2008; Silverstein 2002). Most anthropologists have viewed conspiracy from the perspective of poor and impoverished citizens: as a powerful tool with which marginal citizens understand how power works (Briggs 2004; Marcus 1999; West and Sanders 2003). *Conjuring Crisis* uses these insights to describe how white business and civic leaders used conspiracy to connect their interests with whites across class lines.

8. I do not deny that right-wing and conservative groups have mobilized against civil rights. As Stephen Steinberg points out, there has been a relentless attack on civil rights reforms and protections (1995). However, some of these developments originated in the ways the federal government instituted the civil rights movement (see Dudziak 2000; Reed 1999a; Smith 1996; Steinberg 2007).

9. These types of political reorganizations have had similar consequences in Europe (see Mayer 1994; Peck and Tickell 2002, 2006).

10. Polanyi (1944) argued that free markets stem from political processes that disembed markets from social institutions. Many theorists of neoliberalism have missed Polyani's point that this disembedding results from intense political intervention. Moreover, such imposition of markets requires local politicians and bureaucrats to focus on embedding markets with the necessary infrastructures of schools, roads, and so forth. See Mark Blyth (2002) for a sophisticated discussion of Polyani in terms of the shift from welfare capitalism to neoliberalism.

11. The first and most influential form of this argument came from C. Wright Mills, in his important book *The Power Elite*, in which he railed against how the expansion of the military had negatively affected social policy. He pointed out how "military definitions" of social problems legitimized military power. Historian Michael Sherry (1995) offers a more recent example (1995). Like Mills, Michael Sherry

and Catherine Lutz presume a neat distinction between "militarization" and democratic politics.

12. Despite this deep connection, social science has largely ignored the relationship between democracy and warfare. The tendency to overlook the centrality of militarization stems from how western social science has carried Enlightenment ideals that presume war to be a remnant of prehistory and that modernity should be an age without violence. According to these ideals, democratic societies were to be civil, with belligerent traits forbidden by religion and sublimated by sports and economic competition. Rejection of violence in social science coincides with the neglect of its presence (Hirschman 1977; Joas 1999). Rather than seeing militarization as a recent phenomenon or an American problem, it provided the conditions for the democratic state. See Bensel (1990); Brewer (1989); Katznelson (2002); Kryder (2001); Mann (1993); Skocpol (1992); Skowronek (1982); and Sparrow (1996).

13. See Abrams (1988); Weber (1976); and Lomnitz (2001).

Chapter 1   Narrating a Racial Crisis

1. All names are pseudonyms. I have hidden the identities of everyone involved in this study, including public officials and authors of letters to the editor.

2. Fayetteville Observer, 26 January 1997.

3. "Serving Justice: DWI and District Court," five-part series, Fayetteville Observer, 14, 15, 16, 17, 18 December 1997.

4. "NAACP Report Outlines Allegations of Discrimination Against the Fayetteville Police Department," Fayetteville Observer, 20 February 1997.

5. Many black Fayettevillians speculated that his retirement resulted from his failure to handle the case. Both Ross and his replacement, Floyd Yarborough, denied such a claim. Ross, in his early seventies, told me that he had been the president for twelve years and had planned to step down at the end of 1996.

6. Yarborough's memories reflect what scholars describe as an ironic outcome of advancing civil rights: the resurgence of Ku Klux Klan in eastern North Carolina (Cecelski 1994; Tyson 2004).

7. City of Fayetteville, City Council Minutes, 16 December 1996: 404.

8. City of Fayetteville, City Council Minutes, 16 December 1996: 404.

9. City of Fayetteville, City Council Minutes, 16 December 1996: 402.

10. City of Fayetteville, City Council Minutes, 16 December 1996: 404.

11. City of Fayetteville, City Council Minutes, 16 December 1996: 405–406.

12. City of Fayetteville, City Council Minutes, 16 December 1996: 407.

13. "Police Probe Criticized," Fayetteville Observer, 17 December 1996.

14. Editorial, "Detective Work: The NAACP Should Share Any Evidence," Fayetteville Observer, 18 December 1996.

15. As one of Fayetteville's oldest media institutions, WFNC remained in the powerful Rawls family until 1999. In October of 1999, the Rawls family sold WFNC to a national news service. Fayetteville Observer, 24 September 1999.

16. Jacobs and Simpson handled the debate quite differently. Jacobs was much more sensitive to the issue of race, insisting that callers adhere to substantive details and dispatching callers who were overly racist. Simpson, on the other hand, baited people, and on his show callers ranted a lot more. Also, Simpson was more knowledgeable about the policies and statutes in play and situated the discussions in a more refined historical frame. Both talk show hosts, however, structured their discussions around a logic that presumed the statutes and policies of the council-manager form of government to be rational and neutral.

17. City of Fayetteville, City Council Minutes, 6 January 1997: 431.

18. City of Fayetteville, *City Council Minutes*, 6 January 1997: 431.
19. City of Fayetteville, *City Council Minutes*, 6 January 1997: 432–433.
20. City of Fayetteville, *City Council Minutes*, 6 January 1997: 433.
21. Milo represented the resistance against erosion of community values. However, like most white politicians, he had a well-known friendship with a black preacher with whom he served on city council for several years.
22. City of Fayetteville, *City Council Minutes*, 6 January 1997: 440.
23. I thank Professor Sara Berry for calling my attention to this important point.
24. City of Fayetteville, *City Council Minutes*, 6 January 1997: 443.
25. City of Fayetteville, *City Council Minutes*, 6 January 1997: 444–445.
26. City of Fayetteville, *City Council Minutes*, 6 January 1997: 447.
27. An editorial in the *Fayetteville Observer*, entitled "Dearth of Detail: Proof of FPD Discrimination Is Still Lacking," framed the event, focusing on the NAACP's poor judgment and its reluctance to properly participate with the channels and mechanisms in place (*Fayetteville Observer*, 8 January 1997). It read: "Ever since a long-simmering dispute between the local NAACP chapter and Fayetteville police officials boiled over into the public domain, the debate has centered on specifics—mainly, the lack of them. Chief Dan Proctor said early last month that he had been contacted about alleged discrimination against 10 officers, but had been given too few details to conduct a proper investigation." In response, it argued that the NAACP has "put its own spin on events described in less-than-precise language, clearly worked from the premise that any action taken against a black officer must have been (A) unwarranted and (B) racially motivated. And if that seems too harsh an assessment, remember that the NAACP had already demanded a formal apology to black officers whom Proctor had asked about discrimination, and the rescission of all disciplinary actions taken against black officers. That's the very definition of prejudgment." Criticizing the group for not providing specifics, the editorial continued: "Unfortunately, the NAACP, by its silence, forced council to choose. And even more unfortunately, the council made the wrong choice . . . the council voted by the slimmest of margins to launch its own investigation." The editorial concludes by criticizing both sides for frustrating or circumventing the mechanisms designed to deal with such problems.
28. *Fayetteville Observer*, 10 January 1997.
29. Scholars of conspiracy theories often emphasize fringe elements that are on the edges of power (Marcus 1999). Silverstein (2002) and Rogin (1988) show how political forces at the center of power use conspiracy theorizing and demonology to create enemies to underwrite political projects.
30. Editorial, "Marked Deck: Two Councilmen Should Recuse from Probe," *Fayetteville Observer*, 14 January 1997.

Chapter 2   *Conspiracies and Crises on Cape Fear*

1. Edgar Thompson's conception of the plantation as "frontier institution" shaped Sidney Mintz's classic work on the role of plantations in the Caribbean (see Mintz 1974). For Thompson's formulation of the plantation as a "race-making" institution, see Michel-Rolph Trouillot (2002). For an astute development of the idea of plantations and race-making, see Barbara Fields (1981, 1990). For a powerful analysis of race-making that transcends the Americas, see Anne Stoler (1997).
2. See Greene (1988) for a discussion of how South Carolina planters gravitated to slavery. See Barbara Fields (1981, 1990) for trenchant analysis of how the plantation owners in the New World tried indentured servants and other forms of coerced labor before finally systemizing plantation slavery with the idea of race.

3. As Orlando Patterson has argued, the Sambo stereotype has been universal from the most primitive to the most advanced systems of slavery. The "degraded man-child" stereotype was "an ideological imperative of all systems of slavery" (Patterson 1982, 96).

4. See Kay and Cary on how slave codes intertwined with servitude, which defined slavery by what it was not, freedom (1995, 61). For a broader discussion of the relationship between slavery and ideas of freedom, see Holt (1992) and Patterson (1982).

5. Unlike other North Carolina rivers, the lower portion of the Cape Fear River was deep enough for large ships to navigate for twenty miles upstream (Merrens 1964, 90–91).

6. Most dynamic growth occurred in Fayetteville as its slave population surged to 2,100 at the time of the first census in 1780. With the rise of cotton in the early 1800s, the slave population steadily grew during the antebellum period. On the eve of the Civil War, slaves comprised 41.6 percent of the county's population and 45 percent of the city's population (Parker 1990, 29). Economic development depended on an expanding slave population. By the 1760s, historian Bradford Wood estimates, slaves represented more than 70 percent of the population in Brunswick County (Wood 2004, 37–38).

7. For an examination of the Haitian Revolution, see Dubois (2004), Fick (1990), and James (1963).

8. News of the Haitian Revolution (1791–1804) transformed racial politics in the New World and the American South, as it provided a new model for black politics and contributed to the emergence of a collective black identity. By successfully ousting French slaveholders, Eugene Genovese (1992) has argued, the Haitian Revolution represented a "turning point" in "Afro American" history, as it replaced the idea of petty rebellions and maroons (seeking of autonomy from dominant society) with the idea of revolution whereby blacks seek to be included in political processes as equals. Julius Scott has developed these insights by examining how revolutionary ideas swept through the Caribbean as slaves and free blacks learned about the revolutionary ideas and exploits of Saint Dominguan slaves (Scott 1986). James Sidbury has discussed how the revolt in Saint Domingue sent shockwaves throughout the world by influencing the direction of anti-slavery movements in Britain, France, and the United States. The revolt influenced slaves' struggles for freedom and became a model for black resistance (Sidbury 1997a, 1997b).

9. But mobilizing white solidarity with such scares did not begin with the Haitian Revolution. Since its birth, plantation slavery in the New World had experienced revolts, and planters feared such resistance (see Craton 1982; Wood 1974).

10. Such intense rise in slave insurrection fears has been taken by Herbert Aptheker and many other historians as proof of intense rebellious activity among slaves (Aptheker 1943).

11. Such fears motivated every southern legislature to draw up laws to limit the black population, free and slave alike (Hunt 1988).

12. As James Sidbury has argued in the case of Southampton, Virginia, at the time of Gabriel Prosser's conspiracy, black and white Virginians used the metaphor of "Frenchness" to understand the new situation. Such invocations had more to do with local situations (1997b).

13. For example, Charles Dew argues that the hysteria revolving around the insurrection panic of 1856 was related to the presidential elections, in which southern Democrats feared the emergence of the Republican Party as a major force (Dew 1975, 336).

14. *Fayetteville Observer*, December 1939.
15. It is easy to romanticize the Farmers' Alliance and Fusionists. However radical, they were compromised and eventually destroyed by racism (see Gaither 2005).
16. Future governor Charles Aycock recalled the Fusionist period as one of "chaos of darkness and Negro Domination" (Prather 1998, 21–22).
17. *Fayetteville Observer*, 28 February 1898; see Phillips 2002, 104–106.
18. *Fayetteville Observer*, 22, 27 October 1898.
19. *Fayetteville Observer*, 22, 27 October 1898; Prather (1998, 25).
20. Other military units came to Wilmington to assist the white citizens in establishing white supremacy, including the Fayetteville Light Infantry.
21. *Raleigh News and Observer*, 13 November 1898; Cecelski and Tyson 1998, 4–5.
22. See Grantham (1983) for a description of how disfranchisement was necessary for the New South leaders to impose their economic development plans.
23. It is important to note the similarity in this justification of disqualifying African Americans from public life and the way "the Manning boys" were portrayed as using "the blacks" to take power illegitimately. Moreover, politicians employed this logic to displace the issue of racial discrimination that motivated the NAACP and three black council members during the "Five–Four."
24. Haley (1998, 215); *North Carolina Presbyterian*, 17 November 1898.

Chapter 3   *The Cunning of Racial Reform*

1. Willie Legette, cited in Adolph Reed (1999a, 1). See William Julius Wilson for an important and controversial attempt at assessing these changes. See Steven Gregory (1998) and Adolph Reed (1999) for critiques of Wilson. See Holt (2000) and Jackson (2008) for attempts to build on his insights.
2. See Oates (1950, 422–423) for a contemporary account of this period.
3. Josephus Daniels, quoted in Tyson (1998, 258) and Kousser (1974, 79).
4. *Fayetteville Observer*, 24 July 1918.
5. *Fayetteville Observer*, 17 November 1989.
6. "N.C. Boom Town Called Uncle Sam's Powder Keg," *Baltimore Afro-American*, 8 February 1941.
7. *Fayetteville Observer*, 9 April 1954.
8. Downtown's "death" began before Cross Creek Mall. In the late 1950s and 1960s economic development began following the decentralized model encouraged by the federal highway and road dollars that spurred suburbanization across the United States. Cross Creek Mall represents this national trend.
9. *Fayetteville Observer*, 8 October 1999.
10. "Fayetteville Sticks with All Its Images: From Good to Worst," *Raleigh News and Observer*, 12 March 1989.
11. "From Hanoi to Hay Street," *Fayetteville Observer*, 17 June 2002. In this article a resident recounted as a "little girl" going for ice cream and watching the "spectacle," which included "soldiers hanging out of the windows of the Prince Charles Hotel."
12. "What's Great about Fayetteville?: How This Historic City Shook Off a Bad Reputation and Became All-American," *The State of Fayetteville*, Fayetteville Chamber of Commerce, October 1985.
13. "State to Help Build Housing If City Renews Downtown," *Fayetteville Observer*, 18 April 1996.
14. "Cumberland Commissioners Establish Fund to Help Rebuild Downtown," *Fayetteville Observer*, 2 July 1996.

Chapter 4   Performing Crisis

1. Letter to the editor, *Fayetteville Observer*, 31 March 1997.
2. See Dan Carter (1974) for the rendering of this pattern after the Civil War. See Howard Odum (1997 [1943]) for a sociological analysis of how southern elites adapted this framework to understand the changes wrought by World War II in the South.
3. City of Fayetteville, *City Council Minutes*, 21 January 1997: 470–473.
4. City of Fayetteville, *City Council Minutes*, 21 January 1997: 470–473.
5. Mayor Dawson contracted cancer in 1999. Nevertheless, he ran for one more term. Many voted him in office so he could die as the mayor. Indeed, in 2000 he died in office. He served as council member for ten years. He became mayor in 1987 and served twelve years before expiring.
6. City of Fayetteville, *City Council Minutes*, 21 January 1997: 470–473.
7. Letter to the editor, *Fayetteville Observer*, 2 February 1997.
8. "City Manager Challenges Probe of Office," *Fayetteville Observer*, 24 January 1997.
9. Editorial, "The Next Step," *Fayetteville Observer*, 29 January 1997.
10. Letters to the editor, *Fayetteville Observer*, 2 February 1997.
11. Middle-class white informants watched the council meetings on cable TV, while working-class blacks and whites did not. Residents who followed the event had a bevy of terms to describe the meetings. One informant invited me several times to her house to "watch Laugh- In," while others used circus metaphors to describe the "Five–Four."
12. *Fayetteville Observer*, 2 February 1997.
13. City of Fayetteville, *City Council Minutes*, 17 February 1997, 557.
14. City of Fayetteville, *City Council Minutes*, 17 February 1997, 558.
15. City of Fayetteville, *City Council Minutes*, 17 February 1997, 558.
16. Letter to the editor, *Fayetteville Observer*, 23 February 1997.
17. City of Fayetteville, *City Council Minutes*, 17 February 1997: 551.
18. City of Fayetteville, *City Council Minutes*, 17 February 1997: 551.
19. City of Fayetteville, *City Council Minutes*, 17 February 1997: 551–552.
20. "Recall Bill to Be Filed," *Fayetteville Observer*, 20 February 1997. The bill sought to amend the City of Fayetteville's charter to allow the citizens the right to recall city council members and the mayor. A recall election would require that 15 percent of the voting district's registered voters sign a petition to remove an official from office. An election then would have to be held within sixty days after the county Board of Election certified the petition. If a majority of the voters cast a ballot for recall, the official would be removed and the remaining council members would appoint a replacement. Fayetteville had 47,490 registered voters in 1997, so a recall election for the mayor or an at-large council member would have required 7,124 signatures to have a recall election for mayor or at-large council members. The council's six board members that represented single-member districts, which ranged in population from 6,150 to 9,917, required thresholds ranging from 923 to 1,488.
21. See "Crowd Seeks Right to Recall," *Fayetteville Observer*, 26 February 1997.

Chapter 5   Threatening Images of Black Power

1. The "dozens" refers to the performance whereby contestants insult each other by taunting and kidding. See Abrahams (1962) and Lefever (1981).
2. From interviews with members of the black community, I understand his popularity as coming from working-class and young listeners. I had many working-class

informants, though, who thought he was too "antagonistic" and "militant." Some even described him as a "Black Panther."
3. Locals used the term to talk about middle-class blacks and people in positions of power and authority. Following from this notion of decline, working-class blacks rejected the way the downtown coalition viewed the increasing number of blacks in politics as a sign of progress. Instead, they saw inclusion of blacks as a way local elites could exert control over blacks. As many of the guys at the shoeshine shop would say: "There are no VIP niggers" in Fayetteville. Much like the sociologist E. Franklin Frazier, my informants distinguished status from the type of wealth that reproduced power. During one conversation at the shop, Clay argued that as long as blacks are dependent on a white man for a job, you would have no leaders. Agreeing with Clay, Gerald looked at me and said, "This goes in your book," and described how blacks who move into wealthy white neighborhoods, government positions, and well-paying jobs become controlled. Rather than seeing integration as a sign of progress, many black observers of politics see it as a mode of repression. See E. Franklin Frazier (1957). For recent research on black middle-classes and criticism of Frazier, see Mary Pattillo-McCoy (1999, 2007) and Karyn Lacy (2007).
4. In North American debates about racism, critics often claim "nothing has changed" to direct our attention to the intransigence of racism. Such claims use the term "change" interchangeably with "progress." In contrast, I argue that since the civil rights movement, much has changed, except the terminology and concepts we use to think about it (Reed 1999b; Holt 2000).
5. Interview with a member of the NAACP that was present at the headquarters that day.
6. *Fayetteville Observer*, 9 April 1997.
7. *Fayetteville Observer*, 24 February 1997.

Chapter 6   *Power Shift*

1. Copy of letter from Terrence Puckett to Frank Roberts, 2 October 1996, in the possession of the author.
2. This letter to the editor worked along with FTFR's larger goal of getting rid of people like Mayor Dawson and other elected officials who lacked the expertise to make policy decisions, and hiring professionals who would not be easily controlled by power brokers like Senator Frank Edwards. Drawing on local understandings of the Democratic Party as corrupt, FTFR drew on the national Republican Party's criticism of big government. They focused on low performance in the public schools and Fayetteville's high crime rate, both of which they viewed as products of the city's obsolete political system.
3. Dr. Terrence Puckett, letter to the editor, *Fayetteville Observer*, 26 January 1997.
4. *Fayetteville Observer*, 29 March 1997.
5. City management never accepted Robert Marvin's advice to raze Grove View Terrace. Marvin knew very little about the city's relationship to public housing and was unaware that the city, under the aegis of the Fayetteville Housing Authority, had received over $9 million from HUD since 1992 to rehabilitate the 258 units.

Chapter 7   *Outsiders and Special Interests*

1. For anthropological studies of the way that bureaucratic power masks and conceals the political power, see Handelman (2004), Heymon (1995), and Herzfeld (1993).
2. City of Fayetteville, *City Council Minutes*, 6 March 1997.
3. City of Fayetteville, *City Council Minutes*, 6 March 1997.

4. WFNC Radio, 26 August 1997.
5. WFNC Radio, 26 August 1997.
6. Susan Gannett, 26 August 1997, Investigation of the Fayetteville Police Department.
7. *Fayetteville Observer*, 27 August 1997.
8. *Fayetteville Observer*, 28 August 1997.
9. *Fayetteville Observer*, 30 October 1997.
10. The work of Michel Foucault has helped me develop this insight. In particular, see "On Governmentality" (Foucault 1991). Concerning use of modern political and urban institutions, see Flyvbjerg (1998).
11. *Fayetteville Observer*, 7 October 1997.
12. Letter to the editor, *Fayetteville Observer*, 17 September 1997.
13. Letter to the editor, *Fayetteville Observer*, 23 October 1997.

Chapter 8   Single Slut

1. Letter to the editor, *Fayetteville Observer*, 10 February 1997.
2. This form of voting representation has been outlawed by the U.S. Justice Department in accordance with the Civil Rights Voting Act of 1965. But many cities have complied with this federal law by implementing a mixed system that simultaneously increased minority representation while retaining some at-large seats. Therefore, the Fayetteville city council has six single-member districts, three of which are minority and three of which are at-large. In effect, this plan has ensured that city council will have six white seats to neutralize the three black votes.
3. The relationship between Reynolds and Fayetteville State University Chancellor Harold McLean does not imply that McLean was an "Uncle Tom" or that he did not personally object to the city's approach to the police department controversy. Despite McLean's new relationship to the urban regime, he was very outspoken about Fayetteville's tendency to exclude Fayetteville State from its civic plans. He argued that the college's biggest problem was that a "moat" of poverty separated it from the city. Moreover, once the Fayetteville Partnership and the city announced its new relationship with FSU, McLean made it clear that his involvement with revitalization was a "business" deal, and that he expected something in return for the college's capital projects and its standing in the community.
4. Tony Jefferson, *Powertalk*, WIDU Fayetteville, 17 September 1997.
5. Crab antics have been the object of debates in anthropology about struggles for respectability and reputation in a context of colonialism. See Wilson (1973).

Conclusion

1. *Fayetteville Observer*, 9 November 1997.
2. See John Jackson for a criticism of analyses of contemporary racial problems that views conflict among African Americans with a bifurcated model that interprets the main split along the line between middle-class and poor African Americans (2005).

Epilogue

1. Since the French Revolution, state builders have used military power to integrate large areas of the world—within national boundaries as well as across the oceans—into nation-states and colonial holdings. Military power represented the high point of Enlightenment ideals of bureaucratic efficiency and redistributed the wealth necessary for the capitalist political economy. State power develops with a

myriad of institutions that legitimize its monopoly of violence. With the myth of popular sovereignty, democratic governance has consistently used military power as a key component to producing capitalist society and its complex social hierarchy that cuts across class categories (see Weber 1976).

2. For an examination of the broader impact of the expanding military on the western and eastern portions of the country, see Light (2003), Lotchin (2002), and Markusen et al. (1991).

3. Rather than presuming "sovereignty" to be an objective condition, I see it as a mythic framework whereby the government authorities legitimize the power of the state as emanating from the people. See Giorgio Agamben (1998). Also see J.G.A Pocock (1975) on the importance of military power and citizenship in republican ideals in both Europe and the Atlantic World. See William Sewell (2004) and David Bell (2007) about military and popular rights in France.

Bibliography

Abeles, Marc. 1997. "Political Anthropology: New Challenges, New Aims." *International Social Science Journal* 49 (3): 319–332.

Abrahams, Roger. 1962. "Playing the Dozens." *Journal of American Folklore* 75:209–220.

Abrams, Philip. 1988 [1977]. "Notes on the Difficulty of Studying the State." *Journal of Historical Sociology* 1 (1): 58–89.

Agamben, Giorgio. 1998. *Homo Sacer: Sovereign Power and Bare Life.* Stanford, Calif.: Stanford University Press.

Aptheker, Herbert. 1943. *American Negro Slave Revolts.* New York: Columbia University Press.

Arnesen, Eric. 2001. "Whiteness and the Historians' Imagination." *International Labor and Working-Class History.* 60:3–32.

Austin-Broos, Diane. 1997. *Jamaica Genesis: Religion and the Politics of Moral Order.* Chicago: University of Chicago Press.

———. 2008. *Arrernte Present, Arrernte Past: Invasion, Violence, and Imagination in Indigenous Central Australia.* Chicago: University of Chicago Press.

Baca, George. 2004. "Legends of Fordism: Between Myth, History, and Foregone Conclusions." *Social Analysis* 48 (3): 169–178.

———, ed. 2006a. *Nationalism's Bloody Terrain: Racism, Class Inequality, and the Politics of Recognition.* New York: Berghahn Books.

———. 2006b. "Politics of Recognition and Myths of Race." In *Nationalism's Bloody Terrain: Racism, Class Inequality and the Politics of Recognition,* edited by George Baca, 1–13. New York: Berghahn Press.

———. 2008. "Neoliberalism and Stories of Racial Redemption." *Dialectical Anthropology* 33:719–741.

———. 2009. "Rituals of Racism and the Haitian Revolution," *Ethnoscripts: Analysen Und Informationen Aus Dem Institut Für Ethnologie Der Universität Hamburg* 10 (2): 219–241.

Baker, Lee. 1998. *From Savage to Negro: Anthropology and the Construction of Race, 1896–1954.* Berkeley: University of California Press.

Barrett, John G. 1963. *The Civil War in North Carolina.* Chapel Hill: University of North Carolina Press.

Bell, Catherine M. 1992. *Ritual Theory, Ritual Practice.* New York: Oxford University Press.

———. 1997. *Ritual: Perspectives and Dimensions.* New York: Oxford University Press.

Bell, David A. 2007. *The First Total War: Napoleon's Europe and the Birth of Warfare as We Know It.* Boston: Houghton Mifflin.

Ben-Ari, Eyal, and Sabine Fruhstuck. 2003. "The Celebration of Violence: A Live-Fire Demonstration Carried Out by Japan's Contemporary Military." *American Ethnologist* 30 (4): 532–555.

Bensel, Richard Franklin. 1984. *Sectionalism and American Political Development, 1880–1980*. Madison: University of Wisconsin Press.

———. 1990. *Yankee Leviathan: The Origins of Central State Authority in America, 1859–1877*. New York: Cambridge University Press.

Black, Earl, and Merle Black. 1987. *Politics and Society in the South*. Cambridge, Mass.: Harvard University Press.

Blauner, Robert. 1972. *Racial Oppression in America*. New York: Harper and Row.

Blyth, Mark. 2002. *Great Transformations: Economic Ideas and Institutional Change in the Twentieth Century*. Cambridge: Cambridge University Press.

Bonilla-Silva, Eduardo. 2001. *White Supremacy and Racism in the Post–Civil Rights Era*. Boulder, Colo.: Rienner.

———. 2003. *Racism without Racists: Color-Blind Racism and the Persistence of Racial Inequality in the United States*. Lanham, Md.: Rowman and Littlefield.

Bourne, Joanna. 2006. *Fear: A History of Fear*. New York: Shoemaker and Hoard.

Boyer, Dominic. 2006. "Conspiracy, History, and Therapy at a Berlin Stammtisch." *American Ethnologist* 33 (3): 327–339.

Brash, Julian. 2003. "Invoking Fiscal Crisis: Moral Discourse and Politics in New York City." *Social Text* 21 (3): 59–83.

Brenner, Neil, and Nikolas Theodore. 2002. *Spaces of Neoliberalism: Urban Restructuring in North America and Western Europe*. Oxford: Blackwell.

Brewer, James Howard. 1949. "An Account of Negro Slavery in the Cape Fear Region Prior to 1860." Ph.D. diss., University of Pittsburgh.

———. 1953. "Legislation Designed to Control Slavery in Wilmington and Fayetteville." *North Carolina Historical Review* 30 (2): 155.

Brewer, John. 1989. *The Sinews of Power: War, Money, and the English State, 1688–1783*. New York: Knopf.

Briggs, Charles. 2004. "Theorizing Modernity Conspiratorially: Science, Scale, and the Political Economy of Public Discourse in Explanations of a Cholera Epidemic." *American Ethnologist* 31 (2): 164–187.

Brodkin, Karen. 1999. *How Jews Became White*. New Brunswick, N.J.: Rutgers University Press.

Brokaw, Tom. 1998. *The Greatest Generation*. New York: Random House.

Brooks, Jennifer E. 2004. *Defining the Peace: World War II Veterans, Race, and the Remaking of Southern Political Tradition*. Chapel Hill: University of North Carolina Press.

Brownell, Blaine, and David Goldfield, eds. 1977. *The City in Southern History*. Port Washington, N.Y.: Kennikat Press.

Burran, James Albert. 1977. "Racial Violence in the South during World War II." Ph.D. diss., University of Tennessee.

Carter, Dan T. 1976. "The Anatomy of Fear: The Christmas Day Insurrection Scare of 1865." *Journal of Southern History* 42 (3): 346–364.

Cecelski, David S. 1994. *Along Freedom Road: Hyde County, North Carolina, and the Fate of Black Schools in the South*. Chapel Hill: University of North Carolina Press.

Cecelski, David S., and Timothy B. Tyson, eds. 1998. *Democracy Betrayed: The Wilmington Race Riot of 1898 and Its Legacy*. Chapel Hill: University of North Carolina Press.

Chafe, William. 1980. *Civilities and Civil Rights: Greensboro, North Carolina, and the Black Struggle for Freedom*. New York: Oxford University Press.

Cohen, Cathy. 1999. *The Boundaries of Blackness: AIDS and the Breakdown of Black Politics*. Chicago: University of Chicago Press.

Cooper, Frederick, and Rogers Brubaker. 2000. "Beyond 'Identity.'" *Theory and Society* 29 (1): 1–47.

Corrigan, Philip, and Derek Sayer. 1985. *The Great Arch: English State Formation as Cultural Revolution*. Oxford: Blackwell.

Covington, Howard E., and Marion A. Ellis. 1999. *Terry Sanford: Politics, Progress, and Outrageous Ambitions*. Durham, N.C.: Duke University Press.

Cox, Oliver C. 1949. *Caste, Class and Race: A Study in Social Dynamics*. Garden City, N.Y.: Doubleday.

————. 2000. *Race: A Study in Social Dynamics*. New York: Monthly Review Press.

Craton, Michael. 1982. *Testing the Chains: Resistance to Slavery in the British West Indies*. Ithaca: Cornell University Press.

Crow, Jeffrey. 1977. *Black Experience in Colonial North Carolina*. Raleigh: North Carolina Department of Cultural Resources, Division of Archives and History.

————. 1980. "Slave Rebelliousness and Social Conflict in North Carolina, 1775–1802." *William and Mary Quarterly* 37 (1): 79–102.

Crow, Jeffrey J., Paul D. Escott, and Flora J. Hatley. 1992. *A History of African Americans in North Carolina*. Raleigh: North Carolina Department of Cultural Resources, Division of Archives and History.

Dalfiume, Richard. 1969. *Desegregation of the Armed Forces: Fighting on Two Fronts, 1939–1953*. Columbia: University of Missouri Press.

Das, Veena. 1998. "Official Narratives, Rumour, and the Social Production of Hate." *Social Identities* 4 (1): 109–130.

Davila, Arlene. 2004. *Barrio Dreams: Puerto Ricans, Latinos, and the Neoliberal City*. Berkeley: University of California Press.

Davis, David Brion. 2003. *Challenging the Boundaries of Slavery*. Cambridge, Mass.: Harvard University Press.

Dew, Charles. 1975. "Black Ironworkers and the Slave Insurrection Panic of 1856." *Journal of Southern History* 41 (3): 321–338.

Dominguez, Virginia. 1986. *White by Definition: Social Classification in Creole Louisiana*. New Brunswick, N.J.: Rutgers University Press.

————. 1994. "A Taste for 'the Other': Intellectual Complicity in Racializing Practices." *Current Anthropology* 35 (3): 333–348.

Doyle, Don Harrison. 1990. *New Men, New Cities, New South: Atlanta, Nashville, Charleston, Mobile, 1860–1910*. Chapel Hill: University of North Carolina Press.

Dubois, Laurent. 2004. *Avengers of the New World: The Story of the Haitian Revolution*. Cambridge, Mass.: Belknap Press of Harvard University Press.

Dudziak, Mary. 2000. *Cold War, Civil Rights: Race and the Image of American Democracy*. Princeton, N.J.: Princeton University Press.

Eagleton, Terry. 1991. *Ideology: An Introduction*. London and New York: Verso.

Edelman, Murray. 1988. *Constructing the Political Spectacle*. Chicago: University of Chicago Press.

Eisinger, Peter. 1998. "City Politics in an Era of Federal Devolution." *Urban Affairs Review* 33 (3): 308–325.

Farmer, Paul. 2003. *Pathologies of Power: Health, Human Rights, and the New War on the Poor*. Berkeley: University of California Press.

Fick, Carolyn. 1990. *The Making of Haiti: The Saint Domingue Revolution from Below*. Knoxville: University of Tennessee Press.

Fields, Barbara. 1981. "Ideology and Race in American History." In *Region, Race, and Reconstruction: Essays in Honor of C. Vann Woodward*, edited by J. M. Kousser and J. M. McPherson, 143–178. New York: Oxford University Press.

———. 1990. "Slavery, Race, and Ideology in the United States of America." *New Left Review* 181 (May–June): 95–118.

———. 2001. "'Origins of the New South' and the Negro Question." *Journal of Southern History* 67 (4): 811–826.

———. 2003. "Of Rogues and Geldings." *American Historical Review* 108 (5): 1397–1405.

Flyvbjerg, Bent. 1998. *Rationality and Power: Democracy in Practice*. Chicago: University of Chicago Press.

Foucault, Michel. 1991. "On Governmentality." In *The Foucault Effect: Studies in Governmentality*, edited by G. Burchell, C. Gordon, and P. Miller, 87–104. Chicago: University of Chicago Press.

Frankenberg, Ruth. 1993. *White Women, Race Matters: The Social Construction of Whiteness*. Minneapolis: University of Minnesota Press.

Frazier, E. Franklin. 1957. *Black Bourgeoisie: The Rise of a New Middle Class in the United States*. Glencoe, Ill.: Free Press.

Fredrickson, George. 1981. *White Supremacy: A Comparative Study in American and South African History*. New York: Oxford University Press.

Gaines, Kevin K. 1996. *Uplifting the Race: Black Leadership, Politics, and Culture in the Twentieth Century*. Chapel Hill: University of North Carolina Press.

Gaither, Gerald. 2005. *Blacks and the Populist Movement: Ballots and Bigotry in the New South*. Tuscaloosa: University of Alabama Press.

Gaughan, Anthony. 1999. "Woodrow Wilson and the Rise of Militant Interventionism in the South." *Journal of Southern History* 65 (4): 771–808.

Gavins, Raymond. 1978. "Black Leadership in North Carolina to 1900." In *The Black Presence in North Carolina*, edited by J. Crowe and R. J. Winter. Raleigh: North Carolina Museum of History.

Genovese, Eugene. 1992. *From Rebellion to Revolution: Afro-American Slave Revolts in the Making of the Modern World*. Baton Rouge: Louisiana State University Press.

Geyer, Michael. 1989. "The Militarization of Europe, 1914–1945." In *The Militarization of the Western World*, edited by J. Gillis, 65–102. New Brunswick, N.J.: Rutgers University Press.

Gill, Lesley. 2004. *The School of the Americas: Military Training and Political Violence in the Americas*. Durham, N.C.: Duke University Press.

Gillis, John R. 1989. *The Militarization of the Western World*. New Brunswick, N.J.: Rutgers University Press.

Gilmore, Glenda. 1998. "Murder, Memory, and the Flight of Incubus." In *Democracy Betrayed: The Wilmington Race Riot of 1898 and Its Legacy*, edited by D. S. Cecelski and T. B. Tyson, 73–93. Chapel Hill: University of North Carolina Press.

Ginsburg, Faye. 1989. *Contested Lives: The Abortion Debate in an American Community*. Berkeley: University of California Press.

Gluckman, Max. 1958 [1940]. *The Analysis of a Social Situation in Modern Zululand*. Manchester: Manchester University Press.

———. 1961. "Ethnographic Data in British Social Anthropology." *Sociological Review* 9: 5–17.

———. 1963. *Order and Rebellion in Tribal Africa*. London: Cohen and West.

Goldstein, Daniel M. 2004. *The Spectacular City: Violence and Performance in Urban Bolivia*. Durham, N.C.: Duke University Press.

Gramsci, Antonio. 1971. *Selections from the Prison Notebooks*. New York: International Publishers.

Grantham, Dewey. 1983. *Southern Progressivism: The Reconciliation of Progress and Tradition*. Knoxville: University of Tennessee Press.

Greene, Jack. 1988. *Pursuits of Happiness: The Social Development of Early Modern British Colonies and the Formation of American Culture.* Chapel Hill: University of North Carolina Press.

Gregory, Steven. 1998. *Black Corona: Race and the Politics of Place in an Urban Community.* Princeton, N.J.: Princeton University Press.

Gregory, Steven, and Roger Sanjek, eds. 1994. *Race.* New Brunswick, N.J.: Rutgers University Press.

Guinier, Lani. 1994. *Tyranny of the Majority: Fundamental Fairness in Representative Democracy.* New York: Free Press.

Habermas, Jürgen. 1977. *Legitimation Crisis.* Boston: Beacon Press.

Hackworth, Jason. 2000. *The Neoliberal City: Governance, Ideology, and Development in American Urbanism.* Ithaca, N.Y.: Cornell University Press.

Hadden, Sally E. 2001. *Slave Patrols: Law and Violence in Virginia and the Carolinas.* Cambridge, Mass.: Harvard University Press.

Haley, John. 1998. "Race, Rhetoric and Revolution." In *Democracy Betrayed. The Wilmington Race Riot of 1898 and Its Legacy*, edited by D. S. Cecelski and T. B. Tyson, 207–223. Chapel Hill: University of North Carolina Press.

Hanchett, Thomas. 1998. *Sorting Out the New South City.* Chapel Hill: University of North Carolina Press.

Handelman, Don. 1990. *Models and Mirrors: Towards an Anthropology of Public Events.* Cambridge: Cambridge University Press.

———. 2004. *Nationalism and the Israeli State: Bureaucratic Logic in Public Events.* Oxford: Berg.

———. 2006. "The Extended Case: Interactional Foundation and Prospective Dimensions." *Social Analysis* 49 (3): 65–66.

Handelman, Don, and Galina Lindquist. 2005. *Ritual in Its Own Right: Exploring the Dynamics of Transformation.* New York: Berghahn Books.

Hartigan, John, Jr. 1999. *Racial Situations: Class Predicaments of Whiteness in Detroit.* Princeton, N.J.: University of Princeton Press.

———. 2005. *Odd Tribes: Toward a Cultural Analysis of White People.* Durham, N.C.: Duke University Press.

Harvey, David. 1989. *The Condition of Postmodernity.* London: Blackwell.

———. 2005. *A Brief History of Neoliberalism.* Oxford: Oxford University Press.

Hay, Colin. 1996. "Narrating Crisis: The Discursive Construction of the Winter of Discontent." *Sociology* 30 (2): 253–277.

———. 1999. "Crisis and the Structural Transformation of the State: Interrogating Processes of Change." *British Journal of Politics and International Relations* 1 (3): 317–344.

Herzfeld, Michael. 1993. *The Social Production of Indifference: Exploring the Symbolic Roots of Western Bureaucracy.* Chicago: University of Chicago Press.

Heyman, Josiah McC. 1995. "Putting Power in the Anthropology of Bureaucracy: The Immigration and Naturalization Service at the Mexican–United States Border." *Current Anthropology* 36 (2): 261–287.

Hirschman, Albert O. 1977. *The Passions and the Interests: Political Arguments of Capitalism Before Its Triumph.* Princeton, N.J.: Princeton University Press.

Holland, Dorothy, et al. 2007. *Local Democracy under Siege: Activism, Public Interests, and Private Politics.* New York: New York University Press.

Holt, Thomas C. 1992. *The Problem of Freedom.* Baltimore: Johns Hopkins University Press.

———. 2000. *The Problem of Race in the 21st Century.* Cambridge, Mass.: Harvard University Press.

Holt, Thomas C. 2002. *The Problem of Race in the Twenty-First Century.* Cambridge, Mass.: Harvard University Press.

Huddle, Mark A. 1997. "To Educate a Race: The Making of the First State Colored Normal School, Fayetteville, North Carolina, 1865–1877." *North Carolina Historical Review* 74 (2): 135–160.

Hunt, Alfred. 1988. *Haiti's Influence on Antebellum America: Slumbering Volcano in the Caribbean.* Baton Rouge: Louisiana State University Press.

Igarashi, Yoshikuni. 2000. *Bodies of Memory: Narratives of War in Postwar Japanese Culture, 1945–1970.* Princeton, N.J.: Princeton University Press.

Jackson, John L. 2001. *Harlemworld: Doing Race and Class in Contemporary Black America.* Chicago: University of Chicago Press.

———. 2005. *Real Black: Adventures in Racial Sincerity.* Chicago: University of Chicago Press.

———. 2008. *Racial Paranoia: The New Reality of Race in America.* New York: Basic Civitas.

James, C.L.R. 1963. *The Black Jacobins: Toussaint L'Ouverture and the San Domingo Revolution.* New York: Vintage Books.

Joas, Hans. 1999. "The Modernity of War: Modernization Theory and the Problem of Violence." *International Sociology* 14 (4): 457–472.

Johnson, Michael P. 2001. "Denmark Vesey and His Co-Conspirators." *William and Mary Quarterly* 58 (3): 915–976.

Kantrowitz, Stephen. 1998. "The Two Faces of White Domination in North Carolina, 1800–1898." In *Democracy Betrayed: The Wilmington Race Riot of 1898 and Its Legacy,* edited by D. S. Cecelski and T. B. Tyson, 95–112. Chapel Hill: University of North Carolina Press.

———. 2001. *Ben Tillman and the Reconstruction of White Supremacy.* Chapel Hill: University of North Carolina Press.

Kapferer, Bruce. 1998. *Legends of People, Myths of State: Violence, Intolerance, and Political Culture in Sri Lanka and Australia.* Washington, D.C.: Smithsonian Institution Press.

Katznelson, Ira. 2002. "Flexible Capacity: The Military and Early American Statebuilding." In *Shaped by War and Trade: International Influences on American Political Development,* edited by Ira Katznelson and Martin Shefter, 82–110. Princeton, N.J.: Princeton University Press.

Katznelson, Ira, and Martin Shefter, eds. 2002. *Shaped by War and Trade: International Influences on American Political Development.* Princeton, N.J.: Princeton University Press.

Kay, Marvin L. Michael, and Lorin Lee Cary. 1995. *Slavery in North Carolina: 1748–1775.* Chapel Hill: University of North Carolina Press.

Keith, Jeanette. 2004. *Rich Man's War, Poor Man's Fight: Race, Class, and Power in the Rural South during the First World War.* Chapel Hill: University of North Carolina Press.

Key, V. O. 1949. *Southern Politics in State and Nation.* New York: Knopf.

Kirby, Jack Temple. 1972. *Darkness at the Dawning: Race and Reform in the Progressive South.* Philadelphia: Lippincott.

Klarman, Michael J. 1994. "How Brown Changed Race Relations: The Backlash Thesis." *Journal of American History* 81 (1): 81–118.

Klausen, Jytte. 1998. *War and the Welfare State: Europe and the United States, 1945 to the Present.* New York: Palgrave.

Koselleck, Reinhardt. 1998. *Critique and Crises: Enlightenment and the Pathogenesis of Modern Society.* Cambridge, Mass.: MIT Press.

———. 2006. "Crisis." *Journal of History of Ideas* 67 (2): 357–400.

Kousser, J. Morgan. 1974. *The Shaping of Southern Politics: Suffrage Restriction and the Establishment of the One-Party South, 1880–1910*. New Haven, Conn.: Yale University Press.

Kryder, Daniel. 2001. *Divided Arsenal: Race and the American State during World War II*. Cambridge: Cambridge University Press.

Kyriakoudes, Louis. 2003. *The Social Origins of the Urban South: Race, Gender, and Migration*. Chapel Hill: University of North Carolina Press.

Lacy, Karyn. 2007. *Blue-Chip Black: Race, Class, and Status in the New Black Middle-Class*. Berkeley: University of California Press.

Lassiter, Matthew D. 2006. *The Silent Majority: Suburban Politics in the Sunbelt South*. Princeton, N.J.: Princeton University Press.

Lefever, H. G. 1981. "'Playing the Dozens': A Mechanism for Social Control." *Phylon* 42 (1): 73–85.

Lévi-Strauss, Claude. 1979. *Myth and Meaning: Cracking the Code of Culture*. New York: Schocken Books.

Light, Jennifer. 2003. *From Warfare to Welfare: Defense Intellectuals and Urban Problems in Cold War America*. Baltimore: Johns Hopkins University Press.

Link, William A. 1992. *The Paradox of Southern Progressivism, 1880–1930*. Chapel Hill: University of North Carolina Press.

Lipsitz, George. 1998. *Possessive Investment in Whiteness*. Philadelphia: Temple University Press.

Lomnitz, Claudio. 1992. *Exits from the Labyrinth: Culture and Ideology in the Mexican National Space*. Berkeley: University of California Press.

———. 2001. *Deep Mexico, Silent Mexico: An Anthropology of Nationalism*. Minneapolis: University of Minnesota Press.

———. 2003a. "The Depreciation of Life during Mexico City's Transition into 'the Crisis.'" In *Wounded Cities: Destruction and Reconstruction in a Globalized World*, edited by I. Susser and J. Schneider, 47–70. Oxford: Berg.

———. 2003b. "Times of Crisis: Historicity, Sacrifice, and the Spectacle of Debacle in Mexico City." *Public Culture* 15 (1): 127–147.

Lotchin, Roger. 2002. *Fortress California: From Warfare to Welfare*. Champaign-Urbana: University of Illinois Press.

Luebke, Paul, 1998. *Tar Heel Politics 2000*. Chapel Hill: University of North Carolina Press.

Lutz, Catherine. 2001. *Homefront: A Military City and the American 20th Century*. Boston: Beacon Press.

Malinowski, Bronislaw. 1922. *Argonauts of the Western Pacific*. New York: E. P. Dutton.

Mann, Michael. 1988. *States, War, and Society: Studies in Political Sociology*. London: Blackwell.

———. 1993. *The Social Sources of Power*, vol. 2: *The Rise of Classes and Nation-States, 1760–1914*. Cambridge: Cambridge University Press.

Marcus, George, ed. 1999. *Paranoia within Reason: A Casebook on Conspiracy as Explanation*. Chicago: University of Chicago Press.

Markusen, Ann, et al. 1991. *The Rise of the Gunbelt: The Military Remapping of Industrial America*. New York: Oxford University Press.

Mayer, Margit. 1994. "Post-Fordist City Politics." In *Post-Fordism: A Reader*, edited by Ash Amin. Oxford: Blackwell.

Mbembe, Achille, and Janet Roitman. 1995. "Figures of the Subject in Times of Crisis." *Public Culture* 7 (2): 324.

McCaffrey, Katherine. 2002. *Military Power and Popular Protest: The U.S. Navy in Vieques, Puerto Rico*. New Brunswick, N.J.: Rutgers University Press.

McEnaney, Lauren. 2000. *Civil Defense Begins at Home*. Princeton, N.J.: Princeton University Press.

Mendelberg, Tali. 2001. *The Race Card: Campaign Strategy, Implicit Messages, and the Norm of Equality*. Princeton, N.J.: Princeton University Press.

Merrens, Harry Roy. 1964. *Colonial North Carolina in the Eighteenth Century: A Study in Historical Geography*. Chapel Hill: University of North Carolina Press.

Mills, C. Wright. 1956. *The Power Elite*. New York: Oxford University Press.

Mintz, Sidney W. 1974. *Caribbean Transformations*. Baltimore: Johns Hopkins University Press.

Mintz, Sidney W., and George Baca, eds. 2010. *Southern Classics*. Columbia: University of South Carolina Press.

Morgan, Philip D. 1998. *Slave Counterpoint: Black Culture in the Eighteenth-Century Chesapeake and Lowcountry*. Chapel Hill: University of North Carolina Press.

Mullings, Leith. 2005. "Interrogating Racism: Toward an Antiracist Anthropology." *Annual Review of Anthropology* 34:667–693.

Murphy, Ella Louise. 1960. "Origin and Development of Fayetteville State Teachers College." Ph.D. diss., New York University.

Myers, Andrew. 2006. *Black, White, and Olive Drab: Racial Integration at Fort Jackson, South Carolina, and the Civil Rights Movement*. Charlottesville: University of Virginia Press.

Nietzsche, Friedrich. 1969. *Ecce Homo*. New York: Vintage Press.

Oates, John Alexander. 1950. *The Story of Fayetteville and the Upper Cape Fear*. Charlotte, N.C.: Dowd Press.

Odum, Howard. 1997 [1946]. *Race and Rumors of Race: The American South in the Early Forties*. Baltimore: Johns Hopkins University Press.

Ong, Aihwa. 1999. *Flexible Citizenship: The Cultural Logics of Transnationality*. Durham, N.C.: Duke University Press.

Outland, Robert, III. 2004. *Tapping the Pines: The Naval Stores Industry in the American South*. Baton Rouge: Louisiana State University Press.

Parker, Roy. 1990. *Cumberland County: A Brief History*. Raleigh: Division of Archives and History, North Carolina Department of Cultural Resources.

Patterson, Orlando. 1982. *Slavery and Social Death: A Comparative Study*. Cambridge, Mass.: Harvard University Press.

Pattillo-McCoy, Mary. 1999. *Black Picket Fences: Privilege and Peril among the Black Middle Class*. Chicago: University of Chicago Press.

———. 2007. *Black on the Block: The Politics of Race and Class in the City*. Chicago: University of Chicago Press.

Peck, Jamie, and Adam Tickell. 2002. "Neoliberalizing Space." In *Spaces of Neoliberalism: Urban Restructuring in North America and Western Europe*, edited by N. Brenner and N. Theodore, 33–57. London: Wiley-Blackwell.

———. 2006. "Conceptualizing Neoliberalism, Thinking Thatcherism." In *Contesting Neoliberalism*, edited by H. Leitner, J. Peck, and E. Sheppard, 26–50. New York: Guilford Press.

Phillips, Jonathan F. 2002. "Building a New South Metropolis: Fayetteville, Fort Bragg, and the Sandhills of North Carolina." Ph.D. diss., University of North Carolina, Chapel Hill.

Pocock, J.G.A. 1975. *The Machiavellian Moment: Florentine Political Thought and the Atlantic Republican Tradition*. Princeton, N.J.: Princeton University Press.

Polanyi, Karl. 1944. *The Great Transformation*. New York: Farrar and Rinehart.

Povinelli, Elizabeth A. 2002. *The Cunning of Recognition: Indigenous Alterities and the Making of Australian Multiculturalism*. Durham, N.C.: Duke University Press.

Powdermaker, Hortense. 1993 [1939]. *After Freedom: A Cultural Study in the Deep South*. Madison: University of Wisconsin Press.

Prashad, Vijay. 2006. "Second Hand Dreams." In *Racism's Bloody Terrain: Racism, Class Inequality, and the Politics of Recognition*, edited by G. Baca, 72–84. Oxford: Berghahn Books.

Prather, H. Leon. 1984. *We Have Taken a City: The Wilmington Racial Massacre and Coup of 1898*. Cranbury, N.J.: Associated University Presses.

———. 1998. "We Have Taken a City: A Centennial Essay." In *Democracy Betrayed: The Wilmington Race Riot of 1898 and Its Legacy*, edited by David S. Cecelski and Timothy B. Tyson, 15–42. Chapel Hill: University of North Carolina Press.

Redfield, Peter. 2005. "Doctors, Borders, and Life in Crisis." *Cultural Anthropology* 20 (3): 328–361.

Reed, Adolph L., ed. 1986. *Race, Politics, and Culture: Critical Essays on the Radicalism of the 1960s*. Westport, Conn.: Greenwood Press.

———. 1999a. *Stirrings in the Jug: Black Politics in the Post-Segregation Era*. Minneapolis: University of Minnesota Press.

———. 1999b. *Without Justice for All: The New Liberalism and our Retreat from Racial Equality*. Boulder, Colo.: Westview Press.

Robin, Corey. 2004. *Fear: The History of a Political Idea*. New York: Oxford University Press.

Roediger, David. 1999. *The Wages of Whiteness: Race and the Making of the American Working Class*. New York: Verso Books.

Rogin, Michael P. 1988. *Ronald Reagan, the Movie: And Other Episodes in Political Demonology*. Berkeley: University of California Press.

Schulman, Bruce J. 1991. *From Cotton Belt to Sunbelt: Federal Policy, Economic Development, and the Transformation of the South, 1938–1980*. Durham, N.C.: Duke University Press.

Scott, Julius. 1986. "The Common Wind: Currents of Afro-American Communication in the Era of the Haitian Revolution." Ph.D. diss., Duke University.

Sewell, William. 2004. "The French Revolution and the Emergence of the Nation Form." In *Revolutionary Currents: Transatlantic Ideology and Nation Building, 1688–1821*, edited by Melinda Zook and Michael Morrison, 91–125. Lanham, Md.: Roman and Littlefield.

Sherry, Michael. 1997. *In the Shadow of War: The United States since the 1930s*. New Haven: Yale University Press.

Sidbury, James. 1997a. "Saint Domingue in Virginia: Ideology, Local Meanings, and Resistance to Slavery, 1790–1800." *Journal of Southern History* 63 (2): 531–552.

———. 1997b. *Ploughshares into Swords: Race, Rebellion, and Identity in Gabriel's Virginia, 1730–1810*. New York: Cambridge University Press.

Sider, Gerald M. 1993. *Lumbee Indian Histories: Race, Ethnicity, and Indian Identity in the Southern United States*. Cambridge: Cambridge University Press.

Silverstein, Paul A. 2002. "An Excess of Truth: Violence, Conspiracy Theorizing, and the Algerian Civil War." *Anthropological Quarterly* 75 (4): 643–674.

Simon, Bryant. 1997. "Introduction." In *Race and Rumors of Race: the American South in the Early Forties*, by Howard Odum, vii–xxxii. Baltimore: Johns Hopkins University Press.

Singh, Nikhil. 2004. *Black Is a Country: Race and the Unfinished Struggle for Democracy*. Cambridge, Mass.: Harvard University Press.

Skocpol, Theda. 1992. *Protecting Soldiers and Mothers: The Political Origins of Social Policy in the United States*. Cambridge, Mass.: Belknap Press of Harvard University Press.

Skowronek, Stephen. 1982. *Building a New American State: The Expansion of National Administrative Capacities, 1877–1920.* Cambridge: Cambridge University Press.

Smith, Robert C. 1996. *We Have No Leaders: African Americans in the Post–Civil Rights Era.* Albany: SUNY Press.

Sparrow, Bartholomew. 1996. *From Outside In: World War II and the American State.* Princeton, N.J.: Princeton University Press.

Steinberg, Stephen. 1995. *Turning Back: The Retreat from Racial Justice in American Thought and Policy.* Boston: Beacon Press.

———. 2007. *Race Relations: A Critique.* Stanford, Calif.: Stanford University Press.

Stoler, Ann. 1997. "Racial Histories and Their Regimes of Truth." *Political Power and Social Theory* 11:183–206.

Stone, Clarence. 1989. *Regime Politics: Governing Atlanta, 1946–1988.* Lawrence: University of Kansas Press.

Sugrue, Thomas. 1996. *The Origins of the Urban Crisis: Race and Inequality in Postwar Detroit.* Princeton, N.J.: Princeton University Press.

Taylor, Rosser. 1926. *Slaveholding in North Carolina: An Economic View.* Chapel Hill: University of North Carolina Press.

———. 1928. "Slave Conspiracies in North Carolina." *North Carolina Historical Review* 5:20–34.

Thompson, Edgar. 1955. "The Plantation as a Race-Making Situation." In *Sociology: A Text with Adapted Readings*, edited by L. Broom and P. Selznick, 506–507. New York: Harper and Row.

———. 1975. *Plantation Societies, Race Relations, and the South: The Regimentation of Populations: Selected Papers of Edgar T. Thompson.* Durham, N.C.: Duke University Press.

———. 2010 [1932]. "The Plantation." In *Southern Classics*, edited by Sidney W. Mintz and George Baca. Columbia: University of South Carolina Press.

Trouillot, Michel-Rolph. 1995. *Silencing the Past: Power and the Production of History.* Boston: Beacon Press.

———. 2000. "Abortive Rituals: Historical Apologies in the Global Era." *Interventions* 2 (2): 171–186.

———. 2002. "Culture on the Edges: Caribbean Creolization in Historical Context." In *From the Margins: Historical Anthropology and Its Futures*, edited by K. Axel, 189–210. Durham, N.C.: Duke University Press.

———. 2003. *Global Transformations: Anthropology and the Modern World.* New York: Palgrave.

Turner, Victor. 1957. *Schism and Continuity in an African Village: A Study of Nedembu Village Life.* Manchester: Manchester University Press.

———. 1967. *Forest of Symbols.* Ithaca, N.Y.: Cornell University Press.

———. 1974. *Dramas, Fields, and Metaphors: Symbolic Action and Human Society.* Ithaca, N.Y.: Cornell University Press.

Tyson, Timothy B. 1998. "Wars for Democracy." In *Democracy Betrayed: The Wilmington Race Riot of 1898 and Its Legacy*, edited by David S. Cecelski and Timothy B. Tyson, 253–276. Chapel Hill: University of North Carolina Press.

———. 1999. *Radio Free Dixie: Robert F. Williams and the Roots of Black Power.* Chapel Hill: University of North Carolina Press.

———. 2004. *Blood Done Sign My Name: A True Story.* New York: Three Rivers Press.

Van Velsen, Jaap. 1967. "The Extended-Case Method and Situational Analysis." In *The Craft of Social Anthropology*, edited by A. L. Epstein, 129–153. London: Tavistock.

Verdery, Katherine. 2001. "Seeing Like a Mayor: Or, How Local Officials Obstructed Romanian Land Restitution." *Ethnography* 3 (1): 5–33.

Vincent, Joan. 1990. *Anthropology and Politics: Visions, Traditions, and Trends*. Tucson: University of Arizona Press.

Wacquant, Loïc. 1997. "Decivilizing and Demonizing: The Social Symbolic Remaking of the Black Ghetto and Elias in the Dark Ghetto." *Amsterdam Sociologisch Tidjschrift* 24 (3–4): 340–348.

———. 2005. "Race as Civic Felony." *International Social Science Journal* 183: 127–142.

Wagner-Pacifici, Robin Erica. 1986. *The Moro Morality Play: Terrorism as Social Drama*. Chicago: University of Chicago Press.

Watson, Alan. 1991. *Wilmington: Port of North Carolina*. Columbia: University of South Carolina Press.

Weber, Eugen. 1976. *Peasants into Frenchmen: The Modernization of Rural France, 1870–1914*. Stanford, Calif.: Stanford University Press.

Wedeen, Lisa. 1999. *Ambiguities of Domination: Politics, Rhetoric, and Symbols in Contemporary Syria*. Chicago: University of Chicago Press.

Weiss, Linda. 1998. *The Myth of the Powerless State*. Ithaca: Cornell University Press.

Werbner, Richard. 1984. "The Manchester School in South-Central Africa." *Annual Review of Anthropology* 15:157–185.

West, Harry G., and Todd Sanders, eds. 2003. *Transparency and Conspiracy: Ethnographies of Suspicion in the New World Order*. Durham, N.C.: Duke University Press.

Williams, Brackette F. 1989. "A Class Act: Anthropology and the Race to Nation Across Ethnic Terrain." *Annual Review of Anthropology* 18:401–444.

———. 1991. *Stains on My Name, War in My Veins: Guyana and the Politics of Cultural Struggle*. Durham, N.C.: Duke University Press.

Wilson, Mark R. 2006. "The Politics of Procurement: Military Origins of Bureaucratic Autonomy." *Journal of Policy History* 18:44–73.

Wilson, Peter. 1973. *Crab Antics: The Social Anthropology of English-Speaking Negro Societies of the Caribbean*. New Haven: Yale University Press.

Wilson, William Julius. 1979. *The Declining Significance of Race: Blacks and Changing American Institutions*. Chicago: University of Chicago Press.

Wolf, Eric R. 1956. "Aspects of Group Relations in a Complex Society." *American Anthropologist* 58 (6): 1065–1078.

———. 1999. *Envisioning Power: Ideologies of Dominance and Crisis*. Berkeley: University of California Press.

Wood, Peter. 1974. *Black Majority: Negroes in South Carolina from 1670 to the Stono Rebellion*. New York: Knopf.

Wood, Bradford. 2004. *This Remote Part of the World: Regional Formation in the Lower Cape Fear, North Carolina, 1725–1775*. Columbia: University of South Carolina Press.

Woodward, C. Vann. 1951. *Origins of the New South, 1877–1913*. Baton Rouge: Louisiana State University Press.

———. 1969. *The Strange Career of Jim Crow*. New York: Oxford University Press.

Wyatt-Brown, Bertram. 1982. *Southern Honor: Ethics and Behavior in the Old South*. New York: Oxford University Press.

Index

About the Author

George Baca is research scholar at John Jay College of Criminal Justice, City University of New York. He is the editor of *Nationalism's Bloody Terrain: Racism, Class Inequality, and the Politics of Recognition*, coeditor of *Empirical Futures: Anthropologists and Historians Engage the Work of Sidney W. Mintz*, and associate editor of *Dialectical Anthropology*.

F
264
.F28
B33
2010

Baca, George.

Conjuring crisis.

$25.95

Breinigsville, PA USA
01 June 2010

238938BV00002B/2/P

9 780813 547527